Data Warehousing in the Real World

Data Warehousing in the Real World

A practical Guide for Building Decision Support Systems

SAM ANAHORY

DENNIS MURRAY

 Addison-Wesley

Harlow, England • Reading, Massachusetts • Menlo Park, California
New York • Don Mills, Ontario • Amsterdam • Bonn • Sydney • Singapore
Tokyo • Madrid • San Juan • Milan • Mexico City • Seoul • Taipei

Addison Wesley Longman Limited
Edinburgh Gate
Harlow
Essex CM20 2JE
England

and Associated Companies throughout the World.

Cover designed by Designers & Partners Ltd, Oxford, UK
Text design by Sally Grover Castle
Typeset in 10/12pt Times by 47
Printed and bound in The United States of America

First printed 1997

ISBN 0-201-17519-3

British Library Cataloguing-in-Publication Data
A catalogue record for this book is available from the British Library

Library of Congress Cataloging-in-Publication Data
Anahory, Sam.
  Data warehousing in the real world : a practical guide for
building decision support systems/ Sam Anahory, Dennis Murray.
     368 p. 23×17 cm.
  Includes index.
  ISBN 0-201-17519-3 (alk. paper)
  1. Data warehousing.   2. Decision support systems.   I. Murray, Dennis.
II. Title.
QA76.9.D37A5   1997
005.74 – dc21   97–20862
                                                     CIP

Dedicated to the memory of my father, J. V. Anahory

Contents

PART TWO: DATA WAREHOUSE ARCHITECTURE

PART THREE: DESIGN

PART SIX: FUTURES

APPENDICES

Trademark notice

ASDM and SP/2 are trademarks or registered trademarks of International Business Machines Corporation (IBM)

Alexandria and NUMA-Q are trademarks or registered trademarks of Sequent Computer Systems Inc.

Digital, Open VMS and VAX VMS are trademarks or registered trademarks of Digital Equipment Corporation

Microsoft, Visual Basic, Visual C++ and Windows NT are trademarks or registered trademarks of Microsoft Corporation

Networker is a trademark or registered trademark of Legato Systems Inc.

OmnibackII is a trademark or registered trademark of Hewlett-Packard

Oracle, SQL*Loader and Trusted Oracle are trademarks or registered trademarks of Oracle Corporation

Tandem is a trademark or registered trademark of Tandem Computers Inc.

UNIX is a trademark or registered trademark of Licensed through X/Open Company Ltd.

PART FIVE: CAPACITY PLANNING, TUNING AND TESTING

Preface

Is this book for you? Are you an IT practitioner who is interested in or is about to embark on building an enterprise data warehouse? We work with many IT practitioners who are in a similar position, in most cases somewhat unsure as to why a data warehousing project should be any different from any other IT project.

We have spent a large amount of our time educating practitioners on the design and implementation of data warehouses, either through hands-on experience, or through specific courses. Throughout these encounters we were constantly told "You should write a book about this!" Eventually, we said "Why not?"

This book is designed to answer any question you have on the design and building of enterprise data warehouses and data marts. You should use it as a step-by-step guide as you go through the process, resolving each set of issues as you go along. In order to make this easier, we have structured the book around the delivery process that we have developed to deliver data warehouses. All the suggested solutions are valid to any delivery process, but within this book they are structured in the way we have used time and time again. We suggest you avoid reading this book from cover to cover in one session, because each section goes into a lot of detail, which requires the appropriate context and mind-frame for you to extract the greatest value from this book.

Our focus has been to address the issues in delivering large-scale enterprise data warehouses, because we have found that these solutions can be very complex and prone to failure. Most of the problems that we have encountered have related to the sheer size of the database required, the hardware technology needed to implement large-scale, performant solutions, and the number and complexity of data feeds and data cleanup activities. If you have a requirement to deliver a small data warehouse or data mart (that is using a database less than 20 GB in size), you probably don't *need* this book, but you may find it useful to understand some of the more general issues covered here.

Wherever possible, we have included examples from a specific business area in order to illustrate each point. We have found that most people relate well to the retail sector because they all go shopping. Concepts like "a shopping basket," "basket items," "products," etc., are easy to understand, and are often better to illustrate the design solutions shown in this book. Therefore, we decided to take a larger number of examples from the retail sector, with other examples from the finance and telecommunications sectors. Other sectors are not covered in our examples, because we felt that all the new design concepts were adequately covered without introducing new terms. Similarly, in order to keep terminology simple, we have used technical terms, such as *tablespace*, which are specific to Oracle databases, but which have equivalents in other relational databases. As before, our intent is to refer to common pieces of functionality implied by the term, rather than attach any particular significance to the term itself.

Finally, we would like to thank everyone who made this book possible. It would be impractical to name everyone who has contributed in some way to this book. However, we would like to especially thank a number of people whose support, knowledge, and time made this book possible:

- all our colleagues with whom we have delivered data warehouses on behalf of SHL and Oracle, particularly Dave Pearson, Ben Salama and Bob Walters;
- the companies we have worked with over the years;
- the colleagues that reviewed drafts of the material time and time again, particularly Anthony Power and Ron Jacobs;
- the team at Addison Wesley Longman, particularly our editor Sally Mortimore, who enjoys a good lunch!

Last, but not least, a special word of thanks to Sam's wife Jackie, for putting up with him spending every spare moment in his study tapping away at the keyboard, and for his son Daniel, who insisted on playing "Winnie the Pooh" on his PC whenever he saw him there.

Sam Anahory
Dennis Murray
May 1997

PART ONE

Introduction

CHAPTER 1

Introduction

1.1   BACKGROUND

Over the last 20 years, $1 trillion has been invested in new computer systems to gain competitive edge. The vast majority of these systems have automated business processes, to make them faster, cheaper, and more responsive to the customer. Electronic point of sale at supermarkets, itemized billing at telecommunications companies (telcos), and mass market mailing at catalog companies are just some of the examples of such systems.

In today's world, the competitive edge is coming less from optimization and more from the proactive use of the information that these systems have been collecting over the years. Companies are beginning to realize the vast potential of the information that they hold in their organizations. If they can tap into this information, they can significantly improve the quality of their decision making and the profitability of the organization through focused actions.

The problem for most companies, though, is that their operational systems were never designed to support this kind of business activity, and probably never can be. Even the latest technology cannot be optimized to support both operational and multidimensional requirements cost-effectively. Operational systems also tend to be numerous, with overlapping and sometimes contrary definitions. To meet these needs there is a new breed of system, one that has evolved and matured in recent years and is now known as a **data warehouse**. Industry analysts expect this to represent a substantial percentage of all new spending on computer systems in the next 20 years.

1.2 WHAT IS A DATA WAREHOUSE?

A data warehouse, in its simplest perception, is no more than a collection of the key pieces of information used to manage and direct the business for the most profitable outcome. This could be anything from deciding the level of stock on a supermarket shelf, through focused targeting of customers for loyalty schemes and direct mail promotions, to strategic decision making on major market segments and company profitability.

We need a more precise definition to work with. There is a large body of literature now available on the subject, which contains many different definitions. Most definitions concentrate on the data, saying it should be subject oriented, be consistent across sources, and so on. In our definition the data warehouse is more than just data, it is also the processes involved in getting that data from source to table, and in getting the data from table to analysts. In other words, a data warehouse is the data (meta/fact/dimension/aggregation) and the process managers (load/warehouse/query) that make information available, enabling people to make informed decisions.

1.3 WHY READ THIS BOOK?

We have found that there is a dearth of value-adding information describing detailed solutions to solve the business and technical issues involved in delivering data warehouses. Typically, organizations invest the first few months of a data warehousing project in educating the project team on the risks and issues associated with data warehousing.

In some instances, organizations who try to shortcut the learning process end up having to totally restructure the solution six to nine months down the line. This is when critical issues like query performance, cost of ownership, load window, and extensibility and manageability manifest themselves, often at major cost.

The purpose of this book is to provide data warehousing *practitioners* with information on how to deliver these solutions successfully. This is provided in a "cookbook" format, encapsulating the experience that both authors have in avoiding the pitfalls of this process.

We focus on describing how to deliver data warehousing solutions built on top of open-systems technologies such as UNIX and relational databases. Clearly, data warehouses can be delivered on specialist or proprietary technology (such as Teradata or Tandem), but the details of such environments are outside the scope of this book.

This book provides guidance on:

- identifying the technical, architectural and infrastructure problems, with guidance on solving them;
- identifying the system components that need to be built in order to deliver an effective, low-maintenance solution;

- appropriate designs for the database, system managers, and construction of end-user queries;
- how the process for capturing requirements differs from the approach for delivering an operational system (this information is spread throughout the book);
- the selection of end-user tools (in brief and at an architectural level, not an in-depth comparison), copy management tools, and systems software;
- the operational management of the data warehouse;
- constructing a realistic project plan, staged to minimize risk of failure.

This information is backed up by specific examples, template project plans and functional descriptions, diagrams of the delivery process, database schemas and entity models, system designs, and architectural/infrastructure designs.

I.3.I   WHO SHOULD READ THIS BOOK?

- **Technical architects** who wish to learn what architectures are appropriate, and what criteria determine which is the most suitable solution;
- **systems engineers and analyst programmers** who wish to understand the designs for the various system components that they have to implement;
- **database designers** who wish to understand the various techniques and database designs necessary in order to make a relational database perform well with large data volumes;
- **database administrators** who wish to understand the specific issues that are likely to affect the creation and maintenance of a data warehouse;
- **system managers and operating managers** who wish to understand the issues around managing and operating the typically large, open systems required to support a data warehousing solution.

If you are about to start (or have started) a data warehousing project undertaking one of the above roles, this book will help you to succeed by guiding you round all the pitfalls of the process.

For completeness, we have included information relevant to **project managers** who wish to be aware of the steps, effort, risks, and resourcing of typical projects (see Appendix A). If your project is listed below, you are also likely to benefit, because they are all examples of solutions that use data warehousing technologies:

1   marketing solutions
    - marketing database
    - customer loyalty scheme
    - customer profiling and segmentation analysis
2   retail
    - sales analysis
    - shrinkage analysis
    - promotions analysis
    - space planning

3 insurance
- product profitability analysis
- orphan analysis
4 telephone companies
- individual tariffing through call analysis
- network analysis
5 retail banking
- customer profitability analysis
- customer scoring/loan decisioning

1.4   ROAD MAP

We have structured this book into a number of sections covering the various areas of expertise within a data warehousing solution. Depending on your interest, you should start at the chapter most suitable for you, and work forwards. Wherever possible, we have recapped points that may have been covered in previous chapters that are relevant to the subjects being discussed.

1.4.1   TECHNICAL ARCHITECTS

All technical architects should read the bulk of the book, because it covers all the architectural and design issues that you are likely to experience. **Part Two: Data warehouse Architecture** is the start of the description of the architecture of each component of a data warehouse, and subsequent chapters elaborate on the concepts covered within that section. In other words, technical architects will find it valuable to read the bulk of the information in this book.

1.4.2   SYSTEM ENGINEERS AND ANALYST PROGRAMMERS

Part Three: Design is the start of the detailed design for the database and system components of the data warehouse. We would recommend that you read **Part Two: Data Warehouse Architecture**, even if you are not fully familiar with all the concepts covered, in order to understand the context of the designs. **Part Four: Hardware and Operational Design** should be avoided, because it assumes a fair knowledge of hardware internals.

1.4.3   DATABASE DESIGNERS

All database designers should start off at **Part Two: Data Warehouse Architecture**, and then move on to **Part Three: Design**, where the bulk of the database design issues are described. In addition, **Part Four: Hardware and Operational Design** describes the hardware configuration, security and backup issues within a data warehouse, so it may be appropriate if you are also required to configure the database, implement the backup/recovery strategy, or any access control mechanisms. **Part Five: Capacity Planning, Tuning and Testing** should be read by those responsible for sizing and tuning the data warehouse.

1.4.4   DATABASE ADMINISTRATORS

All database administration activities are primarily covered in **Part Four: Hardware and Operational Design**, but this assumes that you are familiar with **Part Two: Data Warehouse Architecture**, where the overall concepts are discussed. **Part Five: Capacity Planning, Tuning and Testing** should be read if the performance of the data warehouse needs to be optimized.

1.4.5   SYSTEM AND OPERATIONS MANAGERS

Part Three: Design starts off the process of discussing the issues relevant to managing a data warehouse. This is elaborated in **Part Four: Hardware and Operational Design.**

1.4.6   PROJECT MANAGERS

Chapter 2 describes the overall method used to deliver data warehouses. **Appendix A** describes the tasks and deliverables for a typical project and it assumes a degree of familiarization with the system architecture described in **Part Two: Data Warehouse Architecture.**

1.5   ONE FINAL POINT...

Wherever possible, we have used examples from a variety of industry sectors. In a number of cases, we have decided to concentrate on examples from the retail sector, because we have found that most people can relate to them easily (i.e. most people have direct experience of shopping at their local mall). In all these examples, the industry sector is immaterial; it is the underlying concept behind the example that we wish to convey. If you would like to hear of examples in different industry sectors, feel free to contact us directly.

CHAPTER 2

Delivery process

2.1   INTRODUCTION

Data warehousing solutions are fundamentally different from operational systems because they have to evolve and grow as the business requirement for information changes over a period of time. Data warehouses are *never* static, in the same way that business needs are never static. In order to respond to today's requirement for instantaneous access to any corporate information, the data warehouse must also be designed to provide that information in a performant way.

In practice, this means that data warehouses must be designed to change constantly. You may know the main content of the data warehouse, but you are unlikely to know all the detail that may be required. The real problem is that the business itself may not be aware of its requirements for information in the future. As the business grows and changes, its needs will change. Data warehouses are designed to ride with these changes, by always building a degree of flexibility within the system.

In order to provide this flexible solution, we have found that the process that delivers a data warehouse has to be fundamentally different from a traditional waterfall method. The underlying issue with data warehousing projects is that it is very difficult to complete the tasks and deliverables in the strict, ordered fashion demanded by a waterfall method. This is because the requirements are rarely fully understood, and are expected to change over time. The knock-on effect is that architectures, designs, and build components cannot be completed until the requirements are completed, which can lead to constant requirements iteration without delivery, i.e. "paralysis by analysis."

In effect, we have to design and build around what we know today, and what we can guess about the future. The change in mindset that this requires from the practitioners within the project is by far the biggest delivery risk, because the team will constantly battle to understand at what point sufficient information exists to proceed to the next step.

Unless you have a preference for a different delivery process, our advice would be that you adopt the method we have developed. We appreciate that the method differs from a traditional IT systems development approach, but we also know from experience that it minimizes delivery risk. Each step is designed to clarify the point at which the task is sufficiently completed to allow us to proceed to the next step. Above all, we recommend that all the team members are supported as much as possible, while they experience a different way of delivering IT solutions.

The information in the book is structured around the method, in order to aid understanding of the steps and deliverables within the method. However, all the design techniques, mechanisms, and guidelines would apply equally well to any other method. We have tried to show you how to deliver a data warehouse from start to finish, but if you are interested only in a specific technical area, feel free to jump straight in.

2.2 DATA WAREHOUSE DELIVERY METHOD

The delivery method is essentially a variant of the **joint application development** approach, adapted for delivery of data warehouses. The entire delivery process is staged in order to minimize risk, by producing production-quality deliverables, which are designed to grow to a full solution.

Our experience has been that most enterprise data warehousing projects tend to have a development cycle of between 18 and 24 months from start to end. This is clearly difficult to justify, because the required investment is substantial, and no business benefits can be generated until the system is delivered. Clearly, an approach that allows the business to deliver "quick wins" is more attractive.

The approach discussed within this section will not reduce the overall delivery time-scales; however, it does ensure that business benefits are delivered incrementally through the development process. This means that the cost of investment can be offset and measured against the benefits being generated by the data warehouse. If the projected benefits are not being achieved in practice, further investment can be halted, or the project can be redirected to a different business need, minimizing the overall project risk.

Before we discuss the delivery process, bear in mind that this method is designed to deliver an *enterprise* data warehouse, not a point solution. Enterprise data warehouses provide information about many (if not all) aspects of information being used by the business. They are not small databases (that is, 50 GB) or data marts being used to address a specific functional need.

Enterprise data warehouses provide an accurate and consistent view of enterprise information, regardless of which point solutions they may be addressing at a specific point in time. The business benefits that can be derived are clearly much

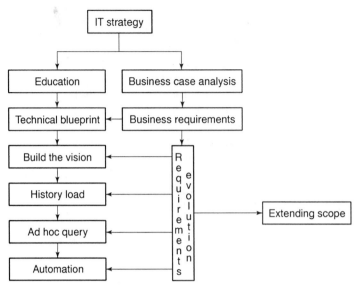

Figure 2.1 The data warehouse delivery process.

greater than those derived from a point solution. If this is not the case, ask yourself very carefully why you are proposing to build a data warehouse.

2.2.1 IT STRATEGY

Data warehouses are strategic investments, which may require business process redesign in order to generate the projected benefits. If there is no overall IT strategy that includes a data warehouse, it can be difficult to procure and retain funding for the project.

2.2.2 BUSINESS CASE

In a data warehousing project, it is critical that we understand the business case for investment. This is necessary to understand the level of investment that can be justified, as hard choices will have to be made regarding the scope and size of the solution.

The purpose of the business case is to identify the projected business benefits that should be derived from using the data warehouse. These benefits may or may not be quantifiable (for example, a $5 000 000 saving per annum), but the projected benefits should be clearly stated. Data warehouses that do not have a clear business case tend to suffer from credibility problems at some stage during the delivery process.

Many organizations justify building data warehouses as "an act of faith." Without exception, these projects have foundered or have been subject to very searching questions within six months of project inception.

2.2.3   EDUCATION AND PROTOTYPING

Typically, organizations will experiment with the concept of data analysis and educate themselves on the value of a data warehouse, prior to determining that a data warehouse is the appropriate solution. In practice, many organizations address this by sponsoring an initial prototyping activity, which is used to further understanding of the feasibility and benefits of a data warehouse. This activity is valuable, and should be considered if this is the organization's first exposure to the benefits of decision support information.

   In some instances, the data warehouse may be the first large-scale client–server solution being implemented within the organization, and will require new skills, experiences, hardware, etc. A prototyping activity on a small scale can further the educational processes as long as:

- the prototype addresses a clearly defined technical objective;
- the prototype can be *thrown away* once the feasibility of the concept has been shown – that is, it does not become "the first bit of the data warehouse";
- the activity addresses a small subset of the eventual data content of the data warehouse;
- the activity timescale is non-critical – that is, it is seen as a timeboxed effort to come to grips with the new technologies being considered.

Unlike prototypes, working models suffer in that they have a tendency to set the expectation that they will grow to the full data warehouse. This may be inappropriate in practice, because the architecture of the model may not scale up to a full data warehouse. If the requirement is to produce an early release of part of a data warehouse, in order to deliver business benefits, we suggest that you:

1   Focus on the business requirements and technical blueprint phases.
2   Understand the short- and medium-term requirements of the data warehouse.
3   Identify an architecture that is capable of evolving.
4   Limit the scope of the first build phase to the minimum that delivers business benefit.

2.2.4   BUSINESS REQUIREMENTS

In order to produce a set of production-quality deliverables that grow to a full solution, we must make sure that the overall requirements are understood, and that the overall system architecture is in place. The *business requirements* and *technical blueprint* phases are designed to address those two points. By understanding the business requirements for both the short and medium term, we can design a solution that satisfies the short-term need, but is capable of growing to the full solution.

   Additionally, at least 20% of the time within the *business requirements* phase should be spent on understanding the likely longer-term requirement. Any less effort than that will affect the feasibility of designing a data warehouse that can grow to satisfy a future requirement.

Within this stage, we must determine:

- the logical model for information within the data warehouse,
- the source systems that provide this data (that is, mapping rules),
- the business rules to be applied to data,
- the query profiles for the immediate requirement.

In some cases, some aspects of the data may not be available from existing operational systems. If this is the case, it is probably not feasible to populate the data warehouse with that data, because manual processes to supplement data captured by the extract and load process are generally unreliable.

2.2.5 TECHNICAL BLUEPRINT

The *technical blueprint* phase must deliver an overall architecture that satisfies the longer-term requirements, and a definition of the components that must be implemented in the short term in order to derive any business benefit. The blueprint must identify:

- the overall system architecture,
- the server and data mart architecture (see Chapter 4) for both data and applications,
- the essential components of the database design,
- the data retention strategy,
- the backup and recovery strategy,
- the capacity plan for hardware and infrastructure (for example, LAN and WAN).

A detailed design of the database is not produced at this stage; rather, the most significant components are identified and sized. In practice, these will tend to be the largest tables that contain information about the business: that is, the major fact tables and associated dimensions (see Chapter 5).

2.2.6 BUILDING THE VISION

Build the vision is the stage where the first production deliverable is produced. This is typically the smallest component of the data warehouse that adds business benefit. For example, this stage will probably build the major infrastructure components for extracting and loading data, but limit them to the extraction and load of one or two data sources, with minimal history.

To a very large extent, the purpose of minimizing the scope of this phase is to reduce project risk, and to timebox the deliverable into a 4–6-month exercise. We recommend that the deliverable satisfies your most pressing business requirement for data analysis. If the time-scales for this activity are significantly longer than 4–6 months, it might indicate that the initial requirement is too complex. In this instance, we suggest that you investigate whether the requirement can be delivered in a number of 4-month phases.

2.2.7 HISTORY LOAD

The remaining phases within a data warehouse delivery can occur in any sequence; that is, they are driven by the specific business drivers. As we have discussed, the purpose of breaking the delivery up into phases is to reduce project and delivery risk. This is achieved by reducing the scope of each phase so that it lasts 3–4 months elapsed. If the projected phase is much bigger than this, it indicates that the scope is probably too large.

In most cases, the next phase is one where the remainder of the required history is loaded into the data warehouse. This means that new entities would not be added to the data warehouse, but additional physical tables would probably be created to store the increased data volumes.

For example, let us consider a case where the *building the vision* phase has delivered a retail sales analysis data warehouse with 3 months' worth of history. This information is probably ample to allow the business user to analyse recent trends and address short-term sales issues. It does not provide sufficient data to identify annual or seasonal sales trends.

The next step could be to backload two years' worth of sales history from archive tape. This would allow the business user to analyse seasonal sales trends year on year. However, the data volumes could be such that the existing relatively small data warehouse becomes a much larger one. For example, a 50 GB database could easily expand to become 400 GB.

Once this happens, the operational management issues become far more complex, and require special strategies and facilities to resolve. For example, backup and recovery procedures become much more complex, disk failures increase dramatically, and load processes take much longer to execute.

In order to resolve these complex issues, we recommend that the activity to backload history is implemented within a separate phase (the *history load* phase). This allows you to focus on resolving the very large database (VLDB) issues without increasing the complexity even further by extending the scope of the data warehouse.

2.2.8 AD HOC QUERY

The next step in the process is where we configure an ad hoc query tool to operate against the data warehouse. These end-user access tools are capable of automatically generating the database query that answers any question posed by the user. The users will typically pose questions in terms that they are familiar with (for example, sales by store last week); this is converted into the database query by the access tool, which is aware of the structure of information within the data warehouse.

The process of generating a database query may sound simple enough, but in practice can be very tricky to get right. The challenge is not to get the user access tool to generate the query; rather, it is to cajole the tool into generating a performant query. Our experience has been that this process is time consuming, and can result in substantial changes to the database in order to force the tool to generate the optimum query. To this end, we can mitigate project risk by performing this activity within a separate phase, after the first benefits are delivered.

We do not mean to imply that you should never perform this activity within one of the other phases. It is our opinion that project risk and complexity will substantially increase, if the user access tool is configured and tuned at the same time that the database is being substantially modified.

2.2.9 AUTOMATION

The automation phase is where many of the operational management processes are fully automated within the data warehouse. These would include:

1 extracting and loading the data from a variety of source systems;
2 transforming the data into a form suitable for analysis;
3 backing up, restoring and archiving data;
4 generating aggregations from predefined definitions within the data warehouse;
5 monitoring query profiles, and determining the appropriate aggregations to maintain system performance.

In most cases, processes 1 and 2 are delivered (at least in part) within earlier stages (*building the vision*); the focus of this phase is to deliver the remaining processes. These activities are complex and time consuming, and should not be performed when other critical issues (such as data load and VLDB) are being addressed.

2.2.10 EXTENDING SCOPE

Within this phase, the scope of the data warehouse is extended to address a new set of business requirements. More often than not, this involves the loading of additional data sources into the data warehouse, although it can just be the introduction of new data marts using the existing information. In either case, the effort and complexity can be substantial, and the phase should be performed as a separate phase.

2.2.11 REQUIREMENTS EVOLUTION

The most important aspect of the delivery process is that the requirements are never static. Business requirements will constantly change during the life of the data warehouse, so it is imperative that the process supports this, and allows these changes to be reflected within the system.

This issue can appear to be a very complex one, but in practice, it is addressed by designing the data warehouse around the use of data within business processes, as opposed to the data requirements of existing queries. The architecture is designed to change and grow to match changing business needs. However, it is critical that the changing requirements are captured and managed through an ongoing requirements capture activity.

In effect, the process operates as a pseudo joint application development process, where new user requirements are continually fed into the development activities. Partial deliverables are produced, fed back to users, and then reworked, ensuring that the overall system is continually updated to meet the business needs.

PART TWO

Data warehouse architecture

CHAPTER 3

System processes

3.1 INTRODUCTION

Years of operational systems development have taught us what techniques are appropriate in order to deliver a typical solution: for example, use normalized data structures, keep the tables small with one table per entity, and so on.

In essence, operational systems are optimized to perform repeatable business functions, while decision support systems do not know in advance the queries and operations that will be executed. This means that all the lessons learned from designing operational systems in the last 20 years may be inappropriate when applied to data warehousing.

Within this section, we will focus on designing data warehousing solutions built on top of open-systems technologies such as UNIX and relational databases. Clearly, data warehouses can be delivered on specialist or proprietary technology (such as Teradata or Tandem), but the details of such environments are outside the scope of this book.

Data warehouses are built to support large data volumes (above 100 GB of database) cost-effectively. The underlying relational database technology has evolved to satisfy the requirements of smaller online transaction processing (OLTP) systems. The size and complexity of data warehouse systems make them very different from these traditional OLTP systems. They therefore require a different approach to the design and development.

On a regular basis, we get called in by organizations that have attempted to develop a data warehouse internally, usually 6–9 months into the project. The usual request would be along the lines of "Can you please come in and tune our database?

We can't get queries to respond fast enough," or "Can you please tell us how to restructure our queries? They are not hitting the performance targets."

By this point, it is often the case that the underlying system and hardware architecture is inappropriate for the business requirements. In many cases, the call is too late, and the only viable option is to start building from scratch – writing off the bulk of the investment to date.

It is essential to the success of the data warehouse that sufficient time is set aside to develop an architecture that can evolve as the business requirements evolve, and will not run out of steam within a five-year period. It is vital not to skimp on this activity. If costs must be cut it is safer to reduce the scope of the phased deliverable (i.e. the *building the vision* phase), but retain the effort to architect the whole solution.

This chapter discusses a number of architectural considerations for a data warehouse, and suggests strategies, components, and designs.

3.1.1   PROCESS

The architecture of a data warehouse is defined within the *technical blueprint* stage of the process (Figure 3.1). The *business requirements* stage should have identified the initial user requirements and have developed an understanding of the longer-term business requirements. This is used within the *technical blueprint* to determine what the overall architecture of the data warehouse should be.

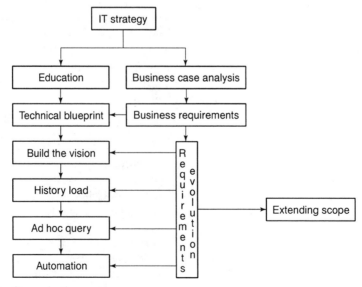

Figure 3.1   Stages in the process.

3.2 OVERVIEW

Data warehouses must be architected to support three major driving factors:

- populating the warehouse,
- day-to-day management of the warehouse,
- the ability to cope with requirements evolution.

These factors are complex, and often require a high degree of cutting-edge technology to deliver such facilities. In many cases, a large proportion of the extraction and data load, and the day-to-day management of the data warehouse, can be automated. The more difficult challenge is to architect systems that automate requirements that are going to change on a continuing basis.

The processes required to populate the warehouse focus on extracting the data, cleaning it up, and making it available for analysis. This is typically done on a daily basis after the close of the business day. A common misconception is that data warehouses are read-only systems. In fact, one of the key challenges for a data warehouse is the daily load and management of new data. It is, however, true that the factual data, once loaded, is usually not updated, but reference information will change on an ongoing basis as new requirements are identified to analyze the factual data in different ways.

The day-to-day management of the data warehouse is different from the management of an operational system, because the volumes can be much larger, and require more active management, such as creating/deleting summaries, or rolling data on/off the archive. In essence, a data warehouse is a database that is continually changing to satisfy new business requirements.

Requirements evolution tends to be the most complex aspect of a data warehouse. This requires the architecture to be structured in such a way as to cope with future changes in query profiles. This evolution will also encompass the addition of completely new subject areas.

In practice, a critical issue to address up front is how big the data warehouse will eventually be. The answer to this question indicates the magnitude of the total solution, and how much headroom is required from the underlying hardware/software.

For example, let us consider a retail sales analysis data warehouse, where the first production phase requires an initial 50 GB of data, which then is likely to grow to 1 TB of data over the following 2 years, through the addition of detailed customer transactions. These daily transactions, often called "basket transactions," represent all the purchases within a basket of goods. In this instance, the underlying hardware must be capable of supporting the eventual database size. It is costly and inefficient to design a solution that calls for a new hardware architecture when the database grows to that size.

3.3 TYPICAL PROCESS FLOW WITHIN

A DATA WAREHOUSE

Before we create an architecture for a data warehouse, we must first understand the major processes that constitute a data warehouse. These processes are depicted in Figure 3.2, and correspond to the data flows within a data warehouse.

These processes are:

1 Extract and load the data.
2 Clean and transform data into a form that can cope with large data volumes, and provide good query performance.
3 Back up and archive data.
4 Manage queries, and direct them to the appropriate data sources.

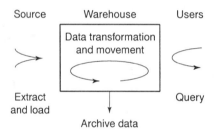

Figure 3.2 Process flow within a data warehouse.

3.4 EXTRACT AND LOAD PROCESS

Data extraction takes data from source systems and makes it available to the data warehouse; data load takes extracted data and loads it into the data warehouse.

Data in operational systems is held in a form suitable for that system. When we extract data from a physical database, whatever form it is held in, the original information content will have been modified and extended over the years, in order to support the data/performance requirements of the operational system. Before loading the data into the data warehouse this information content must be reconstructed.

In essence, information can be defined as data with context and meaning. The data warehouse extract and load process must take data and add context and meaning in order to convert it into value-adding business information.

Within a data warehouse, this is achieved by extracting the data from the source systems, loading it into the database, stripping out any detail that is there to support the operational system rather than the business requirement, adding more context (that is, more reference data), and then reconciling the data with the other sources.

3.4.1   CONTROLLING THE PROCESS

The mechanisms that determine when to start extracting the data, run the transformations and consistency checks and so on, are very important.

For example, it may be inappropriate to start the process that extracts EPOS transactions for a retail sales analysis data warehouse until all EPOS transactions have been received from all stores, and have been audited. In this instance, it may be possible to start the extraction process before all the data has been received. In practice, it may be too difficult to resolve consistency issues if all the data is not available.

In order to ensure that the various tools, logic modules, and programs are executed in the correct sequence and at the correct time, a controlling mechanism is required to fire each module when appropriate.

3.4.2   WHEN TO INITIATE THE EXTRACT

Data should be in a consistent state when it is extracted from the source system. More to the point, the information in a data warehouse represents a **snapshot** of corporate information, so that the user is looking at a single, consistent, version of the truth. Source data should be extracted only at a point where it represents the same instance of time as the extracts from the other data sources.

For example, in a customer profiling data warehouse in the telecommunications sector (telco), it is illogical to merge the list of customers at 7 pm on Friday from a customer database with the customer subscription events up to 7 pm on Thursday from a customer events database. This would mean that we are likely to find customers for whom there are no associated subscriptions.

This problem can be more complex, if the point at which operational data represents the same time period differs between systems. Continuing the previous example, it is very possible that the customer database may not be updated to reflect new subscriptions until 3 hours after the close of business on the customer events system. This is why we typically have to wait until all the data sources are in line before we begin executing consistency checks.

> **GUIDELINE 3.1**   Start extracting data from data sources when it represents the same snapshot of time as all the other data sources.

3.4.3   LOADING THE DATA

Once the data is extracted from the source systems, it is then typically loaded into a temporary data store in order for it to be cleaned up and made consistent. These checks can be quite complex, and identify

> **GUIDELINE 3.2**   Do not execute consistency checks until all the data sources have been loaded into the temporary data store.

consistency issues when integrating data from a number of data sources. In addition, as data changes over time, errors become apparent that have gone unnoticed because the day-to-day discrepancies were too small to detect.

For example, let us take the case in a telco where we amalgamate a customer details database with a customer events database: that is, a database containing a snapshot of all current subscribers, with a database storing all customer transactions.

If 50 customers no longer appear in the customer details database week on week, we would expect to find 50 customer events representing the cancellation of those subscriptions. If this information does not appear in the customer events area of the data warehouse, the user can quite rightly expect this to be a significant inconsistency.

In practice, the likelihood of this error occurring can be quite high, because the two source systems have significantly overlapping data sets. The data warehouse probably is the first time that consistency issues between the two separate systems become apparent. Put another way, if two source systems have overlapping data sets, the effort required to clean them both up will be much higher than twice the effort it takes to clean one up.

> **GUIDELINE 3.3** Expect the effort required to clean up the source systems to increase exponentially with the number of overlapping data sources.

In addition, the process must be capable of fully automatic running: that is, it has the intelligence to report errors in the load and move on, and/or request human intervention. Care should be taken when designing the load process to ensure that the error recovery is an integral part of the design.

For instance, it is very common to discover records during the load process that appear to be incomplete, or contain incorrect values. The load process must have a strategy (which is capable of being fully automated) for dealing with these cases, in order not to prejudice the availability of the data warehouse.

This requirement is more complex in situations where the data warehouse has to be available 24 hours a day, 7 days per week. Realistically, the load process will take a reasonable amount of elapsed time to complete. The only way that the data warehouse can be kept up and running is to perform all the load operations in the temporary data store, and publish the information when ready. This can be achieved using table partitions that extend the size of the existing tables in the data warehouse.

3.4.4 COPY MANAGEMENT TOOLS AND DATA CLEANUP

As we can see, most of the required consistency checks are complex. Most copy management tools do not have the capability of applying these checks directly. Specifically, a number of products that claim to have this facility implement it by allowing users to code the logic in either SQL, stored procedures, or their own programming language. What this means is that a substantial amount of development time is spent just implementing this logic.

This problem leads us to recommend that you investigate the cost–benefit of using a copy management tool, prior to making the purchasing decision. If the source systems do not overlap much, and the consistency checks are simplistic, a copy management tool will cut down the coding effort required. If this is not the case, a copy management tool may not add sufficient value to justify purchase.

3.5 CLEAN AND TRANSFORM DATA

This is the system process that takes the loaded data and structures it for query performance, and for minimizing operational costs.

There are in essence a small number of steps within the process:

1 Clean and transform the loaded data into a structure that speeds up queries.
2 Partition the data in order to speed up queries, optimize hardware performance, and simplify the management of the data warehouse.
3 Create aggregations to speed up the common queries.

3.5.1 CLEAN AND TRANSFORM THE DATA

Data needs to be cleaned and checked in the following ways:

- Make sure data is consistent within itself.
- Make sure that data is consistent with other data within the same source.
- Make sure data is consistent with data in the other source systems.
- Make sure data is consistent with the information already in the warehouse.

Make sure data is consistent within itself

When you take a row of data and examine it, the contents of the row must make sense. Errors at this point are mainly to do with errors in the source systems. Typical checks are for nonsensical phone numbers, addresses, counts, and so on.

Make sure that data is consistent with other data within the same source

When you examine the data against other tables within the same source, the data must make sense. For example, check for the existence of the stock-keeping unit (SKU)/customer/service specified in the transaction, by comparing it with the list of valid SKUs/customers/services.

Make sure data is consistent with data in the other source systems

This is when you examine a record and compare it with a similar record in a different source system. For example, reconciling a customer record with a copy in a customer database and a copy in a customer events database. These checks are the most complex, and are likely to result in the application of complex business rules to resolve any discrepancies.

For example, the business must be able to determine which version of the customer record is more accurate. This determination has to be coded in logic that is automatically executed whenever these discrepancies are spotted.

Make sure data is consistent with the information already in the warehouse

This is when we ensure that any data being loaded does not contradict the information already within the data warehouse. In some cases, the changes could be valid – for example, updating information about the product hierarchy – but the changes need to be controlled carefully, so as not to render meaningless any of the existing information already in the data warehouse.

For example, if we compared the existing customer list with a previous version already in the data warehouse, we would expect inconsistencies to be rationalized by specific customer events. If the events don't exist, we need to determine whether event or customer transactions are missing.

> **GUIDELINE 3.4** Always assume that the amount of effort required to clean up data sources is substantially greater than you would expect.

3.5.2 TRANSFORMING INTO EFFECTIVE STRUCTURES

Once the data has been cleaned, the next task within the clean-and-transform process is to convert the source data in the temporary data store into a structure that is designed to balance query performance and operational cost. The techniques applied to the data to convert it into a form that is suitable for long-term storage are discussed in Chapter 4. Every data warehouse solution will use these techniques to varying degrees; the precise mix will vary depending on the specific business requirements.

Information in the data warehouse must be structured to support the performance requirement from the business, and also to minimize the ongoing operational cost. These requirements essentially pull the design in opposite directions, prompting you either to structure to improve query performance, or to structure to minimize operational management.

3.6 BACKUP AND ARCHIVE PROCESS

As in operational systems, the data within the data warehouse is backed up regularly in order to ensure that the data warehouse can always be recovered from data loss, software failure or hardware failure. Backup and recovery strategies are discussed in detail in Chapter 14.

In archiving, older data is removed from the system in a format that allows it to be quickly restored if required. For example, in a retail sales analysis data warehouse there may be a requirement to keep data for 3 years, with the latest 6 months being kept online. In this sort of scenario there is often a requirement to be able to do month-on-month comparisons for this year and last year. This will require some months of data to be temporarily restored from archive.

It is common to archive data as a flat file extract, where the file is in a format that allows the data to be fast-loaded directly into the relevant fact and dimension tables. One issue that needs to be addressed is the fact that as the data warehouse evolves, the reference data, the structure of the fact data and of any related information may change. To ensure that a restored archive is valid, you may need to extract all related data and structures as well.

3.7 QUERY MANAGEMENT PROCESS

The query management process is the system process that manages the queries and speeds them up by directing queries to the most effective data source. This process must also ensure that all the system resources are used in the most effective way, usually by scheduling the execution of queries. The query management process may also be required to monitor the actual query profiles. This information would then be used by the warehouse management process to determine which aggregations to generate.

Unlike the other system processes, query management does not generally operate during the regular load of information into the data warehouse. This process operates at all times that the data warehouse is made available to end users. As such, there are no major consecutive steps within this process; rather, there are a set of facilities that are constantly in operation.

3.7.1 DIRECTING QUERIES

Data warehouses that contain summary data potentially provide a number of distinct data sources to respond to a specific query. These are the detailed information itself, and any number of aggregations that satisfy the query's information need.

For example, in a retail sales analysis data warehouse, if a user asks the system to "Report on sales of baked beans across Marin County, California, over the past 2 weeks," this query would be satisfied by scanning any of the following tables:

- all the detailed information over the past 2 weeks, filtering in all baked beans transactions for Marin County;
- 2 weeks' worth of weekly summary tables of product by store across the week;

- a bi-weekly summary table of product by region (Marin County is an example of region);
- a bi-weekly summary table of product group by store (baked beans is a product group).

Any of these tables will return the correct result. However, the scan performance will vary quite substantially between each table, because the volumes that have to be read differ quite substantially. The query management process determines which table delivers the answer most effectively, by calculating which table would satisfy the query in the shortest space of time.

Database optimizers are not capable of applying this logic, because it requires a change to the structure of the original query. The determination of which tables to be scanned and which columns to access forms part of the query structure. The optimizer can only work within the bounds of a specific query.

3.7.2 MAXIMIZING SYSTEM RESOURCES

Regardless of the processing power available to run the data warehouse, it is all too possible that a single large query can soak up all system resources, affecting the performance of the entire system. These so called "queries from hell" tend to be the ones that either scan the entirety of detailed information, or are constructed inappropriately and perform repetitive scanning of a large table.

The query management process must ensure that no single query can affect the overall system performance.

3.7.3 QUERY CAPTURE

As users become used to the facilities provided by a data warehouse, they will change the kinds of queries they ask. This is inevitable and should be encouraged, because it indicates that users are exploiting the information content of the data warehouse. This implies that query profiles change on a regular basis over the life of a data warehouse, and the original user query requirements may be nothing more than a starting point. Bearing in mind that summary tables are structured around a defined query profile, if the profile changes, the summary tables need to change as well.

In order to accurately monitor and understand what the new query profiles are, it can be very effective to capture the physical queries that are being executed. At various points in time, such as the end of the week, these queries can be analyzed to determine the new query profiles, and the resulting impact on summary tables. This analysis can be manual or automatic. The mechanism is less significant than the fact that the process has to occur. Query capture is typically part of the query management process.

CHAPTER 4

Process architecture

4.1 INTRODUCTION

Chapter 3 described the major processes that constitute a data warehouse. The aim of this chapter is to outline a complete data warehouse architecture that encompasses these processes. Table 4.1 maps the processes described in Chapter 3 to the system managers shown in Figure 4.1. The nature and constitution of each of these system managers are expanded in the following sections.

It is important to note that Figure 4.1 is an architecture and not a solution. The complexity of each manager will vary from data warehouse to data warehouse. What is important is that the functionality detailed for each manager, in the sections that follow, be present somewhere in the solution. Each manager may consist of a mixture of bespoke and off-the-shelf software.

Table 4.1 Mapping processes to systems.

Process	Function	System manager
Extract and load	Extracts and loads the data, performing simple transformations before and during load	Load manager
Clean and transform data	Transforms and manages the data	Warehouse manager
Backup and archive	Backs up and archives the data warehouse	Warehouse manager
Query management	Directs and manages queries	Query manager

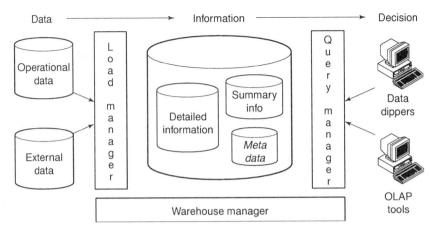

Figure 4.1   Architecture for a data warehouse.

4.2   LOAD MANAGER

The load manager is the system component that performs all the operations necessary to support the extract and load process. This system may be constructed using a combination of off-the-shelf tools, bespoke coding, C programs and shell scripts.

The size and complexity of the load manager will vary between specific solutions from data warehouse to data warehouse but, as an indication, the larger the degree of overlap between source systems, the larger the load manager will be. However, it is worth noting that third-party tools will probably contribute a maximum of 20–25% of the total system functionality.

The bulk of the effort to develop a load manager should be planned within the first production phase. Although the entire system does not have to be built, a significant proportion of the functionality should be provided in the first phase. The precise estimates for effort to develop load managers are covered in Appendix A.

4.2.1   LOAD MANAGER ARCHITECTURE

The architecture of a load manager (Figure 4.2) is such that it performs the following operations:

1   Extract the data from the source systems.
2   Fast-load the extracted data into a temporary data store.
3   Perform simple transformations into a structure similar to the one in the data warehouse.

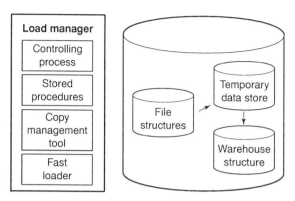

Figure 4.2 Load manager architecture.

Each of these functions has to operate automatically, and recover from any errors it encounters, to a very large extent with no human intervention. This is because this process tends to run overnight at the close of the business day. In a situation where the load manager encounters a major error, it may be necessary for it to flag that human intervention is required. A system that automatically pages system operators/DBAs is fairly typical.

The third-party components that come into play are listed in Table 4.2.

4.2.2 EXTRACT DATA FROM SOURCE

In order to get hold of the source data it has to be transferred from source systems, and made available to the data warehouse. Unless logistics prevent you from doing this, we suggest that the ASCII files are FTPd across the LAN. On the basis that there is sufficient capacity in the LAN to allow this to happen efficiently, this mechanism is probably the most effective way of getting hold of the data.

Current gateway technology operates too slowly to compete with the use of FTP and database load technology. This may change in the future, but given that gateways operate on an SQL basis, it is unlikely that they will ever better the performance of the recommended mechanisms.

Table 4.2 Tools that implement load manager tasks.

Task	Tool
Fast load	Database fast-load facility
Simple transformation	Copy management tool
Complex checking	Stored procedures or C/C++
Job control	UNIX shell scripts and source systems

4.2.3 FAST LOAD

Data should be loaded into the warehouse in the fastest possible time, in order to minimize the total load window. This becomes critical as the number of data sources increases, and the time window shrinks.

The speed at which the data is processed into the warehouse is affected by the kind of transformations that are taking place. In practice, it is more effective to load the data into a relational database prior to applying transformations and checks. This is because most database vendors have very performant facilities to fast-load data from ASCII flat files.

Gateway technology tends to be inappropriate, because gateways tend not to be performant when large data volumes are involved. This technology may be appropriate where the data volumes to be loaded are small, but in practice we have never seen a situation where they have fitted the bill.

Utilities to fast-load data into databases tend to have limited facilities to transform the data at the same time. These facilities usually bypass the SQL layer of the database software, and thus SQL transformations are not possible.

4.2.4 SIMPLE TRANSFORMATION

Before or during the load there will be an opportunity to perform simple transformations on the data. At this point, the purpose of the exercise is to blitz through all the transformations that do not require complex logic, or the use of relational set operators. Once this has been completed, we shall be in a position to start performing the complex consistency checks.

For example, if we were loading EPOS sales transactions into a retail sales analysis data warehouse, we would be performing the following steps:

1 Strip out all columns that are not required within the warehouse (discussed in detail later).
2 Convert all values to the required data types; typically, one would expect differences in data types (length, type, style for dates and numerics) between the EPOS transaction and the data warehouse requirement.

4.3 WAREHOUSE MANAGER

The warehouse manager is the system component that performs all the operations necessary to support the warehouse management process. This system is typically constructed using a combination of third-party systems management software, bespoke coding, C programs and shell scripts.

As with the load manager, the size and complexity of the warehouse manager will vary between specific solutions. Unlike the load manager, the complexity of the warehouse manager is driven by the extent to which the operational management of the data warehouse has been automated.

Third-party tools will probably contribute a maximum of 40% of the total system, with the bulk of the contribution from systems management tools for automated backup/recovery/archiving. It is also possible to procure systems-monitoring tools geared toward tuning data warehouses.

The bulk of the warehouse manager is developed in later development phases. Typically, the bare minimum functional content is implemented in the first build phase, because the focus of that phase is sorting out the data load. The precise estimates for effort to develop warehouse managers are covered in Appendix A.

4.3.1   WAREHOUSE MANAGER ARCHITECTURE

The architecture of a warehouse manager (Figure 4.3) is such that it performs the following operations:

1   Analyze the data to perform consistency and referential integrity checks.
2   Transform and merge the source data in the temporary data store into the published data warehouse.
3   Create indexes, business views, partition views, business synonyms against the base data.
4   Generate denormalizations if appropriate.
5   Generate any new aggregations that may be required.
6   Update all existing aggregations.
7   Back up incrementally or totally the data within the data warehouse.
8   Archive data that has reached the end of its capture life.

In some cases, the warehouse manager also analyzes query profiles to determine which indexes and aggregations are appropriate.

As with the load manager, each of these functions has to operate to a very large extent with no human intervention. In a situation where the warehouse manager

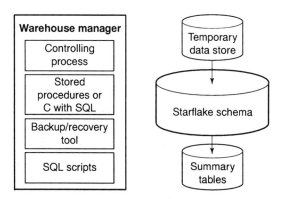

Figure 4.3   Architecture of a warehouse manager.

Table 4.3 Tools that implement warehouse manager tasks.

Task	Tool
Transform into data warehouse	Stored procedures or C/C++
Create indexes, etc.	Stored procedures or C/C++
Generate star schemas	Stored procedures or C/C++
Generate and update aggregations	Stored procedures or C/C++
Backup and archive	Systems management tools
Job control	UNIX shell scripts and C/C++
Query profile analysis	Data-warehouse-specific analysis tools, e.g. MetaCube

encounters a major error, it may be necessary for it to flag that human intervention is required. As before, a system that automatically pages system operators/DBAs is fairly typical.

The components that come into play are listed in Table 4.3.

Using temporary destination tables

Once the data is in temporary tables, we can begin performing the simple conversions to start getting it into shape. The next step is to create a set of tables identical to the destination tables in the data warehouse. For example, if there exists a highly partitioned sales transactions table in the data warehouse, we should create one of those partitions at this point. This allows us to start populating the database in a form that fits the data warehouse requirement.

Because we are about to execute a substantial number of consistency checks at this point, data should not be loaded into the warehouse until it has been cleaned up. If a consistency check fails, then that particular item of data needs to be set aside in a temporary table till later. Although all relational databases provide some form of rollback, in practice it is easier to load data into a temporary area, clean it up, and then publish it to the data warehouse.

On the basis that we have used temporary tables identical to the destination tables, it becomes a simple exercise to publish data to the data warehouse. This can be achieved either by a simple copy operation or, even better, by reassigning the temporary table to become a partition of the destination table.

GUIDELINE 4.1 Do not load data directly into the data warehouse tables until it has been cleaned up. Use temporary tables that emulate the structures within the data warehouse.

GUIDELINE 4.2 Consider partitioning the fact table on the basis of the refresh cycle. For example, if data is loaded on a weekly basis, consider using weekly partitions. Small partitions can be amalgamated into larger partitions on a regular basis: at month end, for example.

4.3.2   COMPLEX TRANSFORMATIONS

At this point, we have a populated set of temporary tables that match the destination tables in the data warehouse. These tables have been populated with the source data, but still without any of the complex transformations that need to take place. The data may not be consistent with itself or with other data in the data warehouse.

Before we can reconcile detailed transactions, we have to ensure that the basis of comparison is the same: that is, the reference information is identical. If this is not the case, we may find that a can of beans today has a different stock-keeping unit (SKU) from the one used yesterday.

In order to avoid this situation, we have to reconcile data in the order in which it makes sense. In practice, this means we start by reconciling the key reference items, and then work our way outwards to related reference items, before addressing the base transaction. This is harder than it sounds, because many of the entities are interrelated to a point where it becomes difficult to decide how to prise them apart.

4.3.3   TRANSFORM INTO A STARFLAKE SCHEMA

Once source data is in the temporary data store and has been cleaned up, the warehouse manager can then transform it into a form suitable for decision support queries. The data is transformed into a form in which the bulk of the factual data lies in the center, surrounded by the reference (dimension) data. Three variations on this theme are commonly used: star schemas, snowflake schemas, and starflake schemas. They are discussed in detail in Chapter 5.

4.3.4   CREATE INDEXES AND VIEWS

At this point, the warehouse manager has to create indexes against the information in the fact or dimension tables. One would expect the index creation time to be significant, even if we need only to create an index against a fact table partition. Because of this, most relational technologies have facilities to create indexes in parallel, distributing the load across the hardware and significantly reducing the elapsed time.

The overhead of inserting a row into a table and indexes can be far higher with a large number of rows than the overhead of re-creating the indexes once the rows have been inserted. Therefore it is often more effective to drop all indexes against tables prior to inserting large numbers of rows. Fact data that tends to have a large amount of data inserted on a daily basis is a prime candidate for dropping indexes before the data load. This method will be

> **GUIDELINE 4.3** Consider dropping all indexes against the fact table partition subject to the load, prior to inserting data into the table. Create the indexes in parallel once data has been loaded.

more effective unless the partition that is being loaded to already contains a substantial amount of data.

Dimension data tends to change or be added to in far smaller volumes than fact data, so unless the dimension is being changed wholesale, retain existing indexes on the dimension tables.

In order to fool user access tools into thinking that the fact table partitions are one large table, at this point in the process the warehouse manager creates views that combine a number of partitions into a single fact table. We would suggest that you create a few views, corresponding to meaningful periods of time within the business.

For example, if we have adopted a monthly partitioning strategy for a Sales Fact table, we could consider creating:

- a view across the last quarter;
- a view across the last six months;
- views corresponding to financial quarters for the business;
- a view across all the partitions – that is, making it look like a single sales table.

There is an overhead for querying through a view, because it is executed whenever a query accesses a view. As long as the number of partitions is not excessive, the system should be able to absorb the overhead.

> **GUIDELINE 4.4** Do not create views that combine large numbers of fact table partitions, because the impact on query performance is substantial.

4.3.5 GENERATE THE SUMMARIES

Once the source data is loaded and structured for access in the data warehouse, the warehouse manager has to create a set of aggregations to speed up query performance. These aggregations operate on the basis that most queries select a subset of data from a particular dimension, for example ladies wear department, and/or aggregate values within a dimension, such as sales last week, sales across the company, and sales across the customer base.

Summaries are generated automatically by the warehouse manager: that is, no human intervention should be required because it is repetitive, and must be executed every time data is loaded. The actual generation of the summaries is achieved through the use of embedded SQL in either stored procedures or C programs, typically using a command sequence such as:

```
create table {...}
as select {...}
from {...}
where {...}
```

This command can create the table in parallel – that is, making full use of system resources – substantially reducing the total elapsed time.

Using metadata

It will be necessary to keep changing the summaries that are produced to match the query profiles at each point in time. If we had to modify the warehouse manager every time we wished to add a new summary or change an existing one, the system would be perpetually in flux.

Metadata can be used to address this issue, by data-driving the generation of summaries. Within the database itself, we store descriptions of the summary tables we require in terms of facts and dimensions (see Chapter 5).

Using query statistics

The warehouse manager has a number of areas of responsibility. One of these areas is maintaining the responsiveness of the system even when the query profiles change over time. This can be achieved by gathering statistics on the queries being physically executed against the data warehouse, and deducing the appropriate summaries to speed up common queries.

Query statistics can be collected by the query manager as it intercepts any query hitting the database. In fact, some relational databases provide facilities to do this as a matter of course. If this information is available, the warehouse manager can be extended to:

1   Convert the SQL queries into star queries (that is, queries that exploit starflake schemas).
2   Analyze the star queries in terms of the facts being used, dimensions being used, level of aggregation, and conditions being applied.
3   Decide how many queries share the same facts and dimensions, and a superset of the conditions.
4   Pick the top $\{n\}$ and determine whether appropriate summaries exist.
5   If they do, do nothing.
6   If they don't, add definitions to summary table metadata.
7   For all remaining summary table definitions that don't match the query profiles, remove from the metadata tables and then remove the associated summary tables; this will clean up summaries that are no longer required.

This process ensures that only relevant summaries are retained by the system on an ongoing basis. New summaries are created to match changing query profiles, and summaries that speed up popular queries are maintained.

This analysis process should run periodically: for example, every weekend. In addition, the metadata should store manual overrides, which allows the system to retain summaries geared toward satisfying specific needs, such as the queries frequently run by senior executives.

4.4   QUERY MANAGER

The query manager is the system component that performs all the operations necessary to support the query management process. This system is typically constructed using a combination of user access tools, specialist data warehousing monitoring tools, native database facilities, bespoke coding, C programs, and shell scripts.

As with the load manager, the size and complexity of the query manager will vary between specific solutions. Unlike the load manager, the complexity of the query manager is driven by the extent to which the facilities are provided by user access tools or native database facilities.

Practically all the query manager is built in later development phases. Typically, the query manager is designed in the first build phase, once the database and user access tool technologies have been determined. The precise estimates for effort to design the query manager are covered in Appendix A.

4.4.I   QUERY MANAGER ARCHITECTURE

The architecture of a query manager (Figure 4.4) is such that it performs the following operations:

1   Direct queries to the appropriate table(s).
2   Schedule the execution of user queries.

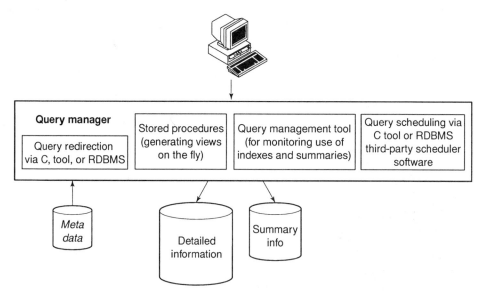

Figure 4.4   Query manager architecture.

Table 4.4 Tools that implement query manager tasks.

Task	Tool
Direct queries to the appropriate table	User access tools, stored procedures or C/C++
Schedule the execution of user queries	Stored procedures or C/C++, native database facilities, user access tools, or third-party scheduler software

In some cases, the query manager also stores query profiles to allow the warehouse manager to determine which indexes and aggregations are appropriate.

The components that come into play are listed in Table 4.4.

4.5   DETAILED INFORMATION

This is the area of the data warehouse that stores all the detailed information in the starflake schema. In many cases, all the detailed information is not held online the whole time, but aggregated to the next level of detail, and the detailed information is then offloaded into tape archive. On a rolling basis, detailed information is loaded into the warehouse to supplement the aggregated data.

For example, it is very common to store transactions at the level of product by store by day for retail sales analysis data warehouses. This information is perfectly appropriate for analyzing actual sales against projected sales. What this degree of detail does not provide is basket analysis: that is, because all transactions for a particular product in a particular store are aggregated to the whole of the day, it is not possible to examine a specific customer basket transaction, or analyze components within the basket.

In order to determine what degree of detail is required, ask yourself the question: What activities within the business process require detailed, individual transactions? This should indicate what user requirements exist to store base transactions.

If the business requirement for detailed information is weak or very specific, it may be possible to satisfy it by storing a rolling three-month detailed history. This could satisfy the need to have some detailed information, without too much impact on the storage requirements.

This style of operation is assisted if all historical changes to dimension data are stored online: that is, dimension tables

> **GUIDELINE 4.5**   Determine what business activities require detailed transaction information, in order to determine the level at which to retain detailed information in the data warehouse.

> **GUIDELINE 4.6**   If detailed information is being stored offline to minimize the disk storage requirements, make sure that the data has been extracted, cleaned up, and transformed into a starflake schema prior to archiving it.

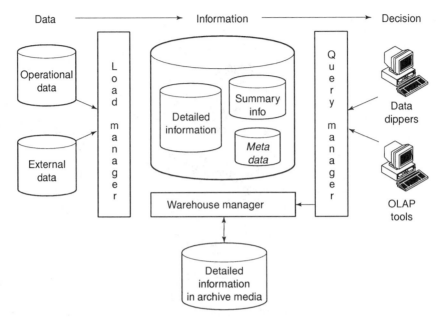

Figure 4.5 A data warehouse with detailed data in archived storage.

are stored with values as they vary over time. This simplifies the process under which a section of detailed data is loaded directly into the data warehouse, and the data can be made immediately available without any further work.

In effect, the architecture for this type of data warehouse is more complex, and looks like that shown in Figure 4.5.

Bear in mind that in order to implement a rolling strategy, historical data will have to be loaded into the data warehouse at regular intervals. For example, data that corresponds to the same period for preceding years, such as "summer sales" for the past five years. This is because queries will tend to focus on year-on-year comparisons; so a rolling strategy must roll data on and off to match year-on-year periods.

4.5.1 DATA WAREHOUSE SCHEMAS

Star schemas are database schemas that structure the data to exploit a typical decision support query. When you examine the components of a typical query, you will find that most queries tend to share similarities:

- The queries examine a set of factual transactions: for example, EPOS transactions, or customer events.
- Queries analyze facts in a variety of ways; by aggregating them on different bases, and/or by grouping them in a variety of ways: for example, EPOS transactions by week, or by store.

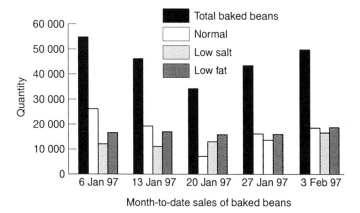

Month-to-date sales of baked beans

Figure 4.6 Typical sales analysis query.

We see that the information to support these queries can be described in a way that places the large volume of factual transactions in the center, and the way in which it is analyzed surrounds it. For example, a retail sales analysis data warehouse (Figure 4.7) may have:

- EPOS transactions in the center, with all the detailed information that has been audited;
- all the information about *products*, such as SKU codes, product hierarchy (section, departments, business units), to one side;
- all the information about *stores*, such as store id, store hierarchy (regions, localities, etc.), store space plans, to one side;
- all the *time* dimension to one side, such as day, week, month, year;
- all the information about *customers*, such as loyalty card numbers, addresses, income and spend, to one side;
- all the information about *suppliers*, such as supplier id, location, discount levels, to one side.

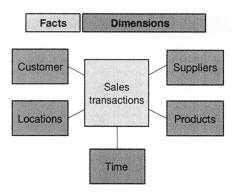

Figure 4.7 A retail sales analysis star schema.

The central factual transaction table is called the **fact table**. The surrounding reference tables are called the **dimension tables**. Put them together and you can imagine them representing a star: hence the name, **star schema**.

The idea is that most queries first of all analyze the data surrounding the fact table to minimize the number of rows that need to be scanned. This is done in order to address the greatest performance hit on queries: specifically, the volume of data that has to be read off disk. By reducing the total volume of data to be scanned, we reduce the time it takes to execute a query.

Because, in most cases, the highest volume of data will be the fact data, it makes sense to reduce it by minimizing the actual set of rows that need to be extracted from the fact table. This is done by ensuring that the much smaller dimension tables are used first, in order to filter out the transactions in the fact table that are not required to satisfy the query.

In relational technology, this is achieved by joining the dimension tables prior to joining to the fact table. If the Cartesian product of the dimensions is not produced before scanning the fact table, the performance of the query will be disappointing.

4.5.2   FACT DATA

Within a data warehouse, information is split into two distinct classes: the basic **factual information** event, and the **reference information** that is used to analyze the factual event (Table 4.5). The factual event contains the physical information that describes a factual event that occurred within the business, examples of which are EPOS transactions, phone calls, and banking transactions against accounts.

Fact data is the major database component of a typical data warehouse, constituting around 70% of the total database volume. Detailed aggregations are treated as fact data as opposed to reference data: for example, a sales table capturing product SKU, by store, by day.

Because the fact data within the data warehouse will form the bulk of the database volume, it is critical that the structure of this information is defined accurately right from the start. Put another way, if the user requirements are not defined to a point where the detailed content of the fact tables is well understood, it will be inevitable that this information will have to be restructured in the future. We recommend you try to avoid this at all costs, because applying even simple restructuring to a large database table is time consuming and costly.

Table 4.5   Characteristics of fact versus reference data.

Fact	Reference
Millions or billions of rows	Tens to a few million rows
Multiple foreign keys	One primary key
Numeric	Textual descriptions
Don't change	Frequently modified

Defining the detailed content of the fact tables should be one of the major focus areas within the *business requirements* stage. Fact data represents a physical transaction that has occurred at a point in time, and as such is unlikely to change on an ongoing basis during the life

> **GUIDELINE 4.7** Ensure that the fact table definitions are accurate prior to starting the bulk population of these tables.

of the data warehouse. The definition of its factual content should be reasonably well understood by the business. If this is not the case in your particular situation, it may be necessary to revisit the architecture of the data warehouse once the information is well defined, to ensure that the architectural assumptions and decisions are still valid.

4.5.3 DIMENSION DATA

Dimension data is the information that is used to analyze the elemental transaction. Examples are a product hierarchy, customers, significant time periods, and all information about locations, such as stores, store groupings, and space plans. The structuring of information in this way makes it possible to optimize query performance.

Dimension data differs from fact data in a number of ways, which affect the way we treat it. First of all, dimension data will change over time. This may be due to changes in the business, such as regional reorganization. Other items like product codes change all the time.

Because it is inevitable that there will be a requirement to change dimension data, it is very effective to structure the dimensions with a view to allowing rapid change. More to the point, it is probably very likely that the initial understanding of dimension data is weak.

Our advice is: don't worry about it. Dimension data in a star schema or snowflake schema is designed to minimize the cost of change, and is typically very low-volume data (that is, under 5 GB), so we suggest you operate on the basis that the requirements will be constantly refined over the life of the data warehouse.

> **GUIDELINE 4.8** Expect dimension information to change on a regular basis, and structure the data warehouse to minimize the cost of change. Specifically, isolate dimension from fact data, and carefully select foreign keys for fact tables.

4.5.4 PARTITIONING DATA

In anything other than a small data warehouse the fact data tables can become extremely large. This poses a number of problems for management, backup, and daily processing. These problems are avoided by partitioning each fact table into multiple separate partitions. To do this effectively you need to ask the question: How active is the information? If we consider how many organizations use decision support data, we shall expect to find that a majority of the questions are asked concerning recent history. This represents the period of time that is relevant to the decision-making process.

This statement is particularly true for canned queries, where the queries themselves tend to be fairly run-of-the-mill and repetitive. For example, in a retail operation, a merchant will tend to ask the same kinds of question day in, day out, such as queries relating the sales performance of the products that he or she is responsible for.

Queries of this nature tend to operate on the basis of year-on-year comparisons of sales transactions over a relatively short historical period. Week to date, month to date, six weeks to date, are all examples of time periods relevant to the business. Bear in mind that the actual week/month will vary at the start of a new week/month. In other words, at the start of every week, "week to date" represents a different set of data.

Data warehouses exploit this style of behavior by partitioning the large-volume data in order to minimize the set of data that needs to be scanned (Figure 4.8). In essence, a partitioning strategy is created to favor queries that scan only recent history, such as week to date and month to date. For example, this can be achieved by segmenting the volume transactions into weekly or monthly partitions. When a query needs to scan data relating to month-to-date figures, it is directed to the table that contains only month-to-date figures. If one week's worth of data is required, that information is read from the appropriate monthly table. If the query requires quarter-to-date figures, the appropriate monthly tables are read in conjunction in order to provide the necessary information.

This technique allows the database to minimize the volume of data scanned, without the overhead of having to use an index. This results in substantially improved query performance, for minimal additional operational overhead. Indexed access is used, but only to supplement the broad subsetting achieved through the partitioning strategy.

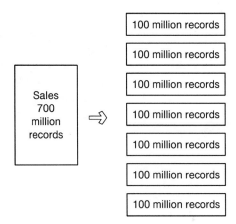

Figure 4.8 An example of a partitioned retail sales fact table.

A word of warning: partitioning the fact data is effective only up to a point. We recommend that you do not partition to a degree where you would end up with large numbers of physical tables, counting each partition as a separate table. A good sanity check is to ensure that the data warehouse does not contain more than 500 tables at any time. Realistically, that is the maximum number of tables that can be managed by a single database administrator.

> **GUIDELINE 4.9** Consider partitioning the large fact tables on the basis of time periods relevant to the business.

> **GUIDELINE 4.10** Avoid a design solution that requires greater than 500 tables in total, unless the business is prepared to accept a much higher operational management cost.

Reasons for partitioning

First let us be clear what we mean by partitioning. Partitioning is where a single logical entity is partitioned into multiple sub-entities. So, in our example, the fact table in the data warehouse could be partitioned into multiple smaller subtables or partitions. How this actually manifests itself within the RDBMS varies from vendor to vendor.

Some vendors have direct support for objects that are partitioned tables; others implement partitioning by having each partition as a separate table and using a union-all view to create the logical table. Each vendor's implementation has its own strengths and weaknesses and can be evaluated along with the other features of the RDBMS.

Whatever method is used to support partitioning, you will need to use it in the data warehouse. The aim in the following pages is to explain why.

Partitioning for ease of management

One reason for partitioning the fact table is to assist the management of the data. A fact table in a data warehouse can grow to many hundreds of gigabytes or even beyond a terabyte in size. This is too large a unit to manage as a single entity: hence the need to partition.

Think of the consequences of having to add a column to a single table of a terabyte in size. What about the problems of archiving data? If you have to extract a month's worth of data from a terabyte table, you will be forced to do a delete, which will not be as efficient as just dropping the oldest monthly partition. Creating and maintaining indexes on an object of that size would be a nightmare. It would be impossible to drop and re-create the index for a data load; this means loading with the indexes in place, which will almost certainly be a slower process.

Partitioning to assist backup/recovery

Backup recovery also forces you toward a partitioning approach. Backing up or restoring a table containing all online fact data would be a major undertaking. The trick with backup in an environment of this size is to cut down on the amount that has to be backed up on a regular basis. If you have not partitioned, you will be forced to back up the whole fact table. The one exception to this is if the RDBMS allows incremental backup, but even then the whole table may have to be scanned to determine which blocks had changed.

> **GUIDELINE 4.11** Mark all inactive partitions read-only, and then back up twice. Further backups are not required, because the data will not change.

To cut down on the backup size all partitions other than the current partition can be marked read-only, and put into a state where they cannot be modified. Then they can be backed up once, although preferably twice, and forgotten. This means that only the current partition is required to be backed up.

Partitioning for performance

Star schemas are a good way of minimizing the set of data that needs to be scanned to respond to a query. Query performance can still be substantially improved, by completely removing large parts of the fact table from the possible set of data that needs to be scanned. This is achieved by breaking up the fact table into partitions, and then requiring the query to scan the partitions that are relevant.

There are challenges to overcome when using this kind of partitioning. How will the query know which partition to access? What about accessing a number of table partitions representing a longer time period? Good performance partitioning strategies are to:

- partition at the appropriate level of detail;
- create user-friendly synonyms;
- create views that amalgamate a number of (possibly all) partitions, to provide a composite view.

Hardware partitioning

A number of hardware architectures operate on the basis that information on disk is not directly accessible to the CPU that is executing the query. All shared-nothing hardware architectures operate on this basis: the information is accessible via a black box called an interconnect, which requests the data to be fetched from a remote disk. Hardware architectures are covered in detail in Chapter 11.

Data warehouses delivered on shared-nothing architectures work best if the data is partitioned to optimize the accessibility of data by each processing node. This type of partitioning may be critical to avoid situations where most queries bottleneck on a single processing node. If this happens, it could be the case that the large proportion of the processing power is idle, waiting for the bottleneck processing node to finish servicing all requests for data.

Any way you cut it you are forced to partition for management and other reasons. So to paraphrase a famous saying: *Partition or die!*

4.6   SUMMARY INFORMATION

This is the area of the data warehouse that stores all the predefined aggregations generated by the warehouse manager. This area of the data warehouse should be treated as transient. It will change on an ongoing basis in order to respond to changing query profiles.

Summary information is essentially a replication of detailed information already in the data warehouse. The implication of this is that summary data:

- exists to speed up the performance of common queries;
- increases operational costs;
- may have to be updated every time new data is loaded into the data warehouse;
- may not have to be backed up, because it can be generated fresh from the detailed information.

In practice, it may not be possible to adopt the last point, because the time taken to completely re-create the aggregations and their indexes may be prohibitive.

Optimal query performance is typically achieved through a high level of aggregations of the base data, which ensures that the bulk of the processing for a query is completed in advance. For example, in a retail sales analysis data warehouse, a common query is to examine corporate sales results year-to-date for each product or product group, such as "How many canned vegetables did we sell across the country year-to-date?" This query requires that each basket transaction is aggregated on a product level across the country, which would require scanning all transactions representing year-to-date sales.

In practice, it is far more effective to predetermine that this type of query is asked often, and create a summary table that contains the aggregated sales across the country, for each product year-to-date. The query can then be executed against this summary table, and needs only aggregate individual product results to create a product group result: that is, all canned vegetable products are aggregated to create a sales figure against canned vegetables year-to-date. If you require a response against all canned vegetables supplied by a particular manufacturer, a possibly different set of products is aggregated.

Because the size of data that needs to be scanned is an order of magnitude smaller, this results in an order of magnitude improvement to the performance of the query. On the negative side, there is an increase in the operational management cost, for creating and updating the summary table on a daily basis.

In some instances, we have seen solutions that have relied on huge numbers of aggregations. These solutions have tended to be barely manageable in the short term, but as query profiles change, and data volumes increase, the tendency is to add new aggregations to address the new query performance issues. Bearing in mind that the load window is also shrinking because of the higher data

> **GUIDELINE 4.12**   Avoid creating a solution that requires more than (approximately) 200 centralized summary tables on an ongoing basis.

volumes, this can result in a situation that spirals out of control. To this end, it is more effective if the solution limits the use of summary tables. At least you'll have a chance of keeping them under control.

This is not to say that an absolute figure of 200 summaries in the data warehouse should ever be considered; rather, avoid using more than around that number. In practice, this number tends to be a good balance. This point is discussed in more detail further on.

> **GUIDELINE 4.13**   Inform users that summary tables accessed infrequently will be dropped on an ongoing basis.

As users grow accustomed to using the data warehouse, it may become inevitable that summary data will exist outside the control of the data warehouse. On many occasions we have seen data warehouses where users have created their own aggregations for very specific reasons. For example, a retail merchant may have created a sales aggregation for a set of stores that he or she uses as an indicator of what is happening in the real world.

These types of aggregation should not be prevented; rather, they should be controlled by providing a reasonable limit to the amount of personal database space given to each user, which is budgeted for in data warehouse sizing calculations. Finally, the user should be made to understand that the management of these summaries is outside the control of the data warehouse.

> **GUIDELINE 4.14**   Allow space in all sizing calculations for a reasonable number of specific aggregations owned by each user, and impose these user limits within the database.

4.7   METADATA

This is the area within the data warehouse that stores all the metadata definitions used by all processes within the data warehouse. Metadata is data about data: it is like a card index describing how information is structured within the data warehouse.

Metadata is used for a variety of purposes. As part of the extraction and load process, metadata is used to map data sources to the common view of information within the data warehouse. As part of the warehouse management process, metadata is used to automate the production of summary tables. As part of the query management process, metadata is used to direct a query to the most appropriate data source.

The structure of metadata will differ between each process, because the focus is different. This means multiple copies of metadata are held within the data warehouse. In addition, most third-party tools for copy management and user access use their own versions of metadata. Specifically, copy management tools use metadata to understand the mapping rules that they need to apply in order to convert source data into a common form. User access tools use metadata to understand how to build up a query. What this means is that the management of metadata within the data warehouse as a whole is a task that should not be underestimated.

4.8   DATA MARTING

Data marts come in many shapes and sizes, and may be created for a variety of reasons. Data marts share a number of attributes, and the design issues that need to be addressed generally apply to all of them.

Essentially, a data mart is a subset of the information content of a data warehouse that is stored in its own database, summarized or in detail. The data in the data mart may or may not be sourced from an enterprise data warehouse: that is, it could have been directly populated from source data. Data marts are very popular in some solutions, where the choice of user access tool requires the use of data marting.

Data marting can improve query performance, simply by reducing the volume of data that needs to be scanned to satisfy a query. In practice, the trick in designing data marts is in making sure that no query requires data not contained within its mart. As designers, if we are almost certain that queries can be satisfied wholly within the data mart, we shall be able to substantially improve the performance of those queries.

Typically, data marts are created along functional or departmental lines, in order to exploit a natural break of the data. This is essential in order to reduce the likelihood of queries requiring data outside the mart.

For example, let us consider a telco marketing function, which is split into three major regional centers: East Coast, West Coast, and Midwest. We are designing a customer-profiling data warehouse to assist the marketing function, and we need to determine whether a data-marting strategy is appropriate. Initially, we would have to investigate whether any marketing executives in each region query information about other regions: that is, do any queries get executed that refer to data outside the region?

If the answer is "no," there could be a strong case to split the content of the data warehouse into three separate data marts, one per region (Figure 4.9). This means that the East Coast marketing function would have customer profiling data about customers within the East Coast, the West Coast marketing function would have customer profiling data about customers within the West Coast, and so on. This design would allow us to improve query performance threefold, by reducing by two-thirds the amount of data being scanned per query.

This technique can even be used when there are a small number of queries that need data across all regions. In real life, it is highly likely that senior executives within each region will wish to examine corporate customer trends. Data marts may still be appropriate if the queries that require corporate trends can be satisfied using summary tables.

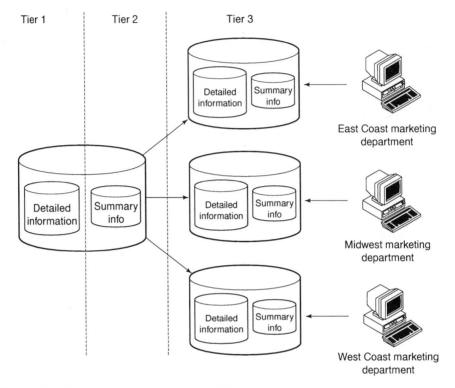

Figure 4.9 Three tiers of decision support information.

Put another way, data subsets are marted into local databases in order to satisfy the majority of the queries, while an additional set of summary tables are replicated into each mart in order to provide a composite view.

A number of user access tools, particularly specialist data mining or multidimensional analysis tools, may require their own internal database structures in order to function. In practice, these tools create their own data mart designed to support their specific functionality, but the issues they encounter are common to most of these tools.

For example, it is very difficult in practice to operationally support more than a handful of data marts. You will find that the time it takes to populate the mart as part of the load process can be significant. If you try to populate more than a handful, you will probably run out of time window. This is a common problem when using a number of user access tools that require data marts.

This problem will exist even if the organization is using multiple copies of a single data-marting user access tool. The issue is the lead time to populate the data in the mart; even if the data structures are identical, the source data will be different and will take time to load.

4.8.1   CAN WE DO WITHOUT AN ENTERPRISE DATA

WAREHOUSE?

One of the reasons for creating a data warehouse is to ensure that information is wholly consistent, regardless of how it is analyzed. Enterprise data can be cleaned and made wholly consistent only if it is compared and resolved against all the information that it is related to. Put another way, it is very difficult to make data consistent with information that may not be present in the same database.

For example, let us consider a situation where a retail outlet has a number of regional product sales data marts, where each data mart contains regional data. In practice, it is more difficult to ensure that the corporate information is consistent across all the data marts, rather than a situation where the corporate information is in the same database. Specifically, we may be able to ensure that the fact data within each region is consistent within itself, but would we be certain that any aggregations at a corporate level are consistent?

We may also find it difficult to ensure that dimension data is wholly consistent, even if it is replicated across all data marts. In real life, dimension data gets out of step, as different users seek to extend their own data marts to allow them to analyze the data in different ways. Even if we start off with identical versions, our experience has been that the data will change over a period of time.

The best solution is where an enterprise data warehouse is used to capture and clean all the data, and ensure consistency. Where appropriate, subsets or summaries are then marted into other databases: if necessary, transforming into different database structures along the way.

This solution is effective because the data is held centrally while all the cleanup and consistency checking is taking place, which simplifies the load process. Subsets or aggregations can then be marted into other databases in order to allow the user access tools to operate on the new data.

> **GUIDELINE 4.15**   Populate data marts via an enterprise data warehouse in order to clean up the data and ensure consistency.

Once the data is in the data mart, it may be possible to avoid retaining the data within the data warehouse, meaning that the data warehouse is used only as a transient storage area. This can provide substantial savings in hardware costs, because the data volume that must be supported will never exceed the peak volume of data captured within a single load process.

If you are considering adopting this strategy, make sure that there is no requirement to analyze detailed information that spans the scope of each data mart. If those requirements exist, investigate whether they can be satisfied by aggregated data.

We recommend that you design for data retention within the data warehouse, if there is any likelihood that a requirement may exist in the future to scan detailed information that spans data marts. Once the appropriate design is in place, it is possible to store the daily detailed fact data in archived form. If and when a

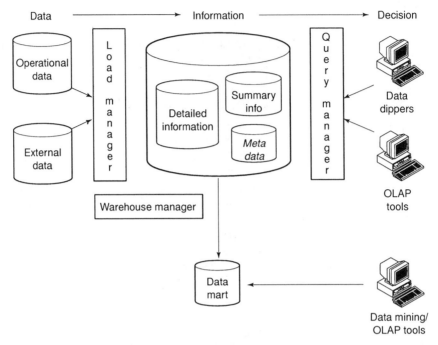

Figure 4.10 A data marting strategy for user access tools.

requirement to analyze detailed data is identified, the archived data will be ready to be loaded directly into the data warehouse.

This strategy is the best compromise, in that you do not need to invest in larger hardware facilities until the requirement is identified. Once this happens, there is minimal cost involved in back-loading the archived data.

GUIDELINE 4.16 When using data marts, always design the data warehouse for full data retention, and consider storing data in archive until a requirement to analyze all the detailed data exists.

4.9 TO SUMMARIZE . . .

We have seen how the major components of a client–server data warehouse support the functional requirements of the system processes described in Chapter 3. The underlying theme is that we must architect a solution that can change over time to keep up with changing business requirements.

As we have discussed, this is achieved by designing flexibility into the data warehouse, and designing around the business processes rather than the business requirements: that is, designing for the way the information will be used, rather than for satisfying specific user requirements. User requirements may change constantly, but the business processes will change far less frequently.

Specifically, starflake schemas are designed to satisfy any query in a performant way, without knowing what the query will be in advance. Summary tables are created to match query profiles that exist at a specific point in time, and will be changed to match any new query profiles. Above all, design for the long-term solution, and don't get caught up in the detailed issues.

PART THREE

Design

3

CHAPTER 5

Database schema

5.1   INTRODUCTION

The objective of this chapter is to explain how to design appropriate data warehouse schemas from the logical requirements model. This is a critical part of designing a data warehouse, and should be covered in detail by any technical architect or database designer. By the end of this chapter, you should be able to design the database component of a data warehouse.

This chapter assumes that you have read Part Two: Data Warehouse Architecture, even if you are not a technical architect. The design guidelines within this chapter follow on from the broad architectural concepts covered in the previous chapters.

5.1.1   PROCESS

This design activity is defined in the *build the vision* stage, after the *requirements analysis* and *technical blueprint* stages are complete (Figure 5.1). All design decisions should be based on the system architecture defined in the technical blueprint. However, this is an iterative process, and it is possible to encounter a number of design issues that may not be resolved without changing the technical blueprint. For this reason the technical architect needs to remain involved in the design process.

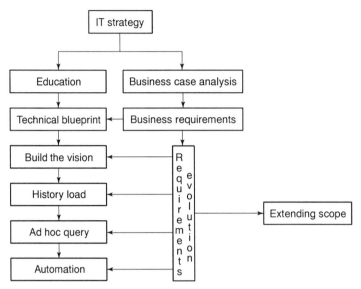

Figure 5.1 Stages in the process.

5.2 STARFLAKE SCHEMAS

One of the key questions to be answered by the database designer is: How can we design a database that allows unknown queries to be performant? This question encapsulates the differences between designing for a data warehouse and designing for an OLTP system. In a data warehouse you design to support the *business process* rather than specific query requirements. In order to achieve this, you must understand the way in which the information within the data warehouse will be used.

In a decision support data warehouse, a large number of queries tend to ask questions about an essential fact, analyzed in a variety of ways. For example, reporting on:

- the average number of sales of beans per store over the last month (Figure 5.2);
- the ten most popular cable programs over the past week (Figure 5.3);
- projected sales of Christmas puddings compared with the actual stock level (Figure 5.4);
- the top 20% spending customers over the past quarter;
- all customers with an average balance in excess of $25 000 month-to-date.

Each of these queries has one thing in common: they are all based on factual data. The content and presentation of the results may differ between examples, but the factual and transactional nature of the underlying data is the same.

Fact data possesses some characteristics that allow the underlying information in the database to be structured. Facts are transactions that have occurred at some

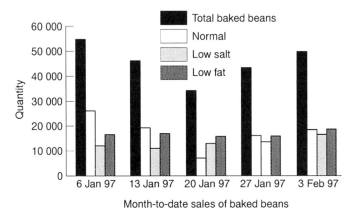

Figure 5.2 Sales of baked beans.

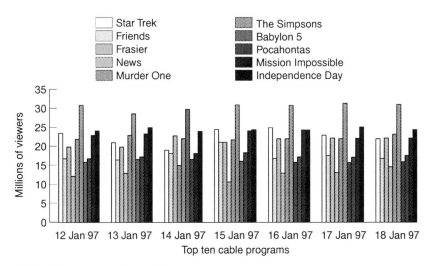

Figure 5.3 Ten most popular cable programs.

point in the past, and are unlikely to change in the future. Facts can be analyzed in different ways by cross-referencing the facts with different reference information. For example, we can look at sales by store, sales by region, or sales by product. In a data warehouse facts also tend to have few attributes, because there are no operational data overheads. For each of the examples described, the attributes of the fact could be as listed in Table 5.1.

One of the major technical challenges within the design of a data warehouse is to structure a solution that will be effective for a reasonable period of time (three to five years). This implies that the data should not have to be restructured when the business changes or the query profiles change. This is an important point, because in

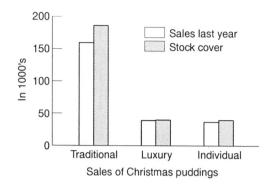

Figure 5.4 Sales and stock coverage of Christmas puddings, week-to-date.

Table 5.1 Example attributes of fact tables.

Requirement	Fact	Attributes
Sales of beans	EPOS transaction	Quantity sold Product identifier (SKU) Store identifier Date and time Revenue achieved
Cable programs	Cable pay-per-view transaction	Customer identifier Cable channel watched Program watched Date and time Duration Household identifier
Customer spend	Loyalty card transaction	Customer identifier Store identifier Transaction value Date and time
Customer account balance	Account transactions	Customer identifier Account number Type of transaction Amount of transaction Destination account number

more traditional applications it is not uncommon to restructure the underlying data in order to address query performance issues.

Star schemas exploit the fact that the content of factual transactions is unlikely to change, regardless of how it is analyzed. Because the bulk of information in the data warehouse is represented within the facts, it can be very effective to treat fact

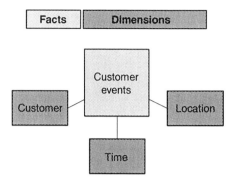

Figure 5.5 A customer-profiling star schema, of the style used in retail banking.

data as primarily read-only data, and reference data as data that will change over a period of time.

If and when reference information needs to change, the underlying fact data should not have to change as well.

Star schemas are physical database structures that store the factual data in the "center," surrounded by the reference (dimension) data (Figure 5.5) The different types of star schemas are discussed in Section 5.6.

> **GUIDELINE 5.1** Avoid embedding reference data into the fact table, because that will protect the fact data from restructuring when the reference data changes.

5.3   IDENTIFYING FACTS AND DIMENSIONS

When we are presented with a large entity model, it can be difficult to determine which entities should become fact tables within the database. Making this determination is not always straightforward. However, because the query performance of the data warehouse will hinge on the correct identification of fact tables, it is very important to get this right.

We have found the following steps and guidelines effective in determining facts from dimensions.

1   Look for the elemental transactions within the business process. This identifies entities that are candidates to be fact tables.
2   Determine the key dimensions that apply to each fact. This identifies entities that are candidates to be dimension tables.
3   Check that a candidate fact is not actually a dimension with embedded facts.
4   Check that a candidate dimension is not actually a fact table within the context of the decision support requirement.

If steps 3 and 4 change the assignment of an entity (fact to dimension or vice versa), the process should be restarted from step 2, in order to ensure that the correct dimensions are identified (Figure 5.6).

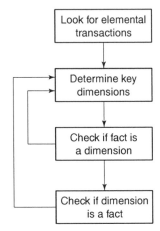

Figure 5.6 Flowchart of fact table identification process.

5.3.1 STEP 1: LOOK FOR THE ELEMENTAL

TRANSACTIONS WITHIN THE BUSINESS PROCESS

The first step in the process of identifying fact tables is where we examine the business (enterprise model), and identify the transactions that may be of interest. They will tend to be transactions that describe events fundamental to the business: for example, the record of phone calls made by a telco customer, or the record of account transactions made by a banking customer. A series of examples are included in Table 5.2, in order to highlight the entities that tend to become facts within a star schema.

For each potential fact ask yourself the question: Is this information operated on by the business processes? Don't assume that the transactions within the operational systems are the sole candidates for fact data transactions. Or, put another way, the degree of detail within the operational system may have more to do with operational constraints or legacy issues, than with the reporting requirements.

For example, let us consider sales information within a small retail operation. It may be the case that the only information being captured at the retail outlets is product sales per day per store. This information at first glance may look like candidate fact data.

> **GUIDELINE 5.2** Always determine the factual transactions being used by the business processes. Don't assume that the reported transactions within an operational system are fact data.

If we examine the business processes more closely, we have to ask whether they operate with daily aggregations of sales, or with actual basket transactions. Obviously, the answer in this case is that the business processes operate on the

Table 5.2 Candidate fact tables for each industry/business requirement.

Sector and business	Fact table
Retail	
Sales	EPOS transaction
Shrinkage analysis	Stock movement and stock position
Retail Banking	
Customer profiling	Customer events
Customer profitability	Account transactions
Insurance	
Product profitability	Customer claims and receipts
Telco	
Call analysis	Call event
Customer analysis	Customer events (e.g. installation, disconnection, payment)

transaction: that is, the sale of individual items. Sales may be being captured or reported at the aggregated level, purely because the operational infrastructure to capture basket transactions is not in place.

The appropriate design would be one in which the basket transaction is identified as the fact, and the daily aggregation is structured to be a large summary table. The load process should be designed to create the daily aggregation from the current operational system, with hooks in place to generate it automatically from basket data once the basket information becomes available.

When considering the level of detail at which to capture transactions, you should design to store the most detailed transaction within the data warehouse, and accept that, initially, only aggregated data may be available. This process will protect the data warehouse design from major restructuring, should the business move to capturing detailed transactions in the future.

5.3.2 STEP 2: DETERMINE THE KEY DIMENSIONS THAT APPLY

TO EACH FACT

The next step is to identify the main dimensions for each candidate fact table. This can be achieved by looking at the logical model, and finding out which entities are associated with the entity representing the fact table. The challenge here is to focus on the key dimension entities, which may not be the ones directly associated to the fact entity.

For example, in a retail banking data warehouse, we may have identified account transactions as a candidate fact table, but the relationship between account transaction and customer may be indirect, such as through the account entity, and the account-owned-by relationship.

At this point, ask yourself what the focus of the business analysis will be. Is it likely to be "analyze account transactions by account," or "analyze how customers use our services"? If the focus of the data warehouse is analysis of customer usage, then structure the dimension to represent the customer entity, not the account entity. By all means, store the relationship between each customer and the accounts they own, but key into the account transaction by the customer identifier.

> **GUIDELINE 5.3** Structure key dimensions to represent the key focal points of analysis of factual transactions. Use the relationships to the fact table within the logical model as a starting point, but restructure where necessary to ensure that you can apply the most suitable foreign keys.

In the same way, apply the same test to each dimension, making sure that what you end up with is a candidate fact table with key dimensions.

5.3.3   STEP 3: CHECK THAT A CANDIDATE FACT IS NOT ACTUALLY A DIMENSION TABLE WITH DENORMALIZED FACTS

We now need to start checking that the candidate facts and dimensions are what they appear to be. In some instances, entities within the operational system can appear to be candidate fact tables, and can turn out to combine both facts and dimensions.

When the source entity represents information held in a single table within the operational system, it is very likely that the table has been designed to capture every operational detail about the source entity. In other words, consider whether the attributes of the table were designed around operational data entry requirements: for instance, data entered in a single screen. It may be the case that some of the attributes turn out to be denormalized facts embedded in the dimension entity.

For example, let us consider the `address` entity in a cable company customer profiling data warehouse. The address table within the source system could contain:

- the street address and zip code;
- dates that stipulate
    - when cables were laid past the address,
    - when a salesperson visited the household at that address,
    - when the household was connected to the cable service,
    - when promotional material was posted to that address,
    - when a subscription service to each product was initiated,
    - when a subscription was cancelled,
    - etc.

If we examine the attributes in detail, we can see that a substantial proportion of the attributes represent dates on which various events took place. In practice, the `address` entity could be mistaken for a fact table, because users will query

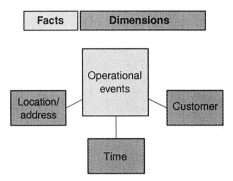

Figure 5.7 Star schema for addresses and operational events.

information about addresses. However, a more accurate representation would be to say that a number of operational events occurred at specific addresses (Figure 5.7).

This means that each date value within an existing row within the address table becomes a row in a new fact table. This will affect the database sizing calculations, but the benefits are that users can now easily query operational events. For example:

- Report on the number of connections quarter-to-date.
- Report the time lag between cables being laid and subscriptions being taken out.
- Report the conversion rate between promotional events and subscriptions.

In addition, we should avoid designs that require fact data to be updated as new transactions take place. Read-only fact tables allow us to make use of very specific database facilities that improve manageability and query performance.

> **GUIDELINE 5.4** Look for denormalized dimensions within candidate fact tables. It may be the case that the candidate fact table is a dimension containing repeating groups of factual attributes.

> **GUIDELINE 5.5** Design fact tables to store rows that will not vary over time. If the entity appears to vary over time, consider creating a fact table that represents events that change the status of that entity.

5.3.4 STEP 4: CHECK THAT A CANDIDATE DIMENSION IS NOT ACTUALLY A FACT TABLE

The final step is to ensure that none of the key dimensions are in themselves fact tables. This is a common problem, because there are a number of entities that at first glance can appear to be dimensions or facts. Table 5.3 contains examples of two entities that could be either facts or dimensions.

Table 5.3 Entities that tend to be structured as either facts or dimensions.

Entity	Fact or dimension	Condition
Customer	Fact	In a customer profiling or customer marketing database, it is probably a fact table
	Dimension	In a retail sales analysis data warehouse, or any other variation where the customer is not the focus, but is used as the basis for analysis
Promotions	Fact	In a promotions analysis data warehouse, promotions are the focal transactions, so are probably facts
	Dimension	In all other situations

As we can see, a guiding principle is to consider what the focal point of analysis is within the business. If the business requirement is geared toward analysis of the entity that is currently a candidate dimension, chances are that it is probably more appropriate to make it a fact table. A good sanity check to assist within this process is to ask yourself the question: By how many other dimensions can I view this entity? If the answer is more than three, it's probably a fact.

For example, in a retail sales analysis data warehouse, when you look at the promotion dimension, ask yourself:

- Can I view promotions by time?
- Can I view promotions by product?
- Can I view promotions by store?
- Can I view promotions by supplier?

If the answer to all four questions is "yes," promotions are fact tables in your situation.

5.4   DESIGNING FACT TABLES

A common question is: How big should a fact table be? In reality, there is no practical, inherent limit to the size of a fact table, given the appropriate hardware architecture, database design, and budget.

For a database designer, the challenge is to recommend a good balance between the value of information made available and the cost of producing it. Factors such as the level of detail stored, and the retention period, need to be weighed against the cost of achieving them. Data warehouses have been built with fact tables larger than 1 TB. This does not mean that we should aim to create large fact tables; rather, the technological limit of database size can generally be ignored, allowing us to focus on the real business requirement.

This section will explain the techniques and mechanisms used in order to reduce the size of fact tables without compromising the value of the data inherent within them. Most solutions will require a number of these techniques to be applied to the database design – unless the business has deep pockets.

Consider the following options:

1 Understand the significant historical period for each supported function. This makes sure that we are only storing in the fact table the period of history that is required for the analyses required.
2 Determine whether statistical samples on subsets of data will satisfy the requirement for detailed data. This impacts on sizing and costs.
3 Select the appropriate columns of data to hold (just because it is there, is no reason to hold it).
4 Minimize the column sizes within the fact table.
5 Determine the use of intelligent or non-intelligent keys.
6 Design time into the fact table. This determines how time should be stored, and the impact of each option on the query performance and size of the fact table.
7 Partition the fact table. This breaks up the fact table into a number of smaller tables in order to aid manageability. This is covered in detail in Chapter 6.

5.4.1 OPTION 1: IDENTIFY THE SIGNIFICANT HISTORICAL

PERIOD FOR EACH SUPPORTED FUNCTION

Initial business requirements on the retention period of data always tend to be aggressive and simplistic: aggressive, in that the requirement may suggest a long retention period, say five to ten years; simplistic, in that the sizing will invariably start off on the premise of storing the most detailed transactions (such as account transactions, telephone call records, or EPOS transactions).

Most data warehouses use a mix of detailed data and different degrees of aggregation to obtain the best balance between query performance and volume of data. In order to achieve the appropriate balance, we need to determine what degree of detail is necessary for each business function.

Broadly speaking, this activity examines the various requirements to retain detailed data, and pins down the minimum retention period for each one. Some guidelines are provided here to assist with this process.

Decision making within organizational functions is effective only if it deals with business patterns that transpired within a reasonable time period.

> **GUIDELINE 5.6** Identify the historical period significant to decision-making processes, and the degree of detail required. This could substantially reduce the volume of data required within the fact table.

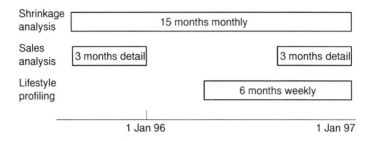

Figure 5.8 Graph showing retention period of functions within a retail operation.

For example, if a retail merchant is trying to decide whether adequate volumes of a product exist to cover next week's sales, it may be inappropriate to examine information on the buying patterns of that product for the last six months. It is more likely that that merchant requires the buying patterns month-to-date and for the equivalent period a year ago.

The significant retention period will vary between each function, but should be readily definable by examining the business processes implemented by those functions. We recommend that you draw a retention period graph showing the period and detail necessary for each business function (Figure 5.8). Once you have the chart, it becomes easier to understand what degree of detail is necessary for what period of time.

After completing this process, you often find that the requirement for detailed information is more limited than was originally requested. Profiles similar to that in Figure 5.8 are not uncommon. Needless to say, as far as the business user is concerned, any switch between detailed data and daily aggregated data should be seamless.

5.4.2 OPTION 2: DETERMINE WHETHER SAMPLES WILL SATISFY

THE REQUIREMENT FOR DETAILED DATA

An alternative mechanism to reduce the volume of detailed information is to retain a sample of detailed information, and daily or weekly aggregations for the rest. As long as the sample is representative (for example, 15% of the total data spread demographically, for customer profiling data warehouses), this should meet the analysis needs.

This technique may be appropriate in situations where the analysis requirement is to analyze trends: that is, analyze detailed information in a variety of ways, in order to spot patterns of behavior

> **GUIDELINE 5.7** If the business requirement does not require all the detailed fact data, consider storing samples and aggregate the rest.

between various conditions. The analysis can be carried out effectively using a subset of the full data. Conversely, sampling may be inappropriate to satisfy campaign management, because it would require access to all the detailed customer records to build up direct mailing lists.

For example, let's take the case of a retail sales analysis data warehouse, where basket transactions are stored for a 15% spread of stores across the US. Although this information can be used to spot trends across all stores, it might be inappropriate to determine product-buying patterns in all stores located at seaside resorts as the statistical sample may be too low.

5.4.3   OPTION 3: SELECT THE APPROPRIATE COLUMNS

The next option is to remove all columns from the fact entity that are not required to answer decision support questions. This will typically be status fields, intermediate values, aggregations, and bits of reference data replicated for query performance.

A good technique is to examine each attribute in turn, and ask yourself the following questions:

- Is this column telling me something about a factual event?
- Is there any other place I can derive this data from?
- Does the business care, or is it for control purposes only?

This should allow you to remove columns that are not required to satisfy the user requirements. Derived data and aggregated data can be produced more effectively on the fly, rather than by storing the aggregated value in the fact table. Performance improvements to queries should be addressed by aggregations within summary tables, not base level tables.

> **GUIDELINE 5.8**   Do not store aggregated columns within fact tables. It is usually cheaper to aggregate the columns on the fly.

For example, in a sales analysis data warehouse, the columns that are typically required are:

- product reference, store reference, date of transaction, number sold (may or may not be a required aggregation), revenue achieved, and optionally,
- customer identifier, time of transaction, till at which the transaction took place, and teller/assistant that carried out the transaction.

The optional items are useful if the basket transaction is being analyzed by customer, for customer-profiling reasons. Till and teller information is used in order to analyze the effectiveness of specific tellers, or the relationship between levels of sales and the positions of tills within a store. The time when a transaction took place would be used in analyses of buying patterns over different periods of time within the day (for example, product peaking during rush hours/after business hours).

In a telco call analysis data warehouse, the columns that are typically required are:

- initiating phone number, destination phone number, date and time of transaction, tariff band, and duration of call.

5.4.4 OPTION 4: MINIMIZE THE COLUMN SIZES WITHIN THE FACT TABLE

Another option is to reduce the size of the row within the fact table. Because fact tables tend to be large because of the requirement to store large numbers of transactions, a small saving per row can have a significant effect on the total table size.

For example, if a fact table for a telco call analysis data warehouse contains 3.65 billion rows (that is, 2 million customers, with 2.5 transactions per day per customer, 2 year retention period), a saving of 10 bytes per row will save us:

$$10 \times 3.65 \text{ billion bytes}$$
$$= 33.99 \text{ GB}$$

This kind of saving is fairly typical in situations where the business requirement calls for large periods of detailed data. This is why care should be taken to consider the value of *every byte* that is designed into a large fact table.

> **GUIDELINE 5.9** Ensure that every byte in the column definitions within a large fact table is needed. Savings here will have a substantial effect on the size and complexity of the fact table.

5.4.5 OPTION 5: DETERMINE THE USE OF INTELLIGENT OR NON-INTELLIGENT KEYS

As with any relational system, foreign keys within a fact table can be structured in two ways:

- using intelligent keys, where each key represents the unique identifier for the item in the real world;
- using non-intelligent keys, where each unique key is generated automatically, and refers to the unique identifier of the item in the real world (Figure 5.9).

For example, in a retail sales analysis data warehouse, the foreign keys could be:

- product SKU, store identifier, and physical date;

or

- product code (which maps to SKU in the *product* dimension table);
- store code (which maps to store id in the *location* dimension table);
- date id (which maps to physical date in the *time* dimension table).

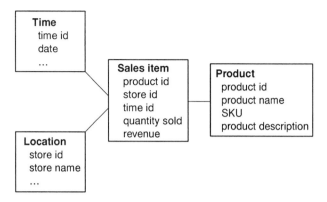

Figure 5.9 Star schema using non-intelligent keys in the fact table.

The use of intelligent keys provides some performance advantages. Specifically, in a situation where the query refers directly to the intelligent key, the query can be satisfied by the fact table alone, which means the dimension table need not be accessed – because the values we are filtering out are already in the same row – and so we avoid a database join.

If a query required the total sales of large diet cola bottles across the company last week, using intelligent keys the query would look like:

```
select sum(quantity_sold)
from sales_item
where SKU='236712'
and date_of_sale between ('17-JAN-97', '21-JAN-97');
```

as opposed to:

```
select sum(quantity_sold)
from sales_item s, product p, time t
where p.SKU='236712'
and t.date_of_sale between ('17-JAN-97', '21-JAN-97')
and p.id=s.product_id
and t.id=s.time_id;
```

As we can see, the first query makes no direct access to any of the dimension tables. This may improve query performance, by avoiding the need to scan and join the product, location, and time dimension tables.

The disadvantage of using intelligent keys is that if any of the unique item identifiers changes or is reassigned over the life of the data warehouse, the fact table will have to be updated to reflect the new identifiers. This exercise can be costly and time consuming, and should be avoided if at all possible.

> **GUIDELINE 5.10** Use non-intelligent keys in fact tables, unless you are certain that identifiers will not change during the lifetime of the data warehouse.

In practice, unless you are absolutely certain that the identifiers will not change or be reassigned in the future, it is safer to use non-intelligent keys. The performance loss of the query can be recovered by other means, such as pre-building appropriate summary tables. The one exception to guideline 5.10 is storing the time dimension, which is discussed next.

5.4.6 OPTION 6: DESIGN TIME INTO THE FACT TABLE

Time information can be stored in a number of ways within the fact table. In most cases, the most appropriate structure is quite different from the way in which the other dimensions are stored.

The starting point for the storage of time within the fact table is the use of a foreign key into a *time* dimension table. Actual physical dates are stored within the dimension itself.

Before we can start designing more effective storage structures, we have to determine whether the business requirement exists for the date of transaction information only, or for the date and time of transaction. This point will have a material effect on the data reduction strategies that we can apply.

For example, in a retail sales analysis data warehouse, we need to determine whether the business will ever need to analyze sales trends through the day, for example looking at the sale of a product during rush-hour. If the requirement to do that does not exist, we can apply options of encoding dates within the fact table.

Possible techniques are:

- storing the physical date,
- storing an offset from the inherent start of the table,
- storing a date range.

Storing the physical date

This option is very effective in situations where the business may require access to the time of transaction, not just the date. Physical dates within a relational database typically contain the time stamp within its structure, which can be ignored within queries if not required. However, the one argument for using non-intelligent keys within the fact table does not apply to dates, because the date specified is not going to be reassigned or changed in the future.

The cost of storing a physical date, as opposed to a unique reference to a time dimension table, is minimal compared with the query performance improvement. That statement holds true in all situations where the bulk of the queries are constrained by time, which is the expected case in all decision support analyses of historical data.

> **GUIDELINE 5.11** Use physical dates in fact tables, rather than foreign keys that reference rows in a *time* dimension table.

Storing an offset from the inherent start of the table

It is highly probable that the fact table is partitioned by time, usually in a unit of time that is meaningful to the business (week, month, quarter, etc.). When we consider storing time within the fact table, we can exploit the period inherent within the partitioned table itself, by referring to dates as offsets from the start date of the table.

For example, in a customer profiling data warehouse, if the fact table that stores customer events is partitioned on a monthly basis, an event that occurred on the 9th of the month can be represented as the number 8 from the inherent start (0 means no offset and therefore corresponds to day 1 of the month).

The advantage of this technique is that the storage costs of the date column are very low: in Figure 5.10 two bytes are large enough to store up to 31 numbers. In a similar vein, weekly table partitions would require only a single byte to store the date offset.

It is worth pointing out that the physical start date need not be stored anywhere, because it can be implied by the table name: for example, `sales_Jan_97`, or `customer_event_1997_week_6`.

The disadvantage of using this technique is that queries would have to be constructed to convert physical dates into date offsets. For example, if we wished to return the sum of all transactions that were completed on 9 January 1997, the query would look like:

```
select count(*)
from customer_events_Jan97
where date_of_event='9-Jan-97' - '1-Jan-97';
```

Note that the offset from the start would have to start from 0 for the first day, 1 for the second, 2 for the third, and so on.

This form of encoding may pose problems for a number of user access tools that generate SQL on the fly. In some cases, they may not be able to cope with these structures, because they don't conform to a simple star schema model. This issue can be addressed by creating a database view that applies the mathematical logic to the row:

> **GUIDELINE 5.12** Consider using date offsets from the implied start date of a fact table partition. If date offsets are used, create a view that looks like the logical table, by adding the offset to the start date.

SKU	Store	No. sold	Revenue	Date offset
6754987	CA_SF_67	8	24.6	6
9284374	CA_LA_32	7	15.75	6
6754778	MA_BO_2	3	1.8	7
7678163	NY_NY_45	1	5.65	10

Figure 5.10 Fact table using date offsets.

```
Create view customer_events_Jan_96
( )
as select { ... }, date_of_event - '1-Jan-97'
from { ... };
```

Storing a date range

If we consider the content of a fact table, it may be the case that the rows report on factual counts which do not vary substantially over time. Date ranges allow us to exploit this relationship, by inserting new records only when a factual count has changed.

For example, in the retail sector, many retailers have a product catalog that is far greater than the number of active products sold every day: that is, not every product will sell every day. The percentage of products sold compared with the product catalog can be as low as 10–15% of the total.

In a shrinkage analysis data warehouse, we can exploit this relationship by only inserting new stock position records every time the stock position is altered. At any point in time, if the stock position for a product has not changed today – that is, it is the same as yesterday's figure – the existing record is updated to reflect this fact. In practice, this is achieved by incrementing a date range within the row (Figure 5.11).

This technique can produce a significant saving in disk capacity and query performance, because it is directly related to the relative proportion of changed records to unchanged records. If changed records account for 15% of the total fact table, the use of date ranges will reduce the table to approximately 18% of its original size (we have added an additional column for the date range).

As with the previous code example, the structure of the query would have to change to take into account the date range. In effect, queries would have to be modified to query against a date range using a between statement.

Following on the shrinkage analysis example, if the user asks a question requiring the stock count of baked beans on 3 February 1997, the query would look like:

```
select sum(sp.stock_count)
from stock_position_fact_table sp, product_dimension p
where p.id = sp.p_id
and p.product_group='baked beans'
and '3-FEB-97' between(sp.start_date, sp.end_date);
```

SKU	Store	Position	Start date	End date
6754987	CA_SF_67	157	13 Jan 97	17 Jan 97
9284374	CA_LA_32	96	14 Jan 97	16 Jan 97
6754778	MA_BO_2	34	14 Jan 97	23 Jan 97
7678163	NY_NY_45	79	15 Jan 97	18 Jan 97

Figure 5.11 Stock position fact table with a date range.

A number of access tools may not be able to process fact tables in this format. In the same way as with storing an offset from an inherent start of the table, this can be addressed by creating a database view to make the fact table appear to have a row for every day within the date range. However, in this case the query itself would also have to change, with the between being replaced by an equals condition, as follows:

```
select sum(sp.stock_count)
from stock_position_view sv, product_dimension p
where p.id=sv.p_id
and p.product_group='baked beans'
and sv.date='3-FEB-97';
```

This view can utilize a time dimension table that has a row for every day of the year, for every year within the data warehouse. This table is joined against the date range in the fact table, in order to produce a Cartesian product. Access tools can then operate against the view in the normal way (Figure 5.12).

Unfortunately, the cost of creating the Cartesian product is very high, requiring significant processing power and temporary space. In effect, the portion of the original fact table required to satisfy the query must be re-created for every query. This means that the processing power to perform the expansion must be available, as well as enough temporary space to accommodate the Cartesian product.

Stock position

SKU	Store	Position	Start date	End date
6754987	CA_SF_67	157	13 Jan 97	17 Jan 97
9284374	CA_LA_32	96	14 Jan 97	16 Jan 97
6754778	MA_BO_2	34	14 Jan 97	23 Jan 97
7678163	NY_NY_45	79	15 Jan 97	18 Jan 97

Time

Date ID
13 Jan 97
14 Jan 97
15 Jan 97
16 Jan 97
17 Jan 97

Cartesian product

SKU	Store	Position	Date
6754987	CA_SF_67	157	13 Jan 97
6754897	CA_SF_67	157	14 Jan 97
6754897	CA_SF_67	157	15 Jan 97
6754897	CA_SF_67	157	16 Jan 97
6754897	CA_SF_67	157	17 Jan 97
9284374	CA_LA_32	96	14 Jan 97
9284374	CA_LA_32	96	15 Jan 97
9284374	CA_LA_32	96	16 Jan 97
..............(etc)...................			

Figure 5.12 View expanding a stock position fact table using date ranges, by joining against a time dimension.

In practice, this may be unacceptably high, and is probably not viable in normal circumstances. We recommend you consider the use of date ranges only if the access tools can cope directly with the structure, without requiring the generation of a Cartesian product.

A word of warning: if an access tool appears to operate directly with the data – that is, without using a combinatory view – check that it does not do the same thing internally. A number of access tools create internal data stores in order to execute queries, which are used as query caches. If the cache store is expanding the data on the fly, the same performance and capacity issues will apply.

> **GUIDELINE 5.13** Consider the use of date ranges in fact tables, where the access tool can cope directly with the structure. If used, make sure that no on-the-fly data expansion is occurring within the access tool.

5.4.7 OPTION 7: PARTITION THE FACT TABLE

This option is extremely detailed, and is covered separately in Chapter 6.

5.5 DESIGNING DIMENSION TABLES

This section will explain the considerations used in designing the dimension tables. These techniques should be applied after the fact tables have been designed, because it helps to know which fact tables exist.

Getting the design for the dimension tables wrong is not a major disaster. The volumes should be relatively small (probably below 5 GB in total), so restructuring costs will be small as long as the primary keys to the fact table(s) are not changed.

5.5.1 CREATING A STAR DIMENSION

Star dimensions speed up query performance by denormalizing reference information into a single table. Star dimensions rely on the perceived use of information by typical queries, where the bulk of the queries are likely to be analyzing facts by applying a number of constraints against a single dimension.

For example, in a retail sales analysis data warehouse, typical queries will analyze sales information by the product dimension. That is, the queries will tend to ask questions about:

- a particular product group, such as ladies' wear;
- attributes of products, such as size, color, style – 16″ collar shirts, or "white shirts," or "dress shirts."

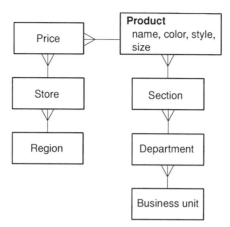

Figure 5.13 Entity model for product information.

Because, in all cases, the query constrains the set of products in a variety of ways, the query can be speeded up if all the constraining information is in the same table. In practice, this is achieved by denormalizing all the additional entities related to the product entity into a single product table (Figure 5.13).

For example, we would take all the product hierarchy information and denormalize it into the same row (that is, one column per level in the hierarchy). Attributes such as size, color, material, style, would be added to each row as well (Figure 5.14).

This technique works well in situations where there are a number of entities related to the key dimension entity, which are accessed often. There is a performance saving of not having to join additional tables to access those attributes.

This technique may not be appropriate in situations where the additional data is not accessed very often, because the overhead of scanning the expanded dimension table may not be offset by the gain in the query. If the bulk of queries don't access those columns, this technique will speed up a minority of queries by slowing down the majority.

Figure 5.14 Product dimension with denormalized attributes.

In order to retain a reasonable balance, insert the columns that are going to be accessed often, based on your understanding of how the information will be used. The star dimension table is generated from the snowflake data, so if you need to change the star dimension in future to add extra columns, it's easy to do. Note that deleting or modifying columns may have an effect on any existing canned queries, and they may have to be modified as well.

> **GUIDELINE 5.14** Denormalize entities accessed often into the star dimension table. All other entities should remain in the snowflake structure.

5.5.2 HIERARCHIES AND NETWORKS

It may not be possible to denormalize all entities into star dimensions. Specifically, all entities that are related through many-to-many relationships should not be denormalized into a star dimension: that is, it is not efficient to denormalize multiple values into a single row.

For example, many retailers use multiple product hierarchies to represent different product views. These could be:

- the product group hierarchies (e.g. business unit, sub-business unit, section, department, SKU);

and a number of hierarchies where each one represents:

- products sold by competitors;
- products supplied by a single, major supplier;
- products that are part of a single promotion (for example, Italian meals);
- specific uses within the business (for example, private hierarchies, products sold during Christmas).

In these situations, it is more effective to determine the hierarchy likely to be used by the largest numbers of queries. This hierarchy is then denormalized into the star dimension table. All queries that require the main product hierarchy should be directed to the star dimension; all other queries should use the snowflake.

For example, the most common hierarchy in the retail product dimension is likely to be the main product hierarchy. That is then denormalized into the star product table, in the same way as described in section 5.5.1. All other hierarchies are accessed through the snowflake.

This technique of finding the common route through hierarchies is effective when the route is unlikely to change in the future. Or, put another way, this technique is effective as long as the query profiles don't change to a point where a different hierarchy becomes the most popular one, or the hierarchy itself is unstable. If there exists a strong possibility that this may occur, it may be more cost-effective not to denormalize any of the hierarchies into the star dimension. This is because the cost of modifying any canned queries may be substantial if the first denormalized hierarchy is removed.

A good compromise is that you start off by denormalizing the most accessed hierarchy, and accept that if the query profiles change in the future, a set of columns representing the new hierarchy are *added* to the star dimension. As long as existing columns are not replaced, there should not be any impact on existing

> **GUIDELINE 5.15** If data in a dimension is networked, denormalize the most commonly accessed hierarchy into the star dimension. If the query profile changes in the future, add columns that denormalize the new (commonly accessed) hierarchy.

canned queries. The cost of updating tools that generate ad hoc queries should be minimal, as only their metadata definitions would need to be updated.

5.5.3 DIMENSIONS THAT VARY OVER TIME

In many cases, some (if not all) of the dimensions will vary over time. This is particularly true for dimensions that use hierarchies or networks to group basic concepts, because the business will probably change the way in which it categorizes the dimension over a period of time.

For example, in the retail sector, the product dimension typically contains a hierarchy used to categorize products into departments, sections, business units, and so on. As the business changes, it is standard practice to re-categorize these products. Tee-shirts could move from menswear into unisex; baked beans could move from canned foods to canned vegetables.

Depending on the business requirement, it may be necessary to support queries that compare facts within a grouping that exists at present, with the grouping that existed at a point of time in the past. These queries tend to be used to understand whether various business policies have been successful (referred to as "as is, as was" queries).

For example, take a case where a department store manager is investigating whether a policy of upgrading the quality of products in the menswear department was successful. In order to address that query, we must examine the revenue and profit generated by the menswear department to date, compared with a year ago.

In order to determine the revenue achieved by the menswear department, we have to sum the sales of all products in the department today compared with a year ago. Because the list of products in menswear will be different today compared with a year ago, two queries have to be executed, where each one looks for a different set of products comprising menswear.

If this requirement exists, it is necessary to store date ranges on the dimension table, which represents the dates in which the values within that row were valid. In other words, if there is a change to any of the values within the dimension, a new row should be *inserted*, rather than updating the values of the old row (the old row is updated in order to complete the date range). Adding a date range to the star dimension table is an effective way of supporting this requirement.

In the menswear example, the basic query structure would be:

```
select sum(s.revenue_achieved)
from sales_year_to_date s, product_dimension pd
where s.product_id = pd.id
and pd.department = 'Menswear'
and pd.end_date > 1-Jan-96
and pd.start_date < 31-DEC-96;
```

This query will extract all transactions for all products that were in the menswear department over any dates in 1996. The result of this query can then be compared against the result from a similar query that examines dates over 1997.

A minor variation on the theme is when the query needs to compare a significant event in the corporate calendar, year on year: for example, if the previous query were constrained to determine profitability in the menswear department during the summer sales. The dates for the summer sales event will vary year on year, so the start and end dates to be applied to the queries will vary. In these situations, we recommend that you store the date range for each event within the *time* dimension.

The previous query would change to:

```
select sum(s.revenue_achieved)
from sales_year_to_date s, product_dimension pd,
time_dimension td
where s.product_id = pd.id
and pd.department = 'Menswear'
and pd.end_date > td.start_date
and pd.start_date < td.end_date
and td.event_name = 'Summer Sales 1996';
```

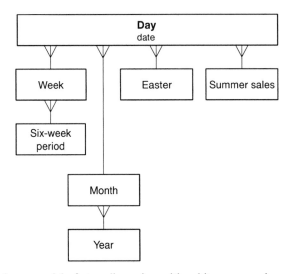

Figure 5.15   Schema model of *time* dimension with arbitrary groupings.

If the query requires more unusual dates – for example, queries against "the last Friday in every month" – we suggest it is addressed by joining the *product* dimension to a *time* dimension table that contains a row for every day of the year (for each year that is covered by the data warehouse).

Any arbitrary grouping of dates can then be supported by creating foreign keys against the set of days required. Avoid using the in statement in SQL, because it can substantially affect query performance (the in statement may cause the database to scan the table being joined, once for every value in the statement).

5.5.4 MANAGING LARGE DIMENSION TABLES

A large dimension table, particularly one that stores values as they change over time, may grow to a size where the table becomes too large to be treated as a dimension table within queries. This point is reached when the dimension table reaches a size similar to a partition of the fact table. Another indication to watch out for is when a full-table scan of the dimension table starts taking an appreciable amount of time.

> **GUIDELINE 5.16** If a dimension table grows to a size similar to a fact table partition, or scanning a dimension table absorbs a signifi- cant percentage of the available query time, consider partitioning the table horizontally and creating a combinatory view.

5.6 DESIGNING THE STARFLAKE SCHEMA

In the preceding sections, we have discussed how, in decision support data warehouses, the most appropriate database schemas tend to use a combination of denormalized star and normalized snowflake schemas. This combination of schema types is referred to as a **starflake schema**, because it contains elements of both concepts, plus a number of additional ideas (Figure 5.16).

To recap, detailed transactions are stored within a central fact table, which may be partitioned horizontally or vertically. In these cases, a series of combinatory database views is created in order to allow user access tools to treat the fact table partitions as a single, large table.

Also, key reference data is structured into a set of dimensions, which are referenced from the fact table. Each dimension is stored in a series of normalized tables (snowflake), with an additional denormalized star dimension table.

In real life, it may be very difficult to restructure all the entities within the enterprise model into a set of distinct dimensions. It is common to come across situations where there are a number of entities or relationships that span one or more dimensions. As we discussed in section 5.5.3, the time dimension is unique in that it almost always applies to most entities within the data warehouse.

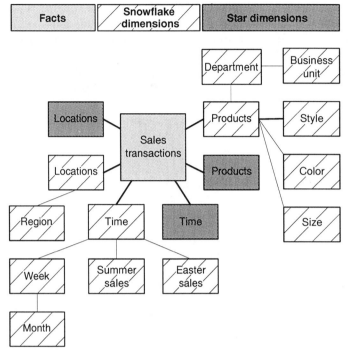

Figure 5.16 Database starflake schema.

For example, in the larger retail operations, it is common to find that stores may apply local pricing to products. So instead of accessing the product dimension in order to determine a product price, we must access the intersection of the product and store corresponding to price (Figure 5.17).

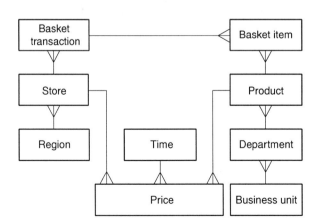

Figure 5.17 Product pricing by store entity model.

Starflake schemas accept that, in the real world, it can be easier and more effective to allow a degree of crossover between dimensions. A number of guidelines are provided here to make sure that you don't allow an entity or relationship to intersect dimensions unnecessarily.

- Intersecting entities should be relatively small. If they are large, check that they are not a separate dimension in themselves.
- Intersecting entities should be clearly understood within the business, and should satisfy a real information requirement.

You should expect the crossovers of the starflake schema to reduce over a period of time, once the system is operational. As requirements become better understood, it

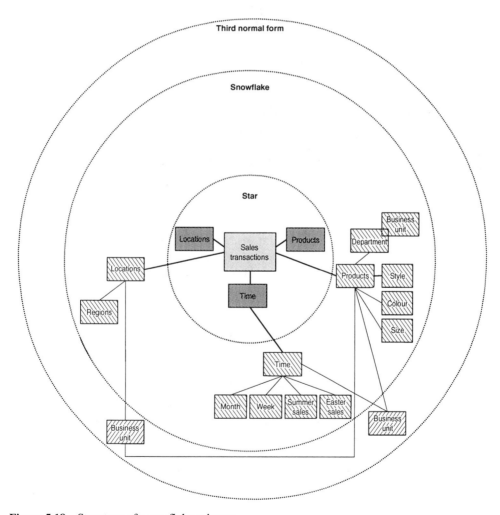

Figure 5.18 Structure of a starflake schema.

will become easier to structure the outlying entities into a more dimensional
basis. This area of the data warehousing
schema is the one where we would expect
the greatest amount of change over a
period of time.

Over the life of the data warehouse
the degree of change within a starflake
schema should vary as we move out of the
center. Fact tables should hardly change at all, key dimensions may change a little,
and outlying entities will probably change a lot.

This, unfortunately, is reality: so our advice is, don't spend too much time trying
to pin down the requirements that use the outlying entities. Expect change, and
accept that all you initially require is a first stab at the requirements.

5.7 QUERY REDIRECTION

Integral to the starflake schema are the techniques that direct a query to the most
appropriate source. These techniques direct queries to the most appropriate partition
of a fact table, or to the star or snowflake dimensions. This is done in order to
optimize the performance of the query, by minimizing the set of data that needs to be
scanned.

In order to operate the data warehouse using this technique, this logic needs to
be embedded into the query tools. This may not be supported by the chosen access
tools. In many cases, it becomes necessary to trick the access tools into thinking that
the various structures defined are in a form that they expect.

Within this section, we shall discuss the various database techniques that can be
used to trick access tools, and guidelines on the style of query that should be directed
to the various table structures in the starflake.

5.7.1 VIEWS AND SYNONYMS ON FACT TABLES

Fact table partitions should be combined in a number of ways, using database views.
The views should represent the significant periods of time within the business – that
is, the time periods that are going to be analyzed most often – for example, month to
date, quarter to date, six weeks to date, last year, this year, and so on.

Each of these views should union the various fact table partitions over the
required period. Try to keep the union statements as simple as possible – that is,
with no unnecessary selection predicates – because this query will be executed every
time the view is accessed.

Synonyms can be used to refer to table partitions in terms that the business will
recognize. For example, in monthly partitioned fact tables, each partition can be
referred to by the period of time it covers (using synonyms), such as `sales-Jan-97`,

or `customer-transactions-August-94`. This allows the use of internal, repeatable names for each fact table partition, which allow them to be reused in a repeatable way.

Views should also be created to combine fact tables that have been vertically partitioned, in order to provide a view of the table with all its columns. Queries that require both segments of the fact table will be less performant, because the increase in data volumes to be scanned will be substantial.

This should not matter too much, because only a small subset of the queries (or low-priority queries) should ever have to scan the vertical partition. If either of these points is not the case, check whether you should have vertically partitioned in the first place.

In a similar vein, consider creating views that combine partitions of two or more fact tables. Many access tools that are structured to utilize star schemas will assume that the query will need only to access a single fact table. Specifically, they will generate multiple SQL queries to satisfy a single user query – that is, a query for every fact table – where a single query joining facts against facts would have been more appropriate.

The only way this can be avoided is by creating a view that joins both fact tables in advance, forcing the access tool to generate only a single SQL query.

An example of this would be a view that combines sales transactions and stock position information within a retail data warehouse. Any user query that seeks to compare actual sales with the level of stock available will benefit from having a view of a single table, combining sales figures and stock positions per product per store per day.

Be careful with this technique. It can be used when the sales table contains EPOS transactions, but would necessitate aggregating all transactions per product per store per day, prior to joining against the stock position table. If this difference of reporting levels exists, it indicates that the combinatory view should be created against the appropriate summary tables instead.

5.8 MULTIDIMENSIONAL SCHEMAS

There is a class of decision support queries that analyze data by representing facts and dimensions within a multidimensional cube. In effect, each dimension is set to occupy an axis, and the values within the cube correspond to factual transactions. This class of query is particularly common in trend analysis.

The purpose of viewing information in a cube is that it lends itself to viewing statistical operations/aggregations, by applying functions against planes of the cube. In addition, the cube can be pivoted, sliced, and diced.

For example, in a retail sales analysis data warehouse, a cubical representation of products by store by day is represented by a three-dimensional cube, with the three axes representing product, store, and day (Figure 5.19). The point of intersection of all axes represents the actual number of sales for a specific product, in a specific store, on a specific day.

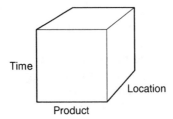

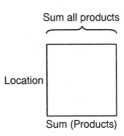

Figure 5.19 Product by store by day cube.

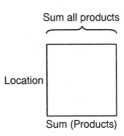

Figure 5.20 Sales by store on a specific day.

Alternatively, if we wished to view the sum of all sales by store on a specific day, the aggregation function would be applied against a slice of the cube (Figure 5.20).

In many user access tools, multidimensional cubes are not just virtual "presentation" concepts, but are created as physical data stores. Bearing in mind that the physical data store should probably be populated from the data warehouse, it is necessary to understand how the specific multidimensional cube extracts data from a star schema.

In most cases, the user access tool will generate SQL queries to populate the data on demand. The design of the multidimensional cube will determine to what extent data is preloaded as part of the load process, and how much data is pulled through on the fly.

If the database design forces the database to constantly access the data warehouse for information, system performance will be low. The most appropriate solution is where the cube is caching the data that satisfies the majority of the queries being asked. This will require substantial design effort, so plan accordingly.

In reality, the specific tool will extract data from the data warehouse according to a predefined strategy. It is worth investigating the specific tool strategy in order to determine whether data will be cached to the required level.

In most cases, as long as the data warehouse is structured around a starflake schema (that is, a schema that is designed to optimize read access performance), the data will be extracted in the most performant way. User access tools that utilize multidimensional cubes are in effect creating their own data mart; architectural issues relating to data marts are discussed in Chapter 8.

CHAPTER 6

Partitioning strategy

6.1   INTRODUCTION

The objective of this chapter is to explain how to determine the appropriate database-partitioning strategy. Partitioning is performed for a number of performance-related and manageability reasons, and the strategy as a whole must balance all the various requirements.

This chapter assumes that you have read Part Two: Data Warehouse Architecture, and Chapter 5 on database design. The design guidelines within this chapter elaborate on the material covered previously.

6.2   HORIZONTAL PARTITIONING

In section 4.5.4 we discussed how, in many organizations, not all the information in the fact table may be actively used at a single point in time. We also explained how horizontally partitioning the fact table was a good way to speed up queries, by minimizing the set of data to be scanned (without using an index).

In practice, if we were to partition a fact table into time segments, we should not expect each segment to be the same size as all the others. This is because the number of transactions within the business at a given point in the year may not be the same as the number of transactions at a different point in the year.

For example, high street retailers would expect much higher transaction volumes at peak periods, such as Christmas and Easter, compared with the rest of the year. This implies that a sales fact table that is partitioned monthly could require a number of partitions that are four to five times as large as the others.

In order to address this possible discrepancy, we need to consider the various ways in which fact data could be partitioned, before deciding on the optimum solution. We must remember that the determination of horizontal partitioning will also have to consider the requirements for manageability of the data warehouse.

6.2.1. PARTITIONING BY TIME INTO EQUAL SEGMENTS

This is the standard form of partitioning discussed earlier. The fact table is partitioned on a time period basis, where each time period represents a significant retention period within the business.

For example, if the majority of the user queries are likely to be querying on month-to-date values, it is probably appropriate to partition into monthly segments. If the query period is fortnight-to-date, consider partitioning into fortnightly segments as long as the total number of tables does not exceed something in the order of 500.

Table partitions can be reused, by removing all the data in them. However, we have to take into account that a number of the partitions will store transactions over a busy period in the business, and that the rest may be substantially smaller.

As will be discussed in section 6.2.6, database tables that represent fact table partitions are reused in a round robin by the warehouse manager. This means that we have to create a number of tables that are sized to contain the expected number of transactions for the period that they represent.

6.2.2 PARTITIONING BY TIME INTO DIFFERENT-SIZED SEGMENTS

In situations where aged data is accessed infrequently, it may be appropriate to partition the fact table into different-sized segments. Typically, this would be implemented as a set of small partitions for relatively current data, larger partitions for less active data, and even larger partitions for inactive data.

For example, in a shrinkage analysis data warehouse where the active analysis period is month-to-date, we could consider (working backwards from the current date):

- three monthly partitions for the last three months (including current month),
- one quarterly partition for the previous quarter,
- one half-yearly partition for the remainder of the year.

These partitions would be created for each year (or part thereof) of history retention (Figure 6.1).

The advantages of using this technique are that all the detailed information remains available online, without having to resort to using aggregations. Also, the number of physical tables is kept relatively small, reducing operating costs.

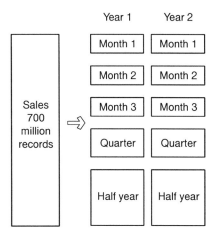

Figure 6.1 Partitioning fact tables into different-sized segments.

This technique may be particularly appropriate in environments that require a mix of data dipping recent history, and data mining through the entire history set.

The disadvantage of using this technique is that the partitioning profile will change on a regular basis. Using this method, a partitioning strategy that differentiates on a monthly basis implies that data must be physically repartitioned at the start of the new month, or at the very least at the start of each quarter.

In effect, you end up moving large portions of the database on a regular basis, and this degree of repartitioning will increase the operational costs of the data warehouse, so before you consider adopting this technique check that the increase is offset by the overall performance improvements.

> **GUIDELINE 6.1** Consider the use of different-sized partitions where the business requires a mix of data dipping recent history, and data mining aged history.

6.2.3 PARTITIONING ON A DIFFERENT DIMENSION

Time-based partitioning is the safest basis for partitioning fact tables, because the grouping of calendar periods is highly unlikely to change within the life of the data warehouse. For example, a month's worth of data is not going to represent more than 31 days' worth of data.

This does not mean that fact tables cannot be partitioned on a different basis. There may be good reasons for partitioning by product group, region, supplier, or any other dimension.

For example, let us consider a marketing function that is structured into distinct regional departments: for example, on a state-by-state basis. If each region tends to query on information captured within its region, it is probably more effective to partition the fact table into regional partitions. This guarantees that all the queries for that region are speeded up by not having to scan information that is not relevant.

Clearly, the benefit of this style of partitioning is that it speeds up all queries regarding a region, regardless of the time period it covers. This technique is particularly appropriate where there is no definable active period within the organization.

When using a form of dimensional partitioning, it is essential that we first determine that the basis for partitioning is unlikely to change in the future. It is important to avoid a situation where the entire fact table has to be restructured to reflect a change in the grouping of the partitioning dimension.

> **GUIDELINE 6.2** Consider partitioning on a dimension other than time, if the user functions lend themselves to that.

To follow on our previous example, if the definition of what constitutes a region within the business changes at any time, the entire fact table would have to be repartitioned to represent the new regional groupings.

In order to avoid this substantial cost, we recommend that you partition only on the time dimension, unless you are certain that the suggested dimensional grouping will not change within the life of the data warehouse. This guideline applies equally well to the time dimension, which is why you should not partition on a time grouping that may change in the future. Examples of groupings to avoid are listed in Table 6.1.

> **GUIDELINE 6.3** Do not partition on a dimensional grouping that is likely to change within the life of the data warehouse.

Table 6.1 Examples of partitioning bases to avoid.

Dimension	Comment
Product	Apt to change product groupings over time. Consider partitioning at a high level, e.g. sub-business unit
Customer	Always changes on an ongoing basis
Location	Avoid if organization is about to restructure geographically
Time – financial or promotional year, e.g. first quarter FY97, summer sales '96, etc.	Could change over time

6.2.4   PARTITIONING BY SIZE OF TABLE

In some data warehouses, there may not be a clear basis for partitioning the fact table on any dimension. In these instances, you should consider partitioning the fact table purely on a size basis: that is, when the table is about to exceed a predetermined size, a new table partition is created.

If we consider a customer event data warehouse in the retail banking area, we could find that the business operates a 7×24 operation: that is, there is no operational concept of the end of the business day, because transactions can occur at any point in time. It may be inappropriate to split customer transactions on a daily/weekly/monthly basis.

If no other dimension is appropriate for partitioning, we may well have to partition by size of table. What this means is that, as transactions are loaded into the data warehouse, we create a new table partition when a predetermined size is reached. This partitioning scheme is complex to manage, and requires metadata to identify what data is stored in each partition.

6.2.5   PARTITIONING DIMENSIONS

In some cases, the dimension may contain such a large number of entries that it may need to be partitioned in the same way as a fact table. Put another way, we need to check the size of the dimension over the lifetime of the data warehouse.

For example, let us consider a large dimension that varies over time. If the requirement exists to store all the variations in order to apply comparisons, that dimension may become quite large. A large dimension table can substantially affect query response times.

The basis for partitioning a dimension table is unlikely to be time. In order to reflect a partitioning basis that fits the business profile, we suggest that you consider partitioning on a grouping of the dimension being partitioned.

For example, if the product dimension contains a large product catalog, of say half a million to a million records, which vary substantially over time, consider partitioning the table into product groupings. Specifically, select the level in the product hierarchy that contains the number of instances that approximates to the number of partitions you desire. If there are 50 departments, create a partition for each department.

In practice, situations where partitioning dimension tables is appropriate are unusual. If the dimension table appears to be very large, always check that it does not contain embedded facts that are causing unnecessary rows to be added.

6.2.6   USING ROUND-ROBIN PARTITIONS

Once the data warehouse is holding the full historical complement of information, as a new partition is required, the oldest partition will be archived. It is possible to archive the oldest partition prior to creating a new one, and reuse the old partition for the latest data.

Metadata is used in order to allow user access tools to refer to the correct table partition. The warehouse manager creates a meaningful table name, such as `sales_month_to_date` or `sales_last_week`, which represents the data content of a physical partition.

This technique also makes it simpler to automate many of the table management facilities within the data warehouse, by allowing the system to refer to the same physical table partitions. The information period they cover will change, but this can be managed by using appropriate metadata.

> **GUIDELINE 6.4** Structure horizontal partitions to round robin. Remember that the size of each partition may vary.

6.3 VERTICAL PARTITIONING

In vertical partitioning, as the name suggests, data is split vertically. This process is shown in Figure 6.2.

This process can take two forms: normalization and row splitting. Normalization is a standard relational method of database organization. It allows common fields to be collapsed into single rows, thereby reducing space usage. For example, Tables 6.2 and 6.3 show a normalization process. In the data warehouse arena the approach tends to be the other way. Large tables are often denormalized, even

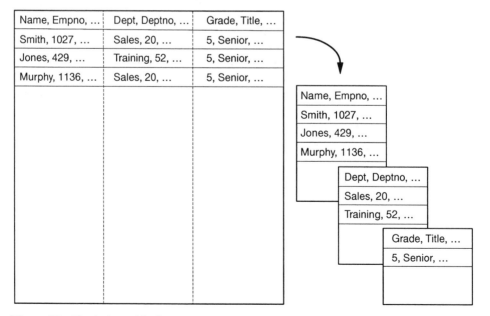

Figure 6.2 Vertical partitioning.

Table 6.2 Tables before normalization.

Product_id	Quantity	Value	Sales_date	Store_id	Store_name	Location	Region
27	5	4.25	21-FEB-96	16	Cheapo	London	SE
32	4	12.00	21-JUN-96	16	Cheapo	London	SE
24	1	1.05	21-JUN-96	64	Tatty	York	N
17	4	2.47	22-JUN-96	16	Cheapo	London	SE
128	6	3.99	21-JUN-96	16	Cheapo	London	SE

Table 6.3 Tables after normalization.

Store_id	Store_name	Location	Region
16	Cheapo	London	SE
64	Tatty	York	N

Product_id	Quantity	Value	Sales_date	Store_id
27	5	4.25	21-FEB-96	16
32	4	12.00	21-JUN-96	16
24	1	1.05	21-JUN-96	64
17	4	2.47	22-JUN-96	16
128	6	3.99	21-JUN-96	16

though this can lead to a lot of extra space being used, to avoid the overheads of joining the data during queries. This is particularly true of the fact data.

> **GUIDELINE 6.5** Normalizing data in a data warehouse can lead to large, inefficient join operations. Such operations should be avoided.

Vertical partitioning can sometimes be used in a data warehouse to split less-used column information out from a frequently accessed fact table. We distinguish **row splitting** from the normalization process, because it is performed for a different purpose. Row splitting also tends to leave a one-to-one map between the partitions, whereas normalization will leave a one-to-many mapping (Figure 6.3).

The aim of row splitting is to speed access to the large table by reducing its size. The other data is still maintained and can be accessed separately. Before using a vertical partition you need to be very sure

> **GUIDELINE 6.6** Consider row splitting a fact table if some columns are accessed infrequently.

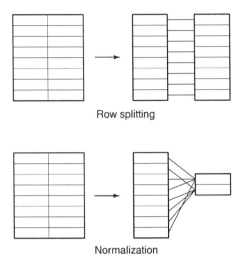

Row splitting

Normalization

Figure 6.3 Normalization versus row splitting.

that there will be no requirements to perform major join operations between the two partitions. This sort of partitioning can be useful, for example, in situations where the split-out data is accessed only by drill-down operations.

6.4   HARDWARE PARTITIONING

As discussed in section 4.5.4, part of the design process is to determine how to maximize the hardware performance by designing the database to fit specific hardware architectures. The precise mechanism used varies depending on the specific hardware platform, but in essence, must address the following areas:

- maximizing the processing power available;
- maximizing disk and I/O performance;
- avoiding bottlenecking on a single CPU;
- avoiding bottlenecking on I/O throughput.

Different hardware-partitioning techniques are used to address each area; solutions will use a mix of the required techniques in order to provide the best overall result.

This section assumes that the reader is familiar with the contents of Chapter 11: specifically, hardware architectures for SMP, MPP, clustered SMP, MPP hybrid, and NUMA machines.

6.4.1 MAXIMIZING PROCESSING POWER AND AVOIDING

BOTTLENECKS

Every data warehouse solution that allows direct query access to data, as opposed to a data warehouse fronted by a data mart, needs to ensure that the best use is being made of the processing power available. This is particularly true when the query performance relies on multiple threads being executed in parallel.

For example, if we would like a query to run five times faster by parallelizing it into five threads, we have to make sure that there are sufficient processors available to execute each thread in parallel.

Shared-everything architectures, such as SMP, maximize processing power at all times, because all disk and memory are fully shareable by all processors. Shared-nothing architectures, such as MPP, will maximize processing power available only if the subprocesses are capable of running on different nodes.

If an available processor does not have access to the data required, a subquery cannot run on that processor. This can lead to situations where the query has been parallelized by the database, but executes serially because the subprocesses are not capable of running on any other processors (Figure 6.4).

Hardware partitioning addresses this problem by ensuring that the data is always available to the other processing nodes. This is achieved using two mutually exclusive mechanisms, either striping data across nodes, or partitioning the tables horizontally where partitions are distributed across nodes.

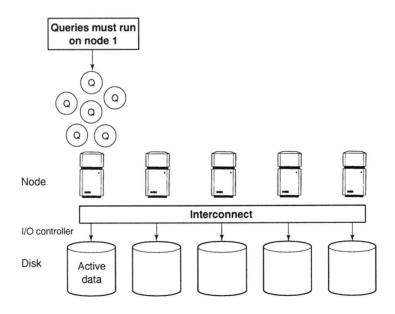

6.4.2 STRIPING DATA ACROSS MPP NODES

This mechanism distributes data by striping a fact table partition into a large number of small data packets on each node. The packet size is determined by the stripe width, and is typically set to optimize the scan performance of the database (Figure 6.5).

Query optimization is achieved on the basis that most queries will not cause the interconnect to become saturated as data is shipped from one node to the other. As long as the throughput of the interconnect is sufficiently high to cope with the data-shipping load, the striping will force all disks containing data to be accessed, and the processors to process in parallel.

For example, if we striped a 10 GB fact table partition across 10 MPP nodes, using a 64 kB stripe width, the data would be stored in 64 kB packets across all 10 nodes. Any query that scans the table will have to read in 64 kB chunks across all the nodes; once it has scanned 64 kB of data, the next 64 kB chunk must be retrieved from the next node. This forces any query that scans that fact table partition to cause the maximum number of disks to be accessed at the same time. If the query is parallelized as well, the other processing nodes will be able to execute the query subprocesses at the same time, and in effect the interconnect is behaving as a disk controller.

It is worth noting that, even if the interconnect is not saturated, all I/Os that are shipped over the interconnect will experience an overhead of typically 10–15%. This can add substantially to query times if large quantities are being shipped.

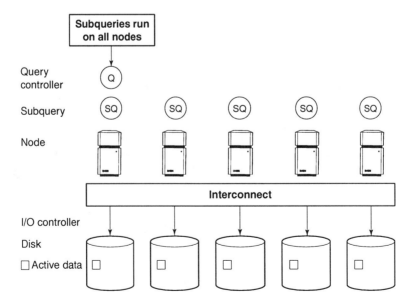

Figure 6.5 Striping data across MPP nodes.

The other problem with this technique is that it tends to work well only when reasonable data volumes are being scanned. Once all queries executing concurrently start accessing large volumes of data across the interconnect, pushing the throughput limit, system performance will degrade as a whole, and there is very little that can be done to improve it once this occurs.

This is why it is critical that you get the striping strategy correct from the start, otherwise you will probably have to redistribute the data in the future. A good pointer is to encourage a solution where some of the concurrent queries use parallel access, and others use index access, in order to spread the load.

If you are measuring the performance of the interconnect, make sure that you test the scan performance of the database across nodes, not the operating system scan time. In essence, the database may not be utilizing the hardware facilities to the best extent, and it is that figure that will determine how fast queries run.

6.4.3   HORIZONTAL HARDWARE PARTITIONING

This technique spreads the processing load by horizontally partitioning the fact table into small segments, and then physically storing each segment in a different node. When a query needs to access a number of partitions, the disks are accessed across the interconnect, in the same way as striping across nodes (Figure 6.6).

If the query is parallelized, then each subquery can run on the other nodes as long as the total number of subprocesses does not exceed the number of available nodes. In this instance, the database may be able to function-ship each subprocess to the node that contains the data in question, which will cut down traffic on the interconnect.

This technique is more effective if we wish to minimize traffic on the interconnect. Consequently, it should be used where the data-shipping volumes are large, or where the latency of the interconnect is affecting system performance.

As may have become apparent, node affinity is probably inappropriate when we are striping across nodes, because the data required by each subprocess is likely to reside on more than one node. In fact, the database technology may not be able to recognize on which node the table partition resides, if the striping is implemented at the operating system level (that is, using logical volumes).

Watch out for a situation where a single partition is in heavy demand by most queries. If this happens, the node containing the partition will probably bottleneck all the queries, either because of lack of processing power to execute multiple queries at the same time, or because of lack of disk throughput to constantly ship data to other nodes.

We suggest you avoid this situation by ensuring that the size of the partition is

> **GUIDELINE 6.7**   Consider striping fact data across nodes where the total, concurrent data to be shipped is well below the throughput on the interconnect. If latency issues are apparent, horizontally partition the fact data across the nodes, and make use of node affinity features.

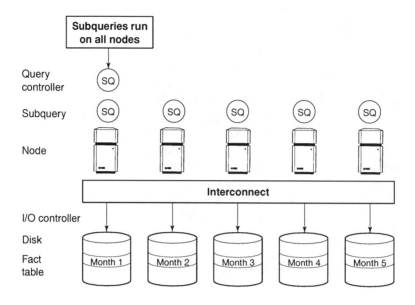

Figure 6.6 Horizontal partitioning of fact data across MPP nodes

sufficiently small. For example, if most queries analyze sales data month-to-date, break up the monthly partition into weekly segments.

A final point to remember: you should always partition fact tables for manageability. So even if you decide to adopt striping across nodes rather than horizontal partitioning, the fact table should still be partitioned horizontally on the basis described in section 6.2.

> **GUIDELINE 6.8** A number of good solutions horizontally partition data to a level meaningful to the business – monthly segments, for example – and then stripe each partition across the nodes.

6.5 WHICH KEY TO PARTITION BY?

It is crucial to make the right decision on which key to partition by. If you choose the wrong key you will eventually end up having to totally reorganize your fact data. For example, let us suppose we have to partition the following table:

```
Account_Txn_Table
  transaction_id
  account_id
  transaction_type
```

```
value
transaction_date
region
branch_name
```

We could choose to partition on any key. Let us look at two of the possible keys:

- `region`
- `transaction_date`

Suppose the business is organized into 20 geographical regions, each with a varying number of branches of different sizes. That gives us 20 partitions, which is not an unreasonable number. This is a nice partitioning scheme because our requirements capture has shown that the vast majority of queries are restricted to the user's own business region.

If we partition by `transaction_date` rather than `region`, this means that all the latest transactions from every region will be in one partition. This is horrible, because now a user who wants to look at data within his or her own region has to query across multiple partitions. So the choice seems obvious: partition by `region`.

Now take a step back and consider what happens when the company reorganizes its regional structure. What happens when a branch is moved from one region to another? If the data is partitioned by `region` we now have data in the wrong partition. Consider also the fact that as new data is added to the database, if the data is partitioned by `region` there will be new data for every partition. This means that no partition can be made read-only, as they will all be changing constantly. It also means that to archive data you will need to remove data from every partition, and not just the oldest partition.

Note that there are none of these problems with partitioning by `transaction_date`, or by any time-based field. This is why in most data warehouse systems partitioning tends to be time based. You have to be extremely careful when you pick your partitioning key: you need to consider every operation, load, backup, archive, indexing, query and so on that can possibly be run against the data. You need to be absolutely clear that the data will never have to be moved.

6.6   SIZING THE PARTITION

One key decision that has to be made is the size of partition to be used. A number of considerations affect this decision. First, what is the size of the largest manageable unit you are prepared to deal with? Remember: you not only have to back it up, but you may also have to manage, monitor, move and restore it. This size will act as the upper bound on the size of the partition.

The service level agreement (SLA) also acts as a limit on the size of any partitioning scheme. A partition will most likely become the unit of backup and recovery. The availability stipulations in the SLA will act as a limit on the size of a partition.

The disk setup used will act as a constraint on the number of partitions you can use. Each partition will need to be separable from the others. The striping policy used will determine the number of separate disk stripe sets that are available and thus the number of non-overlapping partitions you can have. This, in line with the requirements for keeping data online, will determine the minimum set of separable partitions required, which in turn determines the minimum size of each partition. This consideration, though important, should not be allowed to drive you to picking partitions that are too large to manage. The restriction is not absolute, as you can always co-locate partitions that are not likely to be accessed together, but you need to be careful that you are not storing up trouble for yourself later.

Query performance is of course a major consideration. It is important to understand the business and to have a feeling for the time periods that are likely to be accessed, on both an ad hoc and a regular basis. For example, let us take a banking data warehouse, which stores daily ATM and check account transactions. If analysts are looking for trend information they are more likely to run queries against customer by week or month, rather than by day. It is of course possible that they would want to run queries by customer type or profile against a particular day. In this situation the question becomes a case of assessing how much work is involved in extracting a day's work from a monthly partition against how much work is involved in accessing a month's worth of daily partitions.

CHAPTER 7

Aggregations

7.1   INTRODUCTION

The objective of this chapter is to explain how to determine the appropriate aggregation strategy. Aggregation is performed in order to speed up common queries, and must offset the operational costs of creating and managing the aggregations, against the benefits of doing so.

This chapter assumes that you have read Chapter 5 on database design. The design guidelines within this chapter elaborate on the material covered previously.

Though this activity is performed during the database design, it is typically revisited on a regular basis through the operational life of the data warehouse.

7.2   WHY AGGREGATE?

Data aggregation is an essential component of decision support data warehouses. It allows us to provide cost-effective query performance, by avoiding the need for substantial investment in processing power in order to address performance requirements.

Having said that, it is important to note that there is a fine line to walk when designing an aggregation strategy. Too many aggregations will lead to unacceptable operational costs; too few will lead to an overall lack of system performance.

As a guideline, we often advise that the best that can be hoped for is a data warehouse solution where 70% of the queries respond in a reasonable amount of time. The rest will take substantially longer unless the business is willing to make additional, possibly excessive, investments in hardware processing power.

In addition, aggregations allow us to spot trends within the data that may be difficult to see by looking at the detail. The old adage of "not being able to see the wood for trees" is particularly appropriate here.

7.3   WHAT IS AN AGGREGATION?

Aggregation strategies rely on the fact that most common queries will analyze either a subset or an aggregation of the detailed data. A large number of queries in a typical decision support data warehouse will ask questions that analyze data dimensionally. In most instances, you will find that those queries will examine detailed data by either a subset or an aggregation of one or more dimensions. This will be driven by the business need, rather than by the perceived information need.

For example, let us consider a situation where a marketing executive within a supermarket chain wishes to encourage the sales of lamb products in a geographic region he or she are responsible for. Part of this process is likely to involve identifying existing customers who are likely to increase their individual lamb purchases. This could be achieved by offering discounts on existing lamb products, or through special promotions that would encourage customers to switch to lamb from other meat products.

The marketing executive should be able to analyze the customer profiles within a district, and determine the income, spend, and eating preference for customers within that district. It could be rather insensitive for the supermarket to promote

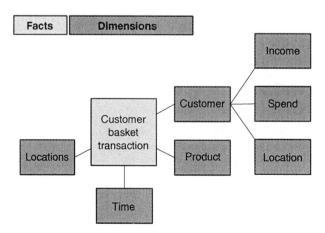

Figure 7.1   Schema for a customer-profiling data warehouse with basket transactions.

lamb sales to customers who have ethical or religious issues with the consumption of lamb.

In this instance, a possible query would examine:

- income,
- spend,
- a district in question aggregated by subdistricts – for example, postal regions within Orange County,
- purchasing trend over a reasonable period of time (for example, 2 years),
- purchasing trend for meat buyers,

against all existing loyalty customers who have made purchases within the past month.

We can see that the query is analyzing customer basket data by five dimensions: income, spend, location, time, and product. At this point, a number of facts are apparent:

- Subdistrict is an aggregation of location.
- District is a subset of location.
- The time period is substantial: that is, it will result in the analysis of the bulk of the detailed basket data.
- Meat buyers are customers who purchase a specific subset of the product dimension.
- Income and spend are dimensions of *customer*, not customer transaction.
- The nature of the query is such that the locations of interest are customer addresses, not store locations.

All these points would lead us to deduce that this query would need to perform the following operations in sequence:

1 Identify customers within Orange County.
2 Identify the subset of customers who purchase meat regularly, by scanning purchases over the past two years.
3 Identify income and spend for each customer.

This all sounds rather complicated and time consuming, and would be greatly simplified by having a pre-aggregated summary table that identifies all meat-buying customers in advance (Figure 7.2). This does not mean to say that the query is changed in any way, but the bulk of the processing is performed in advance of the query, and can be used repetitively, for example to analyze any other trends about this type of customer.

We can see that the appropriate aggregation will substantially reduce the processing time required to run a query, at the cost of preprocessing and storing the intermediate results. We can also see within the example that the advantages of pre-aggregating meat-buying customers could change at short notice, once the business users focus on a different set of conditions.

This highlights the other aspect of pre-aggregating data: the aggregations are geared around the popular queries at a specific point in time. As the business moves on, we have to reapply the analyses that led us to generate our original set of

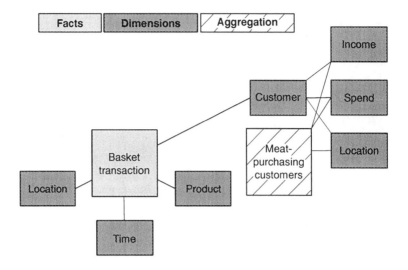

Figure 7.2 Summary table that identifies meat-buying customers.

summaries. This is because summaries are very tightly geared around specific query profiles: as the profiles change, then so should the summaries.

The other point worth noting is that the value of a summary is that the bulk of the processing has been carried out prior to the query's executing. A database view that performs the same aggregation might provide the same interface, but not the same saving of processing time.

For example, a database view that returns a list of meat-buying customers can be used by the marketing executive any time that information is required. However, every time the list is accessed, all the basket transactions will be scanned, incurring the processing penalty. It is far more effective to pre-execute this query and store the results, as long as database storage space is available.

It is worth noting that a number of access tools work by generating various intermediate results on the fly, where they could have been stored as summary tables.

Finally, we can see that the value of having a pre-aggregation is not just the performance saving, but the fact that it allows us to look at a specific set of trends more easily. This highlights the fact that aggregations make trends more apparent, by providing an overview of the whole picture rather than small parts of the picture.

For example, a summary table containing a list of meat-eating customers would allow the marketing executive to analyze other trends about this customer segment. Are they purchasing a particular brand of meat? What additional related products do they purchase?

7.4   DESIGNING SUMMARY TABLES

As we discussed earlier, the primary purpose of using summary tables is to cut down the time it takes to execute queries. As a direct consequence of this, the design strategy for summary tables is substantially different from that for fact tables.

In essence, the overriding objective when using a summary table is to minimize the volume of data being scanned, by storing as many partial results as possible. This is not just about storing aggregated values in columns; it may for example be appropriate to embed reference data into the summary table in order to cut down the time it takes to execute joins.

The following points differ from fact table design when designing summary tables:

- use of intelligent or non-intelligent keys;
- use of abbreviations decoded on the fly;
- use of embedded reference keys;
- which columns to include – that is, vertical partitioning strategy;
- horizontal partitioning strategy.

Summary tables are designed using a similar process to that followed to design fact tables, amended to take into account the differences in strategy. The steps in the process are:

1   Determine which dimensions are aggregated.
2   Determine the aggregation of multiple values.
3   Aggregate multiple facts into the summary table.
4   Determine the level of aggregation.
5   Determine the extent of embedding dimension data in the summary.
6   Design time into the summary table.
7   Index the summary table.

7.4.1   STEP I: DETERMINE WHICH DIMENSIONS ARE

AGGREGATED

As we discussed previously, summary tables should be used as a natural extension of the detailed data. The basic query, which would have used detailed data, is redirected to operate against summaries instead. The underlying structure of the query, in terms of dimensions and facts, is not changed, but is modified to bypass a number of intermediate results.

To this end, summary tables should be created to make full use of the existing starflake schema structures by being designed to act as a pseudo fact table. In other words, the dimension structure is unchanged, but the detailed fact data is summarized. What this means in practice is that summary tables should be designed

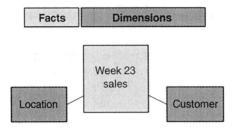

Figure 7.3 Extending a starflake schema to add a summary table.

to retain all the dimensions that have not been aggregated. This technique is sometimes called **subsuming the dimension**.

For example, let us consider a sales analysis data warehouse in which there is a common requirement to aggregate weekly sales of each product or product group. This requires that the summary table can be analyzed by product and store location, with the time dimension aggregated away. The time dimension is buried within the table itself, as the data within the table represents transactions over a specific period.

> **GUIDELINE 7.1** Design summary tables along similar lines as fact tables, making use of existing dimension structures.

In this example, in addition to reducing the number of rows that need to be scanned, we can also reduce the row length itself, because the date column is no longer required (Table 7.1). This technique would be equally valid if we were subsuming a different dimension: that is, the column representing that dimension is no longer required in the table.

Let us consider a case where it is common to aggregate daily product sales data across the country. In this instance the location dimension would be subsumed into the summary table, in that all product transactions across the country are aggregated (Figure 7.4). This means that the store id column would no longer be required in the summary table, since it becomes meaningless (Table 7.2).

Clearly, if this summary table is stored as a single physical table, then the date column is also implied and can be dropped. However, if all daily aggregations are

Table 7.1 Column conversion to a sales summary table aggregated by week.

Sales fact	becomes	Sales summary	Comment on conversion
Product id		Product id	
Store id		Store id	
Date			Date is implied and no longer required
Revenue		Revenue	Aggregated revenue across the week
Quantity		Quantity	Aggregated quantities across the week

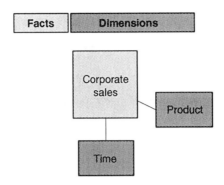

Figure 7.4 Starflake schema for a sales summary table aggregated by location.

stored in a single summary table, possibly partitioned horizontally, then the date column is required to identify when the aggregated transaction took place.

The other variation on the theme is when a dimension is not fully subsumed into the summary table, but each row represents an aggregation of a level within a particular dimension. In this instance, the dimension column needs to remain within the summary table, but probably in a different structure, because it represents a different concept: for example, a product group as opposed to product, or a region as opposed to store identifier. This technique is called **aggregating a dimension**.

Continuing our previous example, if the requirement is to aggregate product sales at a regional rather than a corporate level, then the summary table will require a location column, but not to contain a store identifier. It is highly likely that the structure of regional identifiers will be different from that of store identifiers. If the fact table is using non-intelligent keys, then even though you could consider using non-intelligent keys in the summary, the size of the key is likely to be much smaller, corresponding to the smaller number of regions compared with stores.

Obviously, storing a separate table for each instance within that level – each region, for example – can lead to an inordinate number of summary tables that need to be updated and managed. In order to minimize operational costs, we must ensure that the summary for that instance is warranted.

Table 7.2 Column conversion to a sales summary table aggregated by location.

Sales fact	becomes	Sales summary	Comment on conversion
Product id		Product id	
Store id		Store id	Location is implied, i.e. across the country
Date		Date	
Revenue		Revenue	Aggregated revenue across the country
Quantity		Quantity	Aggregated quantities across the country

It could be the case that a small number of regions are analyzed frequently, while the rest are analyzed infrequently. Clearly, we should summarize only the popular regions. All queries that refer to the less popular regions can be directed to the detailed fact data.

7.4.2   STEP 2: DETERMINE THE AGGREGATION OF MULTIPLE

VALUES

The objective of this step is to fold into the summary table any aggregated values that may be required to speed up queries. This is achieved by analyzing the queries that we are trying to speed up, and seeing what values are being aggregated.

In most cases, the values are likely to be aggregations along one or more dimensions, as discussed in section 7.4.1. However, aggregating a dimension may not be as simple as folding a set of single values into a single aggregation; be prepared to aggregate a number of values related to a dimension into a set of columns.

For example, in a retail sales analysis data warehouse, if we are aggregating product sales by store on a weekly basis, we would probably be interested in the following aggregated values for each product during each week:

- total number of sales,
- peak number of daily sales,
- lowest number of daily sales,
- average number of daily sales.

Each of these items relates to aggregated values along the same dimension; they are simply different ways of looking at the data. Consider using this technique if the basis for calculation is the same: that is, the values represent fact data aggregated on the same basis (in this case, data within one week).

If a significant proportion of queries look at more than one of the aggregated values, store all these aggregations within the same summary table. This will speed up a larger percentage of queries, at the cost of slightly affecting the performance of queries that look at only a single aggregation.

A word of warning: be wary of adding too many aggregated values to the same summary table. Every column added will affect the performance of queries.

As a guideline, we would suggest that you add no more than a handful of aggregated columns. The precise determination has more to do with the size of the columns than with the number, because that will determine the scan-time performance. It is good practice to calculate the achievable query performance if you intend to substantially increase the row size of the summary table. Finally, always bear in mind that you may be aggregating a number of dimensions into the same table, which will exacerbate the problem.

> **GUIDELINE 7.2**   If common queries use more than one aggregated value on the same dimension, aggregate the required values into a set of columns within the same summary table.

7.4.3 STEP 3: AGGREGATE MULTIPLE FACTS INTO THE

SUMMARY TABLE

In some instances, analysis of the queries might identify that a number of facts are accessed within the same query. Typically, this is used to compare a number of related facts within the same basis for aggregation.

In our previous example, the user was interested in product sales aggregated over the week. However, the retail merchant could be interested in the following additional facts:

- number of days where the product ran out of stock,
- shrinkage over the whole week,
- forecast number of sales for that week,
- returns throughout the week.

In other words, this query would need to run against the fact tables listed in Table 7.3.

This means that the query would have executed as four separate queries, or a single query with three union statements, which apply the same selection predicate. This would be costly in performance terms, and does not make use of the fact that, in each case, we are interested in the same products, locations, and time period.

If this style of query is popular, create a summary table that holds aggregations of all the facts required, as long as the aggregations are on the same basis, such as product by store aggregated over the week. This will result in greatly improved query performance, because all the queries are replaced by a single one.

As before, apply this technique only to facts that are clearly used together. The row size of the summary table will become substantial, and may affect the overall query performance.

> **GUIDELINE 7.3** Consider amalgamating a number of related facts into the same summary table.

7.4.4 STEP 4: DETERMINE THE LEVEL OF AGGREGATION

Aggregating a dimension at a specific level implies that any further detail is not available within that summary. As part of this design process, we must make sure that we do not create a huge number of summary tables in total. A total of about 200 summaries is recommended.

Table 7.3 Fact tables and their use for a specific query.

Fact table	Use
Product sales	Analysis of sales transactions
Stock position	Calculate out of stock values
Forecast sales	Compared against actual sales
Stock movements	Shrinkage is a type of stock movement

As designers, we must consider whether the requirement for a summary table can be satisfied by aggregating at a level below the one required, and then aggregate up on the fly. This has the advantage of potentially satisfying an additional set of queries, which require aggregations at a level below the one identified.

For example, in a retail banking data warehouse, a common query could be the calculation of customer profitability on a monthly basis. This is done by:

1   counting all customer transactions over the period;
2   calculating the cost of each transaction;
3   calculating the direct or indirect fees being charged to the customer;
4   deducing the net profit or loss to the bank.

Clearly, there exists a requirement to produce a monthly aggregation of customer transactions. However, we could consider creating weekly aggregations, which are aggregated up to a month as and when required. This gives us the advantage that the weekly aggregation is available, if and when users decide to drill down to weekly detail from the monthly figures.

This technique is particularly appropriate where the degree of aggregation on the fly is minimal. We would advise against using this technique if the ratio of the number of detail rows to aggregated rows is high.

In the previous example, the four- or five-weekly figures are aggregated in order to produce monthly figures. The cost of producing this aggregation is likely to be four or five times the optimum performance. This is probably acceptable if the query response requirements are not aggressive.

However, it would probably be inappropriate to store daily aggregations that are aggregated on the fly to monthly figures, as performance of that query is likely to be 30 times slower than the optimum figure.

In this instance, it may be appropriate to create two summaries, one at the monthly level to address monthly values and above, and another at the daily level to address daily and weekly values. This determination should be driven by an investigation into the popularity of daily results.

> **GUIDELINE 7.4**   Consider aggregating at the level below the level required for known common queries.

7.4.5   STEP 5: DETERMINE THE EXTENT OF EMBEDDING

DIMENSION DATA IN THE SUMMARY

Unlike fact tables, summary tables are re-created on a regular basis, possibly every time new data is loaded. The purpose of the summary is to speed up queries, and database joins with dimension data that take significant amounts of time. If a strategy of using non-intelligent keys within the summary table has been adopted,

Table 7.4 Intelligent keys.

Dimension	Value stored
Product	SKU
Location	Store id
Time	Physical date

these joins would be necessary every time a query accesses dimension data, which is probably most of the time.

The argument for using non-intelligent keys in fact data was in order to prevent the need to restructure the fact data if the keys were changed in future. Because the summary table will be re-created on an ongoing basis, it is more appropriate to use intelligent keys, which will cut down the number of joins that need to take place.

For example, in a retail sales analysis data warehouse, the keys would be as listed in Table 7.4.

Use of intelligent keys will not remove the need to join the dimension tables against the summary data. Any query that accesses information only held in the dimension tables will need to execute a join.

> **GUIDELINE 7.5** Always use intelligent keys in a summary table.

In these instances, consider whether this type of query is executed regularly. If it is, we recommend that you store the most popular values within the summary table itself. This will ensure that the fastest response time can be achieved by a query accessing the summary table.

Let us consider a case where users are regularly querying a weekly aggregation of product sales by store. If users regularly query against product groups, it is probably appropriate to denormalize all the levels of the hierarchy into the same summary table: that is, you should add a column for every level in the product hierarchy, as we would do in a star dimension table.

The disadvantage is that the summary table can end up with very wide rows. In principle, this should not be a problem, because the number of rows should be relatively small. However, we recommend that you calculate the achievable query performance using the proposed table structure. This should highlight any situations where the width of the table will affect overall system performance.

A good guideline is not to use this technique when the summarized level of detail is low, as in daily aggregations.

> **GUIDELINE 7.6** Consider denormalizing the dimension into the summary table, in order to speed up queries by removing the need to join tables. Don't use this technique if there are large numbers of rows in the summary.

7.4.6 STEP 6: DESIGN TIME INTO THE SUMMARY TABLE

As with fact tables, time can be stored in a variety of ways to speed up query performance. Within this subsection, we shall discuss the appropriateness of each technique described for fact data, when applied to summary data. This implies that you are familiar with all the techniques covered in section 5.4.6.

In broad terms, the focus of summary data is to speed up query response times, so each technique is amended in order to provide the best overall performance.

Storing a physical date

This option should always be used unless the level of aggregation is very low. As already discussed, summary tables should always use intelligent keys, in order to reduce the need to join. This means that the physical date is stored within the summary table, in preference to a non-intelligent key to the date dimension table.

One point to bear in mind is that when the time dimension is being aggregated at some level, even at a daily level, any time-of-day information is aggregated away, which implies that this aspect of date storage is hardly ever used in summaries.

We recommend that if you are using database date structures that embed the storage of time, you should always set the time of day to an amount that makes it clear that the value should be ignored.

> **GUIDELINE 7.7** Always store physical dates within summary tables.

Storing an offset

Clearly, summary tables that aggregate time have implied start dates, which can be utilized to store date offsets from the start. However, because the summary table is much smaller than a fact table, the processing time necessary to convert the date offset to a physical date could form a substantial percentage of the total time.

If this is the case, we recommend that you do not use date offsets within the summary table. Disk I/O rates become less of an issue when the data volumes are small, and processing time becomes more significant.

> **GUIDELINE 7.8** Date offsets are probably inappropriate within a summary table.

Storing date range

Date ranges are useful in that they can represent a significant aggregation of rows within the table. As before, this technique will increase the processing time, because it makes use of the between statement to satisfy the query.

If the degree of aggregation caused by use of the date range is high, the scan time saved by reducing the data volumes will still outweigh the additional processing time. However, if the degree of aggregation is low, it may be more appropriate to expand all rows represented by a date range into individual rows.

At this point, it is also worth considering the requirements for specific user access tools. Many tools are unable to execute queries against fact tables that utilize date ranges, because they expect a key to a time dimension table.

Storing date ranges within the fact table can result in significant savings in data storage and query performance. The saving within summaries will be proportionately less, because there will be a much smaller number of rows. Because of this, it is typically more effective to avoid the use of date ranges within summaries.

> **GUIDELINE 7.9** Avoid the use of date ranges within summary tables, unless the user access tools can operate effectively with them.

7.4.7   STEP 7: INDEX THE SUMMARY TABLES

One key decision that has to be taken is the level of indexation of the summary tables. As the aim is to direct as many queries as possible to the summary tables, it is worth investing some system resource and time in making each summary as usable as possible. The size of most summary tables makes the creation and maintenance of many indexes on each table feasible.

Our advice is to maximize the query potential of the summary tables by indexing all the likely access paths to each summary table. Queries that access the bulk of the rows in a large summary table are more likely to scan the table in parallel rather than use an index, but it is likely that the majority of the queries will be more focused, with only a small percentage of the rows in the summary table being accessed.

> **GUIDELINE 7.10** Consider using a high level of indexation on the summary tables.

7.5   WHICH SUMMARIES TO CREATE

Identifying which summary tables are required is a complex and ongoing process. As query profiles change, the determination of which summaries are necessary will change as well. However, it is necessary to initiate the process by identifying the first set of summaries that are created within a new data warehouse.

If the data warehouse is replacing an existing MIS, it could be the case that a set of summaries already exist. In this instance, create those summaries within the data warehouse, in order to allow you to seamlessly cross over the existing user population. However, in most instances, you will have to determine what the likely query profile will be, possibly with no statistics on which to base your decision.

One technique is to examine the various levels of aggregation within each key dimension, and determine the most likely combinations that may be of interest. This can be done by creating a table with the key dimensions, and looking for the

Table 7.5   Aggregation levels of key dimensions in a retail sales analysis data warehouse.

Product	Location	Time
Business unit	Region	Year
Sub-business unit	County	Quarter
Department	District	Month
Section	Store identifier	Week
SKU		Day
		Actual time of day

combinations that match our understanding of the user interest. For example, in a retail sales analysis data warehouse, we would first create a table of the key dimensions. This could look like Table 7.5.

The next step would be to consider the combinations based on our understanding of the kinds of queries the business is likely to ask. In our example, let us say that the users are merchants, who are responsible for maximizing the sales of product departments on a regional basis.

We see that an initial combination might be department by region by day. Because there are five regions, this implies that we need five summary tables at this level. After some reflection, we might decide to amend that to SKU by region by day in order to give us more flexibility to address a wider range of queries.

This process is continued until we have identified no more than 50 summary tables. These should seed the system, on the basis that this figure will increase as query profiles become better understood. This process can be automated by the warehouse manager.

7.5.1   WHEN IS A SUMMARY TABLE TOO BIG TO BE USEFUL?

The whole purpose of a summary table is to minimize the amount of data that needs to be scanned to satisfy a query. Clearly, if that figure is high, the query will take longer to respond.

Before you can answer this question, it is important to understand that the significant factor is the volume of data typically scanned, as opposed to the full size of the table. In most cases, we would expect a proportion of the table to be needed within a query; it will be unusual for the majority of the queries to be scanning the bulk of the data within the summary tables.

If we have a range of summary tables aggregating product sales over different time periods, product ranges, and locations, we would assume that:

- Most queries that look at corporate results will scan the bulk of those tables.
- Most queries that look at regional results will scan a proportion of the tables that store more detailed information.

Table 7.6 Degrees of aggregation within summary tables.

Level of aggregation	Example	Comment
High	Weekly corporate sales, i.e. weekly sales by product	Provides an overview of the business
Medium	Weekly sales by product by store	Next level of detail: overview of a region or product group
Low	Daily sales by product by store	Detailed data; almost pseudo fact data

● Most queries that look at detailed aggregations (such as daily sales) will analyze a small proportion of the large summary table.

It becomes clear that, broadly speaking, there are three distinct classes of aggregations (Table 7.6).

Summary tables with low degrees of aggregation are so large that they warrant being treated as fact data. This means that their design should follow the guidelines recommended for fact data, using column reduction strategies, horizontal and vertical partitioning strategies.

Summary tables with high degrees of aggregation will be so small that they should be designed to contain all the information required within a query, with dimensions denormalized into the summary.

Summary tables with medium degrees of aggregation are the ones that will be borderline when it comes to deciding how much to put into each row. These tables should be sized carefully to prevent the total row length from affecting the overall scan time.

As a guideline for medium aggregated summary tables, if the data to be scanned is more than 1–2 GB in size, the table is probably too large. You should expect highly aggregated summary tables to be no more than a few hundred megabytes in size.

> **GUIDELINE 7.11** Consider applying fact table design techniques to large summary tables.

CHAPTER 8

Data marting

8.1 INTRODUCTION

The objective of this chapter is to explain how to design data marts, and to decide whether a data mart is appropriate for your particular situation. Data marts hive off a subset of the data in the data warehouse, into a separate database, possibly in a different location.

This chapter assumes that you have read Part Two: Data Warehouse Architecture and Chapter 5 on database design. The design guidelines within this chapter elaborate on the material covered previously.

This activity is performed as an integral part of the database design, and is typically revisited on a regular basis through the operational life of the data warehouse.

8.2 WHEN IS A DATA MART APPROPRIATE?

Data marts are created for the following reasons:

- to speed up queries by reducing the volume of data to be scanned;
- to structure data in a form suitable for a user access tool;
- to partition data in order to impose access control strategies;
- to segment data into different hardware platforms.

We recommend that you do not data mart for other reasons, because the operational costs of data marting can be high, and once a strategy is in place, it can be difficult to change without incurring substantial redevelopment costs.

Before you start designing a data mart, you must make sure that a data-marting strategy is appropriate for your particular situation. If you follow the steps below and determine that a data mart appears to fit the bill, move on to designing the data mart. Our experience has been that many people data mart when there is no need to, and could make substantial savings in costs by not doing so. The steps are:

- Identify whether there is a natural functional split within the organization.
- Identify whether there is a natural split of the data.
- Identify whether the proposed user access tool uses its own database structures.
- Identify whether any infrastructure issues predicate the use of data marts.
- Identify whether there are any access control issues that require data marts to provide Chinese walls.

In all cases, we recommend that you allow for data to be loaded into an enterprise data warehouse, and then to be data marted. In most cases, it will be appropriate to have an enterprise data warehouse in addition to the data marts, which implies a substantial degree of data replication.

If access control issues are involved, it may be necessary to purge the data from the enterprise data warehouse, after the data has been data marted. This strategy is described further in section 8.2.3.

8.2.1 IDENTIFY FUNCTIONAL SPLITS

Within this step, we must determine whether the business is structured in such a way as to benefit from functionally splitting the data. Look for departmental splits, and then determine whether the way in which the departments use information tends to be in isolation from the rest of the organization.

For example, let us consider a retail organization in which each merchant is responsible for maximizing the sales of a group of products. Their brief could be to maximize sales by ensuring adequate stock levels for a store, and sales levels that meet or exceed targets.

In practice, this means that the information in a data warehouse that would be of value is:

- sales transactions on a daily level, to monitor actual sales;
- sales forecasts on a weekly basis;
- stock positions on a daily basis, to monitor stock levels;
- stock movements on a daily basis, to monitor supplier or shrinkage issues.

All this information can form very substantial data volumes when, by the nature of the role, the merchant is not interested in products that he or she is not responsible for. In this instance, we can consider data marting the subset of the data dealing with the product group of interest, because the merchant is extremely unlikely to query

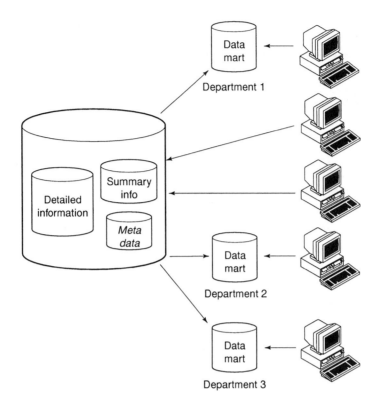

Figure 8.1 A data-marting strategy in the retail sector.

information about other products. Note, however, that consideration needs to be given to future changes. If the departmental structure changes, how will the data marts be affected? What happens if products are switched from one department to another? When identifying the functional split these issues need to be taken into account.

On further investigation we may determine that the departmental splits are valid, but that additional information is required about other departments. In this case, consider whether the additional data can be provided as highly aggregated summary tables, which have minimal storage costs and can be replicated into all data marts.

Continuing the previous example, it could be that the merchants query sales trends of other products in order to understand more fully what is happening to sales or to shrinkage in general. It may be appropriate to continue with a data-marting strategy, but it would have to add a number of highly aggregated summaries that can provide the wider sales and shrinkage information.

Examples of the required summaries are sales transactions month-to-date, aggregated at a weekly level, such as sales by product by store by week, or shrinkage month-to-date, aggregated at a corporate level, such as stock movements by product by day.

Finally, at this point we need to determine the business benefits and technical feasibility of using a data mart. Ask yourself whether the additional hardware cost is going to offset the performance improvements. In many instances, the hardware costs cannot be justified, because performance could be improved by other means, such as higher numbers of summary tables, or more processing power for the data warehouse platform.

In addition, the implied number of data marts may not be feasible within the available load window. We recommend that you do not support more than a handful of data marts for a data warehouse that has an overnight load process. Higher numbers of data marts are likely to lead to load window problems.

> **GUIDELINE 8.1** You should not have more than a handful of data marts for a data warehouse with an overnight load process, because the processing time is likely to exceed the load window.

8.2.2 IDENTIFY USER ACCESS TOOL REQUIREMENTS

Data marts are required in order to support any user access tools that require internal data structures. Data within those structures is outside the control of the data warehouse, but they need to be populated and updated on a regular basis.

Some of these tools are often populated directly from source systems, on the basis that they are satisfying the existing requirements to analyze data. This may be true initially, but it is highly likely that additional requirements outside the scope of the tool are identified in future.

In practice, this data should be populated from a data warehouse, not directly from the source data, in order to ensure consistency across all user access tools, even if they each have their own data mart. More to the point, even if we start with a single, very specific user access tool, we must remember that analysis requirements could change in the future. An additional access tool may be required, or a new requirement may exist to analyze detailed data that may not be held in the appropriate structures in the existing data mart.

In order to avoid problems in the future, we recommend that you adopt a data-marting strategy as described in section 8.2.1. User access tools may come and go, but the underlying information will be held in a form suitable for analysis. This could be populating a new user access tool, or simply making the detailed data available for other analyses.

> **GUIDELINE 8.2** Populate multiple data marts from an enterprise data warehouse. This will ensure data is consistent across all data marts.

8.2.3 IDENTIFY ACCESS CONTROL ISSUES

In a number of cases, information within the data warehouse may be subject to privacy laws, which restrict access to data. The extreme case of this is where there must be a complete Chinese wall between different segments of the data warehouse. This situation occurs in the financial sector, where legislative controls may restrict access to data relevant to that organization.

For example, if you are designing a data warehouse for a retail banking institution, check that all the accounts belong to the same legal entity. It may be the case that accounts are owned by a number of retail banks wholly owned by a holding bank. Privacy laws could force you to totally prevent access to information that is not owned by the specific bank.

Clearly, we may not be able to utilize database facilities to apply this degree of access control. If we place all account transactions in a single fact table, we may not be able to provide the appropriate level of access control. The database may be able only to restrict access to specified tables per user, as opposed to specified rows per user.

Data marts allow us to build complete Chinese walls by physically separating data segments within the data warehouse. The detailed data can then be removed from the data warehouse in order to avoid possible privacy problems.

Within the data warehouse, we can retain aggregations that have been created at a level of detail where privacy laws no longer apply. They can be generated from the detailed data loaded as part of the load process, by updating existing summary tables. Alternatively, the aggregations can be generated from each individual data mart, and stored centrally.

Continuing our previous example, we could create a data mart for each legal entity, and load it via the data warehouse, with detailed account data. In other words, the detailed data is loaded into the data warehouse, cleaned up and made consistent. Subsets of the detailed data are then downloaded into each data mart, corresponding to detailed information about each legal entity.

Once the detailed data resides within the data marts, it is used to update any summary tables within the data warehouse. At this point, we are able to remove the detailed data if necessary, avoiding potential data privacy issues.

8.3 DESIGNING DATA MARTS

8.3.1 DATA SUBSETS AND SUMMARIES

Data marts that are not created to satisfy the requirements of user access tools should be designed to match the database design of the data warehouse. It is good practice to design the data mart as a smaller version of the starflake schema within the data warehouse.

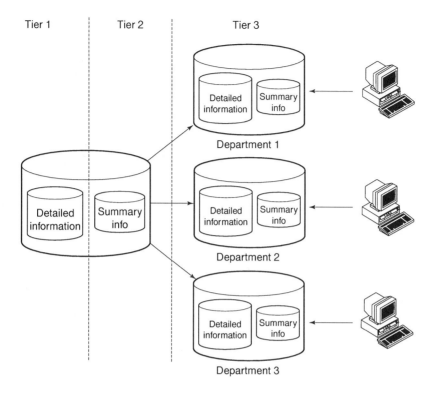

Figure 8.2 Design of data marts that are created to support functional groups.

This allows us to maintain greater control on the database instances, by ensuring that the same design is replicated on each data mart. Clearly, the data volumes within each data mart will be substantially smaller than for the data warehouse, but the complete database design, possibly excluding partitioning, can be applied to each data mart.

Summaries are data marted in the same way as they would have been designed within the data warehouse; in other words, each summary table is designed to utilize all the dimension data in the starflake schema.

For example, in a retail sales analysis data warehouse, let us say that we have decided to adopt a starflake schema and a horizontal partitioning strategy based on monthly partitions. We have also decided to data mart product group segments into departmental data marts, physically on other hardware.

These data marts should use the same starflake schema, making the fact and dimension tables identical. However, the fact table contains only the data that is relevant to the department that is being data marted.

Summary tables are copied from the data warehouse. Each summary may incorporate data from other departments, but is structured to operate against the same dimension data.

8.3.2 DIFFERENT DATABASE DESIGNS

If we have to populate a database design specific to a user access tool, we shall probably have to transform the data into the required structure. This could simply be a transformation into different database tables or, alternatively, we may have to transform into structures that exist outside the data warehouse database.

For example, if the user access tool operates against the data warehouse database, we would only have to transform from one database schema to another. This is less complex than transforming into flat file structures, or to a non-relational database.

Typically, database transformations involve a degree of aggregation. This should be created from the detailed data in the normal way, as the data in the starflake schema is designed to be aggregated quickly and effectively.

Complex transformations should be designed using the guidelines discussed in sections 3.5.2 and 3.4. There is a great deal of similarity between the load and warehouse management process that loads and transforms into the data warehouse structure, and a data mart load process that transforms from the data warehouse into the data mart structure.

Because these transformations may be complex, the bulk of the transformations may have to be implemented by stored procedures. Data cleaning and consistency will not be an issue, because the data will already have been cleaned by the load process into the data warehouse.

The use of copy management tools may be appropriate, because they may be able to perform the data transformations into the data mart. As discussed in section 3.4, we recommend that you check that the bulk of the transformations can be carried out by the copy management tool. If this is not the case, there is likely to be a substantial degree of hand-crafting to get the tool to perform the appropriate transformations. As a result, the cost–benefit case for the copy management tool may be weak.

8.4 COSTS OF DATA MARTING

Data-marting strategies incur costs in the following areas:

- hardware and software
- network access
- time-window constraints

8.4.1 HARDWARE AND SOFTWARE

Data marts require additional hardware and software, even if they are sited on the same physical hardware that is running the data warehouse. Essentially, the data mart database will require additional processing power and disk storage to handle the user queries. Having said that, we have to bear in mind that the total processing requirement may not have substantially changed, because the data marts may be off-loading queries from the enterprise data warehouse.

On the whole, the data mart is likely to require additional processing power, but it is unlikely to be substantial unless we plan to retain detailed data within the data warehouse as well. If there exists a requirement to retain detailed data within the data warehouse and the data mart, we shall incur additional costs to store and manage the replicated data.

This will be true even if the data mart is placed on the same MPP hardware that is running the enterprise data warehouse. The additional nodes running the data mart may be within the same cabinet, but they will be operating as separate systems.

In all cases, data marts should not be used to avoid the need to store aggregations. Data marting is more expensive than aggregating, and so it should be used as an additional strategy, not as an alternative strategy. Also, aggregations can provide an overview of corporate information, which may not be available by data marting detailed fact data.

> **GUIDELINE 8.3** Avoid using data marts as an alternative to aggregation. Costs will be higher, without providing the "overview" capability of aggregations.

8.4.2 NETWORK ACCESS

Clearly, the process of loading data into each data mart will be affected by the available capacity of the physical connections between both items of hardware. In many cases, each data mart will be in a different geographical location from the data warehouse, so you will need to ensure that the LAN or WAN has sufficient capacity to handle the data volumes being transferred within the data mart load process.

This may not be an issue when the data marts are within the same database as the data, or when data marting onto a different set of nodes within an MPP or cluster architecture, where the node-to-node communication speed is high.

8.4.3 TIME WINDOW CONSTRAINTS

The data-marting load process will eat into the available time window, the extent of which will depend on the complexity of the transformations, and the data volumes being shipped. In all cases, it is impractical to populate more than a handful of data marts within an overnight window, unless the data marts are extremely small.

The determination of how many data marts are feasible will vary, depending on a number of factors:

- time window available,
- network capacity,
- volume of data being transferred,

- mechanisms being used to insert the data into the mart.

We recommend that you calculate the approximate time necessary to complete the data mart loads, in order to determine if the proposed architecture is feasible.

In essence, you have to:

1 Calculate the data volumes being shipped to each data mart.
2 Calculate elapsed time to transfer across the LAN or WAN into each mart (hardware).
3 Calculate elapsed time to load the data into each mart (database).

Allow additional elapsed time, if the load process is performing data transformations, in order to convert into the internal structure of the data mart.

CHAPTER 9

Metadata

9.1 INTRODUCTION

Designing the metadata for the data warehouse is one of the more difficult and least well-defined design tasks. What exactly is metadata? The word *meta* comes from the Greek, and means *among*, *beside* or *after*. In the context of metadata it means data about something else. Metadata is, in essence, information that describes something else.

In a data warehouse the term **metadata** is used in a number of different situations. This is part of the confusion that surrounds metadata. Two people may talk about metadata and mean two different things.

To help clarify the situation we shall break the discussion down by the different functions for which metadata is required. Metadata is used for:

- data transformation and load
- data management
- query generation

Each of these functional areas is discussed separately in the pages that follow.

9.2 DATA TRANSFORMATION AND LOAD

Metadata may be used during data transformation and load to describe the source data and any changes that need to be made. Whether or not you need to store any metadata for this process will depend on the complexity of the transformations that are to be applied to the data, when moving it from source to data warehouse. It will also depend on the number of source systems and the type of each system.

The more sources that are used to feed the data warehouse, the more likely it is that you will need to store metadata about the process. Likewise, the greater the difference in the nature of the source system and the data warehouse system, the greater the requirement to store metadata.

The advantage of storing metadata about the data being transformed is that as source data changes the changes can be captured in the metadata, and transformation programs automatically regenerated.

For each source data field the following information is required:

- source field
  - unique identifier
  - name
  - type
  - location
    - system
    - object

The source field needs to be uniquely identified and described. A **unique identifier** is required to avoid any confusion occurring between two fields of the same name from different sources. The other attributes of name, type and location describe where the data comes from. The **name** is its local field name. The **type** is the storage type of the data, such as character, integer, floating point and so on. The **location** is both the system it comes from and the object that contains it. Some example source fields are shown in Table 9.1.

The destination field needs to be described in a similar way to the source:

- destination
  - unique identifier
  - name
  - type
  - tablename

Again, a **unique identifier** is needed to help avoid any confusion between commonly used field names. The **name** is the designation that the field will have in the base data

Table 9.1 Source field types in various formats.

Unique ID	Name	Type	Location	
			System	Object
accid001	Account_id	Alphanumeric	Online Txn system	Tnx file
val004	Value	Pic 999999.99	Online Txn system	Txn file
accbal012	Account_balance	Float(10,2)	Account system	Account table
Cnam010	Cust_name	Varchar	Customer system	Cust_det table

Table 9.2 Destination descriptions.

Unique ID	Name	Type	Tablename
accid001	Account_id	Varchar2(18)	Acc_Txn
val004	Value	Number(8,2)	Acc_Txn
accbal012	Account_balance	Number(10,2)	Acc_Detail
Cnam010	Cust_name	Varchar2(30)	Customer

within the data warehouse. The term **base data** is used here to distinguish between the original data load destination and any copies, such as aggregations, in which the data may later appear. Metadata will be required for both the fact data and the dimension data, and base data refers to both, and not just to the fact data.

The **destination** type is the database data type, such as Char, Varchar, Number and so on. The **tablename** is the name of the table the field will be part of. Some examples of destination descriptions are shown in Table 9.2.

The other information that needs to be stored is the transformation or transformations that need to be applied to turn the source data into the destination data:

- transformation(s)
  - name
  - language
    - module name
    - syntax

These transformations can be anything from a simple field-type conversion to a complex suite of procedures and functions that need to be applied. The **name** is a unique identifier that differentiates this from any other similar transformations. The **language** attribute contains the name of the language that the transformation is written in. The other attributes are **module name** and **syntax**. Generally these will be mutually exclusive, with only one being defined. For simple transformations such as simple SQL functions the syntax will be stored. For more complex transformations the name of the module that contains the code is stored instead.

This all seems straightforward, but even this process is not as simple as it seems. There are many complications, such as different data type notations. If the source systems are non-relational the data will have data types that are different from those of the relational system that you are using. Many legacy systems will have data fields that are described in COBOL notation.

Even between two different RDBMS vendors you will get differences. For example, some vendors store date and time data in different fields while others store date and time in the same field. Any transformation between the two may be further complicated by the units of storage used. One may store time down to hundredths of a second, while the other stores time down to thousandths of a second.

What one system means by Char fields another system would call Varchar. Numbers, even if defined the same way, will often be stored differently internally. Different systems have different binary representations of numbers, depending on whether they are byte swapped or not. Different systems have different encoding schemes, such as ASCII and EBCDIC. Then there are different national language character sets that need to be catered for. What is worse is that potentially every source system is differently encoded with different data types, and so on.

> **GUIDELINE 9.1**   Adopt a common notation to describe source and destination data. Ideally, this notation should be a superset of the destination data types.

What is needed is a common notation that you can translate everything to. Ideally you should use the notation and data types of the destination database as the common notation. However, this may not be rich enough to cover all variants of all types of every data source. You may need to extend the data type notation of the destination system to allow a coherent and consistent definition of the source data.

Another common difficulty is how to deal with many-to-one, one-to-many, and many-to-many mappings from source to destination. If there are many of these mappings you should probably be using a CASE tool or a third-party transformation mapping tool to handle the data transformations. There is no point in reinventing the wheel.

The advantage of transformation and mapping tools is that they will do all the work described above and more. Generally they will handle all aspects of the data transformation and load, even generating the programs required.

The main disadvantage of these tools is their cost. They can prove to be prohibitively expensive, and the decision as to whether to invest in such a tool needs to be well costed. Even with a transformation and mapping tool there will be man-days of effort required to perform the mapping. Any cost–benefit analysis needs to take this into account.

> **GUIDELINE 9.2**   The more data sources that need to be mapped, the more valuable a transformation and mapping tool becomes.

The other prime disadvantage of many transformation tools is that the code they generate is not efficient.

9.3   DATA MANAGEMENT

Metadata is required to describe the data as it resides in the data warehouse. This is needed by the warehouse manager to allow it to track and control all data movements. Every object in the database needs to be described. Metadata is needed for all of the following:

- tables
  - columns
    - name
    - type

- indexes
  - columns
    - name
    - type

- views
  - columns
    - name
    - type

- constraints
  - name
  - type
  - table
    - columns

All this information is fairly self-explanatory; it will already be available in the database's data dictionary, and does not need to be duplicated. There are, however, data warehouse specific requirements on what metadata is stored, and not all will be found in the data dictionary. One of the main requirements is to be able to cross-reference columns in different tables that contain the same data, even if they have different names. Some of this information may be contained in foreign key and primary key constraints, but this information is likely to be incomplete.

It is particularly important to be able to track the same column through the aggregations. To this end you will need to store metadata like the following for each field:

- field
  - unique identifier
  - field_name
  - description

where the unique identifier is an identifier assigned to the column to distinguish it from any other column with the same name. The field_name and description attributes are there to allow a full description of the data field.

For each table the following informa-tion needs to be stored:

> **GUIDELINE 9.3** To choose the correct source for a query you need to be able to track all occurrences of each data field through every aggregation, index and table.

- table
  - table_name
  - columns
    - column_name
    - reference identifier

The table_name is the table name as stored in the data dictionary. The column_names are again the names as found in the data dictionary. The column reference identifier is the unique identifier described in section 9.4. This allows the column to be linked with the columns in aggregations, even if they are named differently.

Aggregations are a special case of tables, and they require the following metadata to be stored:

- aggregation
  - aggregation_name
  - columns
    - column_name
    - reference identifier
    - aggregation

This is identical to the table metadata except for the aggregation field, which should contain a description of the aggregation that has been performed. This could be a clear text field, but ideally should contain the actual aggregation function applied. This needs to be handled consistently, because this field will be used for comparisons to check whether aggregations contain information that is aggregated similarly or differently. The functions listed below are examples of aggregation functions:

- min
- max
- average
- sum

This information is not complete; as well as the function, you need to store any group-by information. For example, if the aggregation was built on the sum of sales data aggregated by the sale date, you need to capture that fact. So instead of sum you will store sum by sale_date.

If an aggregation is calculated by compounding multiple fields from the table or from multiple tables, this information needs to be captured in the metadata. For example, if an account attracts multiple types of interest, and each is tracked separately in the fact data, but in a particular aggregation you are only interested in the total, in this case you need to record the fact that the field is calculated from interest A+interest B.

Partitions are subsets of a table, but they also need the information on the partition key and the data range that resides in that partition:

- partition
  - partition_name
  - table_name
    - range allowed
    - range contained
    - partition key
      - reference identifier

The table_name refers to the table that the partition is part of. The partition key is the column or columns on which the table is partitioned, and the reference identifier

is the unique identifier from the column metadata. The range values specify the range
of data that is allowed in the partition and the range of actual values contained.

9.4   QUERY GENERATION

Metadata is also required by the query manager to enable it to generate queries. The
same metadata used by the warehouse manager to describe the data in the data
warehouse is also required by the query manager.

The query manager will also generate metadata about the queries it has run.
This metadata can be used to build a history of all queries run and generate a query
profile for each user, group of users and the data warehouse as a whole.

The metadata that is required for each query is:

- query
  - tables accessed
    - columns accessed
      - name
      - reference identifier
  - restrictions applied
    - column name
    - table name
    - reference identifier
    - restriction
  - join criteria applied
    - column name
    - table name
    - reference identifier
    - column name
    - table name
    - reference identifier
  - aggregate functions used
    - column name
    - reference identifier
    - aggregate function
  - group by criteria
    - column name
    - reference identifier
    - formula
  - sort criteria
    - column name
    - reference identifier
    - sort direction
  - syntax
  - execution plan
  - resources

- disk
  - read
  - write
  - temporary
- CPU
- memory
- start date and time
- end date and time
- user name

The list of tables accessed should be the actual tables and not just view names; the view should be expanded and the underlying tables identified. The fact that views were used will still be recorded by saving the original syntax. Anywhere columns are referenced, both the name and the unique identifier should be used. Again, this will allow later analysis of the query history data to identify any possible aggregations that could be useful.

The select clause of an SQL statement may contain compound columns that are constants or expressions. These expressions may contain multiple column names from different tables, or may contain no column names at all. You can also get pseudo columns such as rownum in the select clause of the query. This information also needs to be captured.

The restrictions information is gathered from the where clause of the SQL statement. The column restricted and the actual restriction applied should be captured. Note that, if the query is a complex SQL statement with views that themselves are complex, you may find that multiple restrictions are present for the same column.

The join information may join the same column to multiple other columns. The reference identifier will usually be the same for the joining and the joined column. If they are not you will have identified either a meaningless conjunction of data, or a new connection between data items that you had not recognized before.

The join metadata consists of the same pieces of information twice, once for each side of the join. Any aggregate functions may involve multiple columns. For example, you may average the sum of two columns from different tables. That information needs to be captured along with the function. The same applies to the group by clause, as the statement may be grouped by more than just a simple column name.

For the sort information you need to capture whether the result has to be sorted in ascending or descending order.

The syntax should be stored in a text field as a direct lookup for comparing statements. Note that hard-coded values in the SQL will make two statements that are essentially the same textually different. If you want to avoid this you should substitute variable names for the values before storing the data. However, if you do this you should store the values separately, because they are useful information in themselves. Note also that the order of table names in the from clause, the order of the where clause, the use of different table aliases and so on will cause similar statements to appear different. It may be best to store the syntax as it was specified and to clean up the statement programatically before performing any analysis. You also need to be careful that changing the order of the `from` clause or the `where` clause does not affect the actual optimization and execution of the statement in the RDBMS you are using.

Along with the syntax you will need to capture the execution plan used to run the query. This is vital to understanding any query that is run more than once. It is important to be able to see whether the execution plan changes as the data and the data volumes change, or if more partitions or a wider range of data is queried.

Capturing the resources used by every SQL statement may cause extra overhead on the system. It may also prove extremely difficult to exactly match resource to a particular statement. However, this is extremely useful information, and should be captured if it is possible and does not create too much of an overhead. Even if it has a large overhead it may be useful to be able to switch on and off the gathering of this information on occasions.

When capturing the I/O statistics for a query it is important to capture the write statistics as well as the read. Even though a query is essentially read-only it can generate writes in a number of ways. First, it may be requested to write the result set of the query to a table in the database or to a file. Second, temporary space may be used for doing sort operations, or for intermediate results.

The memory and CPU usage statistics are extremely useful data when it comes to planning for increasing capacity as users are added and the query load is ramped up. They can also be used for tuning and for query prediction. The start date and time plus the end date and time are also essential to tuning and prediction. The main time statistic used is the elapsed time, but it is still useful to have the start and end times to be able to tell which queries overlapped, and how they overlapped daily and nightly processing.

> **GUIDELINE 9.4** Gathering of resource statistics can cause overheads. Where possible, statistics should be gathered passively.

This is a lot of information to generate and store, and may have an adverse effect, especially on very short queries that are submitted via the query manager. However, the information gained on user and resource usage will probably be worth it. It is also possible to build most of the information later from the statement syntax, which means that all you have to save initially is the execution plan and the SQL itself.

> **GUIDELINE 9.5** Most required data can be extracted from the SQL syntax and the execution plan. This means that the analysis can be performed any time at your convenience.

This data, as well as being used to generate query profiles, can also be used to tune the data warehouse performance. It can tell you what new aggregations would be useful. It will also indicate where new indexes may be required.

9.5 METADATA AND TOOLS

Metadata is used by many tools, and it is possible that you will end up with a number of sets of mutually exclusive metadata that describe the same data.

Once you have established the exact metadata requirements for the data warehouse, you will probably need to define some mechanism for creating and maintaining it. You could design your own programs to do this, and you will need to write code for the warehouse manager and the query manager to enable them to create and update their metadata.

CASE tools are designed to perform the sorts of operations that you will require for the creation and management of the metadata. You may want to investigate the use of such a tool. Having such a tool would also help if the metadata needs to be made visible outside the data warehouse.

Being able to export or externalize the metadata effectively opens up an interface to the data warehouse, in particular on the query side. This would theoretically allow any tool or program that uses that interface to access the data warehouse in the desired way. More importantly, it would allow any query tool to work via the query manager.

The problem is that, as mentioned above, each query or reporting tool will have its own metadata, and unfortunately at the moment they do not conform to a standard. There is currently no recognized standard for metadata in the industry, although a number of vendors are working on one. Therefore, to get query tools to work via the query manager is a major task.

One seemingly obvious solution to this problem is to use the metadata format of one of the query tools you are using. This is not a real solution, because the query tools will almost certainly change over time, and any new tool is not likely to be able to use the metadata of the older tool. The upshot is that, until there is a standard that all tools comply with, you are probably better off defining your own metadata.

CHAPTER 10

System and data warehouse process managers

10.1 INTRODUCTION

It is worth taking a moment here to talk briefly about what we mean by a manager in this context. First, note that when we use the term "manager" we are not talking about people. In this instance a manager is used to describe a process or part of the data warehouse application as a whole. The system managers refer to areas of management of the underlying hardware and operating system or systems themselves, such as scheduling and backup recovery. The data warehouse process managers refer more specifically to the data warehouse itself and to the previously identified components of the data warehouse architecture (see Part Three). A specific manager will consist of the tools and procedures required to manage its area of responsibility. To avoid tortuous use of language in the discussions that follow, the terms "manager" and "tool" will sometimes be used interchangeably, but it should be borne in mind that the term "manager" has a wider meaning.

10.2 WHY YOU NEED TOOLS TO MANAGE A

DATA WAREHOUSE

Data warehouses are not just large databases; they are large, complex environments that integrate many different technologies. As such, they require a lot of maintenance and management. If the data warehouse is not to become a financial black hole, and a drain on system and database administration resources, sophisticated tools will be needed.

The traditional approach of having a large team of administrators to manage a large system does not work well in the data warehouse arena. The system usage is generally too ad hoc and unpredictable to be manually administrated. Therefore, intelligent tools are required to help the system and database administrators to do their job properly.

The added complication is that, as the chosen tools will need to communicate and work together, they must integrate properly. There are tools of all flavors, shapes and sizes in the marketplace today, and new tools are being announced every day. Because of this, any list of tools covered here would already be out date even as you were reading this book. Therefore, the approach taken here is to indicate the areas where tools are required, and to outline the criteria that such tools must meet to be of use.

The tools required can be divided into the following two categories:

- system management tools,
- data warehouse process management tools.

Each category is detailed separately in the sections that follow.

> **GUIDELINE 10.1** Because of the size and complexity of the system, tools will be required to manage the data warehouse efficiently.

10.3 SYSTEM MANAGERS

There are a number of areas of system management that are crucial to the success of a data warehouse. The most important managers are:

- configuration manager
- schedule manager
- event manager
- database manager
- backup recovery manager

There are other areas of system management, such as resource and performance monitoring, but these are either less critical or are subsumed into other areas. For instance, resource and performance monitoring falls under the auspices of the warehouse and query managers and is discussed later.

10.3.1 CONFIGURATION MANAGER

The configuration manager is responsible for the setup and configuration of the hardware. There are a number of different aspects that need to be addressed, ranging from the configuration of the machine itself through to the configuration and management of the disk farm. How the configuration manager is structured varies from operating system to operating system, and with UNIX it varies from vendor to vendor. Most configuration managers have a single interface that allows control of all aspects of the system, while others will have many different tools, each with their own interface.

From the data warehouse perspective, the single most important configuration tool is the I/O manager. For a detailed discussion on the requirements of the I/O manager see section 12.3.

10.3.2 SCHEDULE MANAGER

Behind every successful data warehouse there is a good solid scheduler. Almost all operations in the data warehouse will require some scheduling control. Even the daily ad hoc query load has an element of scheduling. As explained in section 18.3.2, the trick to making the data warehouse perform under the ad hoc query load is to use queuing to make the load predictable.

Every operating system will come with its own scheduler, and with some form of batch control mechanism. However, the operating system tools are often lacking in features. For example, in UNIX, commands such as cron which allow jobs to be scheduled for a certain time are not sufficiently rich in features to handle the requirements of a data warehouse. Here is a list of the features that the scheduling software must have:

- Handle multiple queues.
- Deal with inter-queue processing.
- Work across cluster or MPP boundaries.
- Maintain job schedules across system outages.
- Deal with international time differences.
- Handle job failures.
- Restart or re-queue failed jobs.
- Support job priorities.
- Support the stopping and starting of queues.
- Log queued jobs.
- Notify a user or process when a job has completed.
- Re-queue jobs to other queues.

This list can be used as a feature checklist for any scheduling software that you are evaluating. Not all features may be required by every data warehouse, but it is important to consider future requirements when making a decision.

For example, suppose the data warehouse is a local initiative and has no requirement for being able to handle different time zones. Let us further suppose that the company later opens an international office in another time zone. If this new office becomes another data source, and feeds back and forth need to be coordinated, the software will need to be capable of dealing with the time differences.

Some of the jobs the scheduler has to be able to handle are:

- overnight processing
  - data load
  - data transformation
  - index creation
  - aggregation creation
  - data movement operations
  - backup
- daily ad hoc query scheduling
- execution of regular report requirements

The schedule manager will need to be able to handle the interactions and dependencies between jobs, as well as dealing with any errors or problems that occur. If the operating system software is not up to the job, a third-party tool will be required.

> **GUIDELINE 10.2** If the data warehouse is running on a cluster or MPP architecture, the schedule manager must be capable of running across that architecture.

10.3.3 EVENT MANAGER

The first question most people ask when the event manager is raised as a topic is: What exactly is an event manager? An event manager is a piece of software that deals with defined events on the data warehouse system. It will monitor continuously for the occurrence of any events, and deal with them.

The next question people generally ask is: Why should they use an event management tool? This is an easy question to answer, but as event management software is not cheap the answer is often hard to explain or justify. The primary reason such a tool should be used is because a data warehouse environment is just too complex to be managed manually. The event manager is needed to track the myriad of things that can go wrong on such a large and volatile system.

Yes, but why do you need software to do this? Traditionally this job would be performed by the system manager, and in the case of the database, the database administrator (DBA). Every DBA and system manager has their favorite hand-crafted scripts for checking for problems. These scripts can be run regularly; they could even be scheduled to run automatically. This is all well and good, but in a terabyte-plus system, where it could take hours or even days to recover from a serious problem, you just do not have that luxury. If a problem occurs you need to know about it immediately. Ideally, you need to know about it before it happens, so it can be prevented. That is why you need event-tracking software.

Having an event manager will free the DBA and the system manager to manage the data warehouse proactively, rather than reactively. This allows them to get on with planning for changes to the data warehouse, such as new users, new data sources, software or hardware upgrades, and system tuning.

Events

Having established the requirement for the tool, we need to discuss what the tool needs to be capable of doing. First we need a definition of the term event:

> An event is a measurable, observable occurrence of a defined action.

Any event manager tool used must be based on that definition. Observability is an obvious attribute requirement, as it would be impossible to detect something that was not observable. Likewise, measurability is also a fairly obvious attribute, as the event manager needs to be capable of capturing the details of the event. The fact that an event is a defined action is crucially important. The event manager software must have an interface that allows you to define events.

Below is a list of the most common events that need to be tracked within a data warehouse environment:

- running out of space on certain key disks
- a process dying
- a process using excessive resource (such as CPU)
- a process returning an error
- disks exhibiting I/O bottlenecks
- hardware failure
- a table reaching its maximum size
- a table failing to extend because of lack of space
- CPU usage exceeding an 80% threshold
- excessive memory swapping
- usage of temporary or sort area reaching a certain threshold
- buffer cache hit ratios exceeding or falling below thresholds
- any other database shared memory usage
- internal contention on database serialization points

The event manager should ideally be capable of handling events automatically. Most event management packages allow procedures to be defined for each event. Scripts can be associated with an event, and the scripts will be executed if the event occurs.

Scripts that automatically resolve problems have to be well designed, if they are not to cause more problems than they solve. Any automated problem-resolution process has to be completely self-contained. It must not be able to affect other processes.

For example, if you have an event manager that detects when a certain table has insufficient room to expand, the procedure that goes with that event could have the ability to automatically expand the tablespace for that table. To do this it would have to expand a current data file or add a data file to the database. The question is: Where does the space for the data file come from? It should come from a pool of scratch disk space that is kept just for that purpose. The scratch space could be made available as temporary workspace to users rather than just sitting idle, but if that is the case the event manager must have the ability to clear down space if it needs to. This in itself is not a problem, as long as people clearly understand that the temporary workspace has no guarantees for continued existence of anything they put there. The problem arises if some other data warehouse process relies on this space to do its work. This opens the possibility of that process failing.

Clearly the event manager must also be able to report the error. This is particularly important in environments like data warehouses, where many of the operations are automated and "lights out."

The event manager must also be able to raise alerts. An alert is a heads-up message to warn of an impending event. For example, an alert could be raised whenever a key disk becomes more than 75% full. The alert must be captured somewhere, like on a console screen or in an alert log file. However, in the case of more serious alerts, such as a process failing, you may want the alert to be highly visible. It would be useful if the event manager could, either directly or indirectly via other software, ring a pager or mobile phone. This allows serious problems to be detected as they develop, and often major outages can be avoided.

> **GUIDELINE 10.3** An event manager is required to track the myriad of things that can go wrong on such a large and volatile system.

10.3.4 SYSTEM AND DATABASE MANAGER

The system and database manager will probably be two separate pieces of software, but we have lumped them together here because they do essentially the same job. The system manager will help the system management team to maintain and manage the system. Likewise, the database manager will help the DBAs to maintain and manage the database. We shall talk about them as a single manager, as it should be clear when something applies only to the operating system, or only to the database.

The purpose of each of these tools is to automate certain processes, and to simplify the execution of others. The system and database manager will generally have a menu system or GUI front end that allows structured access to the management functions. When choosing a system and database manager the criteria you should check for are:

- ability to add and remove users
  - user password management
- ability to maintain users
  - increase users' quotas
  - assign and deassign roles to users
  - assign and deassign profiles to users
- ability to maintain roles and profiles
  - create, maintain and delete roles
  - create, maintain and delete profiles
- ability to perform database space management
  - monitor and report on space usage
  - tidy up fragmented and unused space
  - add and expand space

- ability to perform system space management
  - monitor and report on space usage
  - clean up old or unused files or directories
  - add and expand space
- manage summary or temporary tables
  - assign or deassign temporary space to and from a user
  - reclaim space from old or out-of-date temporary tables
- ability to manage error and trace logs
  - ability to browse log and trace files
  - ability to redirect error or trace information
  - ability to switch on and off error and trace logging

User management should not be an onerous task in a data warehouse, because there are generally not a large number of users. However, each user has the potential to use huge amounts of system resource, and so user management is important. It is particularly important to be able to easily manage the roles and profiles that control the resource usage of each user. Whatever tool you choose to perform these functions must be flexible, and most importantly it must clearly display any role and profile dependencies.

Roles provide a very simple example of how things can get out of hand in a data warehouse. Let us suppose that a role X is created to be a low-level administration role, and role Y is created to allow unlimited space usage. If it is discovered that certain of the low-level administration tasks require a lot of space to perform, it is easy to see how role Y may at some stage get assigned to role X. This is not a problem as long as role X is used for its intended purpose. If, however, role X is assigned to a user who wants to do some work after hours or over a weekend, when no administrators are around, you may have a problem. You now have a user with unlimited space usage and the potential to use it. This was probably not the intention of assigning role X to the user. The tool used to perform the assignment operation needs to be capable of explicitly displaying the fact that X has Y and what that means.

Being able to manage space both inside and outside the database is a critical success factor in the performance of the data warehouse. In such an environment small changes can make huge differences. A simple change, such as specifying the fill or packing factor on a block, can save an enormous amount of space. Suppose we change the fill factor from 90% to 91% to allow another 1% of data into a database block. If we are using 8 kB blocks, that means about 80 extra bytes of data per block. This does not seem like much, but if the average record length is 70 bytes, and it happens that with the current fill factor we waste 65 + bytes of space, that change means two extra rows per block. Allowing for block overheads this change will on average increase the number of rows per block from 102 to 104. That is a saving of 150 + kB on 100 000 rows of data. If you load 100 000 000 records per day that becomes a daily saving of 150 MB, which becomes 13 GB over three months.

For similar reasons it is important to be able to reclaim unused space, and to unwind any space fragmentation that leaves small chunks of unusable space. The tool you choose has to be capable of displaying clearly how and where space is used, so the right decisions can be made.

The ad hoc demands placed on the data warehouse will often require the use of temporary tables to store interim results. Space will need to be set aside for this purpose. That space needs to be efficiently managed. The consequence of not managing it efficiently is that either the space required will be many times larger than necessary, or everything will grind to a halt. If the system and database management tool allows this space to be efficiently monitored, and allocated space to be dated and tracked, the space can be kept to a minimum, saving many tens of gigabytes of disk space.

As ever, it is the size and complexity of the data warehouse that is the issue here. Large numbers of error log and trace files will be produced. These need to be regularly and automatically scanned for errors or problems. This is one of the functions of the event manager. These files also need to be managed, with old log and trace files being purged to save space and make it easier to deal with the current logs.

Logs that contain significant data should be archived. Logs such as the database log, which contains all major changes, should be kept to maintain a history. This could prove to be important in a crisis situation, where the thread of events over the last number of weeks or months can become important. Any log files that contain errors that have not yet been explained should also be kept until the cause of the error is understood. The tool should allow such indicated log files to be archived, while others are deleted.

10.3.5 BACKUP RECOVERY MANAGER

As most backup packages have their own tools for managing backup and recovery, the requirement for a backup recovery manager will probably be met by the backup software itself. Nonetheless, it is worth outlining here the abilities that a tool should have. We shall concentrate on the management features here; for a wider list of requirements see section 14.4.

There are three main features required for the management of backups:

- scheduling
- backup data tracking
- database awareness

It must be easy for operations and management staff to control backup schedules via the tool. The backup recovery manager will need to integrate with whatever schedule manager software is being used. You should check how easy it is to schedule a one-off backup of part of the data warehouse.

At the end of the day, backups are taken for one reason and one reason only: protection against data loss. Backups are useless if they cannot be used when they are required. There are a number of questions that you need to be able to answer with confidence. For any given database data file or any file external to the database, do you:

- know when it was last backed up?
- know where the tape, or other medium, it was backed up to is located?
- know where any related files, such as journal files, are located?

These questions must be instantly answerable via the backup recovery manager. The backup software will keep some form of database of where and when each piece of data was backed up. The backup recovery manager must have a good usable front end to that database. If it does not, it will be a nightmare trying to find anything to perform a recovery. It is not advisable to get into a situation where you have to trawl through hundreds of tapes trying to find various bits of a file. This would be a very uncomfortable position, particularly if users and management were breathing down your neck.

It is useful for the backup software and the backup recovery manager to be database aware. Being database aware means that the software can be addressed in database terms, and will not perform backups that would not be viable. For example, in an Oracle database objects reside in tablespaces. It is no use backing up a single tablespace on its own unless you have roll-forward journal archiving enabled. If roll-forward journal archiving is not enabled, restoring tablespaces from different times will mean that they are out of sync and could corrupt your database. If the tool is database aware it can prevent mistakes like this happening. The exception to this rule is a read-only tablespace, which can be backed up and restored separately from the rest of the database. Again, a database-aware tool will know this.

The other useful feature of having a database-aware backup recovery manager is that the different parts of the database can be addressed by their database names, and not by the often abbreviated and unreadable file names.

One last point worth mentioning: ideally, the backup software used should work across clusters or MPP platforms if that is the environment being used. The backup recovery manager should also be capable of this.

> **GUIDELINE 10.4** Ensure that the backup software you use is database aware and integrates with your RDBMS.

10.4 DATA WAREHOUSE PROCESS MANAGERS

The data warehouse process managers are pieces of software responsible for the flow, maintenance and upkeep of the data, both into and out of the data warehouse database. There are three different data warehouse process managers:

- load manager
- warehouse manager
- query manager

These are dealt with in the following sections. Each process manager has its own responsibilities and complexities, and there are potential overlaps between the responsibilities of each process. It will help to avoid any ambiguities if we draw some strict boundaries within which each process will work.

Figure 10.1 shows the overall architecture of the data warehouse. If we change the diagram slightly to outline the territory of each of the process managers (Figure 10.2), it will be become clear that the load manager's responsibility for the data ends once the data has been delivered into the database. It is also clear that the warehouse manager is responsible for all the data while it exists within the data warehouse. Finally, the query manager is responsible for the management and scheduling of all user access to the data warehouse.

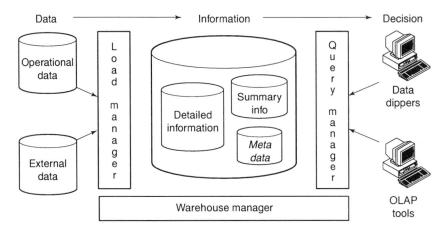

Figure 10.1 Data warehouse architecture.

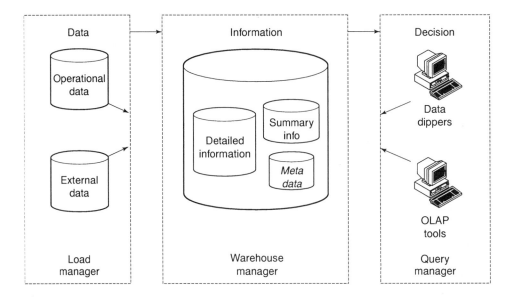

Figure 10.2 Boundaries of data warehouse process managers.

10.5 LOAD MANAGER

10.5.1 FUNCTIONAL DESCRIPTION

The load manager is responsible for any data transformation required and for the loading of data into the database. These responsibilities can be summarized as follows:

- data source interaction
- data transformation
- data load

The depth and complexity of the requirements placed on the load manager by each of these areas vary radically from data warehouse to data warehouse. This means that the load manager can vary from the simplicity of a few simple load scripts to an enormously involved development involving data transformation tools, database-to-database gateways and complex load programs.

It is not uncommon for the load manager to start out simple and to grow in complexity as data sources and user requirements are added. It is also possible for the development to go the other way, as data sources merge or are replaced. In particular, if the organization has multiple data warehouses, one can often become a greatly simplified source of data for another.

10.5.2 DATA SOURCE INTERACTION

The load manager will need to be capable of interacting with the source systems to verify that it has received all the data from the source. This is a major issue, and if not addressed data will get lost, leading to invalid results in the database. This interaction can be handled in many ways. The level of interaction possible will depend on the compatibility of the source and data warehouse systems.

The simplest level of interaction is if the source system packages control information into the files being transferred, or into separate control files. This information is then transferred with the rest of the data. The load manager can use this control information to ensure that it has all the files, and that each file contains the relevant data. Control information such as checksums of the file contents can be used.

If a higher level of interaction is possible between the source system and the data warehouse system, the load manager might exchange messages with the source system to ensure that each file is transferred correctly. If there are any problems, the data warehouse system could request that the file be sent again.

If a copy management tool is being used to transfer the data from the source system, this task becomes the responsibility of the copy management tool. In this case you need to ensure that the tool is carrying out the relevant checks. For example, you need to ensure that the tool verifies that the whole of a day's data gets transferred, and not just part of it.

If the data is being transferred directly via a gateway product into the database rather than by file, the load manager can use the gateway product itself to check how many records are to be transferred. It can then check at the data warehouse end that the correct number of records have been transferred.

However it is done, these checks must be implemented to ensure that all the correct data makes it from source to data warehouse. You also need to ensure that no data gets loaded twice.

> **GUIDELINE 10.5** Make sure that there are control checks to ensure that all data gets loaded, and no data gets loaded twice.

10.5.3 DATA TRANSFORMATION

An amount of data transformation will almost certainly need to be performed. For example, the source may supply more fields than are required; these fields will need to be stripped during the load. The source fields may be in formats different from that of the RDBMS you are using, requiring the format to be changed. There is often a requirement for a single field to be broken into two, or for multiple fields to be compacted into one. Extra fields, such as a sequence number to be used as a unique identifier, may need to be added.

Other fields may need to be derived from some combination of the supplied data and data already in the data warehouse. If more complex data mapping or transformation is required, you will need programs to carry out the transformations. You may need to look at using a copy management or transformation tool (see sections 3.4 and 3.5.

10.5.4 DATA LOAD

The ultimate goal and the responsibility of the load manager is to get data loaded into the data warehouse database. There are a number of different methods for getting the data from the source into the data warehouse. Some of the more commonly used approaches are:

- loading from flat files,
- 3GL programs for extracting and loading data,
- gateway products for connecting different RDBMSs,
- copy management tools.

Some of these tools, such as the gateway products and some of the third-party tools, are designed to select data directly from the source system itself. Others rely on the data being transferred from the source system as a file.

If large amounts of data need to be loaded, then it is likely that you will need to use the RDBMS's own loader software. These loader programs will sometimes have direct path load mechanisms, which bypass the SQL layer of the RDBMS and build whole database blocks directly. This will greatly improve the performance of the load.

Generally, the load performance can be further improved if there is a no-logging option. This option switches off journaling for the load operation. Note, however, that if this option is used it needs to be taken into consideration in your backup recovery strategy. If no-logging is to be used you also need to design the load jobs to be re-startable.

10.6 WAREHOUSE MANAGER

The warehouse manager is responsible for maintaining the data while it is in the data warehouse. This layer of software also creates and maintains the metadata that describes where everything resides within the data warehouse. The responsibilities of the warehouse manager are listed below:

- data movement
- metadata management
- performance monitoring and tuning
- data archiving

Given the size and complexity of most data warehouses it is important to automate as many data management operations as possible. The warehouse manager should be designed to deal with all the tasks mentioned above automatically. Extensive reporting capabilities are a must for the warehouse manager; in particular, it should be able to report any failures of data movement, such as aggregation creation failures.

10.6.1 DATA MOVEMENT

The warehouse manager is responsible for any data movement within the warehouse, such as aggregation creation and maintenance. Any tables, indexes or other objects required will also be created and maintained by the warehouse manager.

Aggregation creation and maintenance is a process that should be automated. The warehouse manager needs an interface that allows new aggregations to be requested, and old aggregations to be removed. This mechanism can be controlled via tables in the database. Database procedures can be used to insert a row into a table for each new aggregation to be created. The warehouse manager will also need to know what fields are required in the aggregation and what fields to aggregate on. From this information it can build the aggregation and the metadata to describe it.

Most aggregations can be created by a single query. However, the query is often complex and not necessarily the most efficient method of generating the aggregation. It may be possible to generate the aggregation from other aggregations, or by a multiple-stage process with interim result tables. These interim results can often be used as the basis of multiple aggregations, thereby saving time and resource overall. The warehouse manager needs to be capable of taking advantage of these optimizations.

There is no warehouse manager software currently on the market that can do this automatically, which means that human input is required. One suggestion to work around this problem is to allow a program or procedure to be associated with each aggregation. If one exists, the warehouse manager can use it instead of directly generating the aggregation from a single query.

> **GUIDELINE 10.6** Associate a creation procedure with each aggregation. This allows aggregation creation to be tailored without changing the warehouse manager software. If the procedure does not exist, the aggregation can be created directly using the relevant SQL.

To make the best use of system resources, the warehouse manager may need to use parallelism for any given operation. It may also need to run multiple operations side by side. To ensure that the system is neither underutilized nor swamped with work, this process can be driven via the queuing mechanisms of the schedule manager. To achieve this the aggregations may need to be prioritized. They may also need to be sequenced if one aggregation is to be built from another. This means that the warehouse manager needs to integrate with the queuing mechanism of the schedule manager.

The warehouse manager is also responsible for creating and maintaining the indexes on the fact and dimension data and on the aggregations. The indexes on the fact data will need to be created as soon as the data load completes. Likewise, the indexes on the aggregations will need to be created as soon as a new aggregation is built.

If data marts are being used, the warehouse manager will be responsible for maintaining them. It will schedule any refreshes of the data marts, and may also be responsible for pushing the data out to the different data mart machines.

10.6.2 METADATA MANAGEMENT

The warehouse manager is responsible for managing the metadata. Metadata is used to describe the data that resides within the data warehouse; it also describes where each piece of data resides. For a detailed discussion on metadata see Chapter 9.

If new data is loaded, old data is archived or current data is moved within the data warehouse, metadata needs to be generated or updated to keep track of where that data resides. For example, if the fact data is partitioned into multiple tables for management reasons, the warehouse manager will need to be aware of the partitioning key, and the range of key values that each partition contains.

This metadata will be required by the query manager to allow it to generate queries. The query manager will also need to be able to identify when different tables contain the same data, but possibly as different levels of aggregation. The warehouse manager needs to generate this information when it creates or updates aggregations.

10.6.3 PERFORMANCE MONITORING AND TUNING

The warehouse manager is responsible for monitoring the performance of any operation it runs. It should also manage the storage of the performance statistics produced by the query manager. These statistics, along with the query history of all queries, should be stored in the database, so that they can be analyzed.

These statistics need to be kept for as long as possible. For each query the statistics could be averaged over time to reduce storage space. However, it is important to keep a time trail for these statistics, so that changing trends can be identified. Therefore, the data should not be aggregated over too large a time period, or it may mask trends. Older data can be aggregated over a greater time period if the averages do not change, but recent data should be averaged over a day or at most a week.

The warehouse manager is responsible for the creation of aggregations and indexes: therefore, any tuning that requires either an aggregation or an index will need to be passed on to the warehouse manager. Ideally the warehouse manager itself should be capable of identifying the need for new aggregations, and automatically creating them. There is no such predictive software on the market today, but software is beginning to appear that can perform that function at a basic level, and it is inevitable that more sophisticated software will follow.

10.6.4 DATA ARCHIVING

As data ages, it will need to be purged to clear room for more current data. There is often a desire to hold data online for long periods of time, but usually the practicalities of working with such huge volumes of data dictate a reasonable cutoff point. Most companies have a natural cycle of data that will indicate how long data remains immediately useful.

These times will often conflict with business rules or legal requirements for how long data should actually be maintained. This generally means that data will need to be archived off the data warehouse, either to nearline storage, or to tape. Which method should be used will depend on how likely old data is to be retrieved. It is worth mentioning here that data warehouses rarely generate new fact data; they normally load fact data from other sources. This means that the source system will already have the data archived. This is often a sufficient argument to avoid archiving on the data warehouse.

If archiving is required it needs to be factored into the capacity planning and the overnight window design from the beginning. This is important even though archiving may not be required for some years. If it is not designed in from the beginning it may become a serious problem when it is required to run for the first time. It will probably increase the overheads of the overnight process and may even delay the start of the process by having to clean off space to allow new data to be loaded.

If designed properly, the load process will not depend on the archiving process being run first. Sufficient space should be made available to allow the archiving to occur later than immediately required. This allows the archiving to be performed at a more convenient time.

When designing the archiving process there are a number of details that need to be established:

- data life expectancy
  - in raw form
  - in aggregated form
- data archiving
  - start date
  - cycle
  - workload

The **data life expectancy** is the amount of time that data is expected to remain in the database. You need to establish the requirement for how long fact data needs to be held online at the fact level. Older fact data can often be held online in aggregated form, reducing the amount of space it requires. This is a useful trick, but it has a cost. Rolling up the data requires processing power, and can require more space in the short term. This needs to be designed into the warehouse manager's processing schedule.

For archiving there are three figures that need to be established. First, you need to establish the start date: that is, when archiving is required to begin. For example, if the aim to keep 3 years' worth of data online, and the data warehouse is to start off with 18 months of historic data loaded, you will need to begin archiving 18 months after the go-live date.

The second figure that needs to be decided is the archive cycle or frequency. How often is data archived? Even if data is loaded daily, you may not want to run archiving on a daily cycle. It is often better to use a longer cycle, such as a week, a month, or even a quarter. This will increase the storage requirement to a cycle beyond the life expectancy, but it also makes the archiving more flexible, and gives you room to spread the load over more convenient times.

Finally, you need to estimate the load that **archiving** will place on the system. This is important to know accurately, as it tells you how much leeway you have in scheduling the archiving of a set of data. It also tells you when the process can be run. For example, if the archiving is to be on a monthly cycle, and archiving a month's worth of data takes several hours, it is not likely that you can do the archiving during a normal overnight run. You may need to put it off to a weekend and use the daily scheduling time to get the job done.

> **GUIDELINE 10.7** Design and test the archiving process into the data warehouse from the beginning, even if it will not be employed for some time. This will avoid any nasty shocks down the line.

10.7 QUERY MANAGER

The query manager has several distinct responsibilities. It is used to control all of the following:

- user access to the data
- query scheduling
- query monitoring

These areas are all very different in nature, and each area requires its own tools, bespoke software and procedures. The query manager is one of the most bespoke pieces of software in the data warehouse. The tools required to perform the query manager's tasks are not yet available, but are beginning to appear. They will become increasingly important as data warehouse user populations grow. Indeed, if the future dream of large user communities running against enormous data warehouses is to be realized, these tools are both essential and inevitable.

10.7.1 USER ACCESS TO DATA

The query manager is the software interface between the users and the data. It presents the data to the users in a form they understand. The query manager also controls the user access to the data. In a data warehouse, the raw data will often be an amalgamation of data from many disparate data sources. The disparate and often contradictory data needs to be tied together somehow; to achieve this the raw data is often abstracted. Data in this raw format can often be difficult to interpret. This, coupled with the fact that data from a single logical table is often partitioned into multiple real tables, can make ad hoc querying of raw data difficult.

The query manager's task is to address this problem by presenting a meaningful schema to the users via a friendly front end. The query manager will at one end take in the user's requirements, and in the background using the metadata it will transform these requirements into queries against the appropriate data.

Ideally, all user access tools should work via the query manager. However, as a number of different tools are likely to be used, and the tools used are likely to change over time, it is probable that not all tools will work directly via the query manager. Any restrictions on the users' access will need to be imposed by the tool itself. The tool also needs to be capable of presenting the coherent picture of the data warehouse that the query manager would have presented.

If users have access via tools that do not interface directly through the query manager, you should try setting up some form of indirect control by the query manager. Certainly no large ad hoc queries should be allowed to be run by anyone other than the query manager. It may be possible to get the tool to dump the query request to a flat file, where the query manager can pick it up. If queries do bypass the query manager, your query statistics gathering will be less accurate.

10.7.2 QUERY SCHEDULING

Scheduling of ad hoc queries is a responsibility of the query manager. Simultaneous large ad hoc queries, if not controlled, can severely affect the performance of any system: in particular if the queries are run using parallelism, where a single query can potentially use all the CPU resource made available to it. Typically this will be achieved using queuing mechanisms to ensure that large jobs do not clash. For details on how this is done see section 18.4.

This means that the query manager has to integrate with the schedule manager. The query manager will need to be able to issue commands to queue, abort and re-queue query jobs. It will also need to be able to deal with multiple queues and queue priorities.

One aspect of query control that is glaringly visible by its absence is the ability to predict how long a query will take to complete. Some RDBMSs have a prediction facility, but to date they have been notoriously unreliable. Prediction tools are a new field, and the first of them is only just arriving on the market. In the absence of a good predictive tool, the best that can be done is to use the experience of similar queries, but to do this requires a lot of historic query data.

10.7.3 QUERY MONITORING

One of the main functions of the query manager will be to monitor the queries as they run. This is one of the reasons why all queries should be run via, or at least notified to, the query manager. The gathering of statistics is vital if the data warehouse is to be successful. As the usage of the data warehouse grows, and the number of concurrent users and the number of ad hoc queries grow, the success of the data warehouse will depend on how these queries are managed.

One of the keys to that success is the tuning of the ad hoc environment to meet the users' needs. To achieve this, the query profiles of the different groups of users need to be known. This can be achieved only if you have long-term statistics on the queries run by each user and the resources used by each query. The query execution plan needs to be stored along with the statistics of the resources used, and the query syntax itself. For details on what information needs to be collected see section 9.4.

The query manager has to be capable of gathering these statistics, which should then be stored in the database for later analysis. It should also maintain a query history. Every query created or executed via the query manager should be logged. This allows the query profiles to be built up over time. This history enables the identification of frequently run queries, or types of queries. These queries can then be tuned, possibly by adding new indexes or by creating new aggregations.

> **GUIDELINE 10.8** Ideally all query access to the data warehouse should go via the query manager.

PART FOUR

Hardware and Operational Design

4

CHAPTER 11

Hardware architecture

11.1 INTRODUCTION

The aim of this chapter is to cover the issues raised by the choice of hardware. Any data warehouse solution will contain many different pieces of hardware, ranging from the database server to the network and the user front-end hardware. This chapter deals primarily with the possible server environments, covering them in some depth. Network and client-side issues are generally outside the scope of the data warehouse design team. However, there are still some network and client-side issues that need to be considered, and these are covered below.

11.2 PROCESS

The hardware architecture of a data warehouse is defined within the *technical blueprint* stage of the process (Figure 11.1). The *business requirements* stage should have identified the initial user requirements and given an indication of the capacity-planning requirements. The hardware architecture is determined once a broad understanding of the required technical architecture has been achieved. The backup and security strategies are also determined during the *technical blueprint* phase.

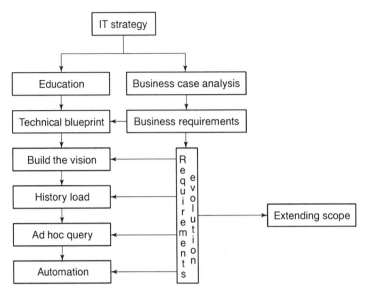

Figure 11.1 Stages in the process.

11.3 SERVER HARDWARE

The server is a crucial part of the data warehouse environment. To support the size of the database, and the ad hoc nature of the query access, warehouse applications generally require large hardware configurations. There are a number of different hardware architectures in the open systems market, each of which has its own advantages and disadvantages. The different architectures are discussed below.

11.3.1 ARCHITECTURE OPTIONS

There are two main hardware architectures commonly used as server platforms in data warehouse solutions: **symmetric multi-processing** (SMP), and **massively parallel processing** (MPP). There is a lot of confusion about the distinction between these architectures, and this is not helped by the existence of hybrid machines that use both.

The primary distinguishing feature between SMP and MPP is as follows. An SMP machine is a set of tightly coupled CPUs that share memory and disk. An MPP machine is a set of loosely coupled CPUs, each of which has its own memory and disk. Bear this in mind as we discuss each of the architectures in detail below.

To add to the confusion, new and emerging technologies, such as extremely high-speed memory connections and non-uniform memory architecture (NUMA), are adding variants of the SMP architecture, allowing them to scale to much higher levels.

11.3.2 SYMMETRIC MULTI-PROCESSING

Figure 11.2 illustrates a typical SMP configuration. SMP machines are the natural progression of the traditional single-CPU midrange servers. SMP, along with the growth of clustering technology, has made possible the support of larger and larger databases. They are also the base technologies that enable the downsizing of mainframe systems. SMP gives the CPU bandwidth needed to support the large ad hoc queries of decision support systems.

An SMP machine is a set of CPUs that share memory and disk. This is sometimes called a **shared-everything environment**. Unlike some of the earlier multi-CPU machines, where there existed a master CPU with a number of slave CPUs, the CPUs in an SMP machine are all equal. The operating system contains special code to allow the different CPUs to access central structures, such as memory address tables and job schedule queues, in a controlled manner. This means that a process can run on any CPU in the machine, and indeed it will often be run on different CPUs at different times. For example, a process that is performing I/O will not need CPU time. Its context – the memory and register information associated with the process – will be switched out of the CPU it is currently using. When the I/O is complete and the process needs a CPU to perform its next instruction, it gets queued by the process scheduler and will be run in turn on the next available CPU.

Having said this, most vendors have the facility to allow processes to have CPU affinity. This is where the process runs only on certain CPUs. Indeed, those CPUs can be dedicated to specific tasks. This can be useful when there are processes, such as real-time processes, that require immediate response. It can also help to avoid heavy context switching for busy processes.

The length of the communications bus connecting the CPUs is a natural limit to the scalability of SMP machines. As the bus gets longer the interprocessor communication speeds become slower. Add to this the fact that each extra CPU imposes an extra bandwith load on the bus, increases memory contention, and so on.

These problems eventually cause a tail-off in the CPU scalability curve, reaching a point where the benefit of adding any extra CPUs is negated by the increased overheads. Clearly, the actual scalability of different vendors' hardware will differ, but all SMP boxes display a tail-off in scalability similar to that shown in Figure

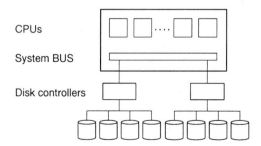

CPUs

System BUS

Disk controllers

Figure 11.2 SMP machine.

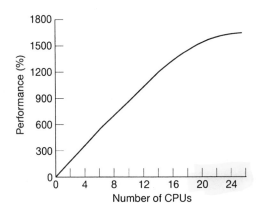

Figure 11.3 Typical SMP scalability curve.

11.3. This limit in the in-box scalability of CPU bandwidth can be overcome by the use of clustering technology.

Having multiple CPUs available allows operations to be processed in parallel. For example, if the database software supports parallel queries, a single query can be decomposed and its separate parts processed in parallel. This makes query performance scalable. In other words, a given query can be speeded up by throwing more hardware at it. This is crucial, as it makes it possible to run queries today that yesterday would have been considered impossible. It is exactly this software technology, in conjunction with bigger, faster SMP and MPP systems, that is driving the current data warehousing boom.

11.3.3 CLUSTER TECHNOLOGY

Figure 11.4 illustrates a typical cluster system. A cluster is a set of loosely coupled SMP machines connected by a high-speed interconnect. Each machine has its own CPUs and memory, but they share access to disk. Thus these systems are called **shared-disk systems**. Each machine in the cluster is called a **node**. The aim of the cluster is to mimic a single larger machine. In this pseudo single machine, resources such as shared disk must be managed in a distributed fashion. A layer of software called the **distributed lock manager** is used to achieve this. This software is run on each machine, and communicates over the high-speed interconnect. The distributed lock manager maintains the integrity of each resource by ensuring that the resource can be changed on only one node of the cluster at a time.

The distributed lock manager and the interconnect become the factors that limit the scalability of the cluster itself. The scalability differs from hardware vendor to hardware vendor, but clusters generally will scale only to somewhere between four and eight nodes.

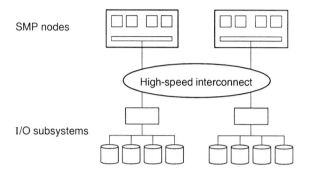

SMP nodes

High-speed interconnect

I/O subsystems

Figure 11.4 Cluster of SMP machines.

Clustering technology was first introduced by Digital on VAX VMS machines back in the 1980s. In the last few years the main UNIX vendors have introduced clustered systems. These systems have had many teething problems but have now begun to prove themselves. However, they still suffer from some fundamental issues that affect design. One of the main problems is the inability of the UNIX clusters to support proper file system sharing. Sharing is currently limited to raw devices (see section 12.4. This is a nuisance, as it requires, amongst other things, the database software to be installed multiple times. However, this is already changing, as some UNIX vendors are now bringing out shared-file systems.

11.3.4 MASSIVELY PARALLEL PROCESSING

Figure 11.5 illustrates a typical MPP system. Massively parallel processing is the "new kid on the block." Like any new technology, MPP has had its teething problems, not least of which is the lack of tools to manage, monitor and support these massive machines. This is starting to change as the MPP market shakes itself out.

Most of the myriad MPP start-up companies have failed, leaving only a few serious players in the MPP business. However, MPP has for the most part failed to get a toehold in the IT strategies of general business. This is likely to be compounded by the advent of the new SMP architectures that are emerging, which allow much greater SMP scalability. So, for the foreseeable future, MPP is likely to be concentrated in certain niche markets.

An MPP machine is made up of many loosely coupled nodes. These nodes will be linked together by a high-speed connection. The form that this connection takes varies from vendor to vendor. Each node has its own memory, and the disks are not shared, each being attached to only one node. However, most MPP systems allow a disk to be dual connected between two nodes. This protects against an individual node failure causing disks to be unavailable.

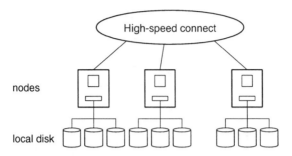

Figure 11.5 MPP machine.

These types of environment are generally referred to as **shared nothing**. There are many different models of MPP. Each will have nodes that consist of one or more CPUs. For example, some MPP machines have nodes with two CPUs, where one CPU is dedicated to handling I/O. Others have nodes that are genuine SMP machines in their own right. Yet others have single CPU nodes, where some will be dedicated to handling I/O and others to processing. However, all these configurations have one thing in common: nothing is shared directly.

The level to which systems are shared nothing varies from vendor to vendor. For example, the IBM SP/2 is a fully shared nothing system. An extra layer of software called the **virtual shared disk** (VSD) needs to be added to allow disks to be shared across nodes. This contrasts with the **Pyramid mesh** machine, where although disks are localized on nodes, each disk is still visible via the normal UNIX I/O subsystem. Any MPP system will suffer overheads if an I/O is issued and data has to be shipped from node to node to satisfy the request.

Like a cluster, MPP machines require the use of a distributed lock manager to maintain the integrity of the distributed resources across the system as a whole. The distributed lock manager needs to be able to track which node's memory holds the current copy of each piece of information. It also needs to be able to swiftly satisfy any requests for that information, getting the data rapidly from node to node. It is primarily in the method of implementing this communication that the MPP vendors differ.

The advantage of MPP systems is that because nothing is shared they do not suffer the same restrictions as SMP and cluster systems. For example, because a disk can be shared on a cluster, each shared disk must be connected to each node that shares it. This connection takes up a disk slot on each node and thus limits the amount of disk that can be connected. In an MPP system the amount of disk that can be supported is limited only by the number of nodes that can be connected. There is great variability in these systems, with SMP/cluster solutions supporting anywhere from 1 to 50 TB, and MPP systems supporting from 10 to 100 + TB.

Likewise, the amount of CPU power that can be made available in an MPP system is dependent on the number of nodes that can be connected. The scalability of the MPP system will depend on its internal connection method. The available systems vary radically, some scaling to 64 nodes while others scale up to thousands of nodes.

While shared nothing gives MPP its scalability, it is also its Achilles' heel. Because nothing is shared, MPP is a much more difficult environment on which to design and develop. Data location becomes crucial. To make use of the CPU power of the MPP system while avoiding vast amounts of data shipping, data needs to be spread across many nodes. Getting this data partitioning correct is critical to the success of the system. In a data warehouse where ad hoc queries are allowed it is almost impossible to come up with a partitioning strategy that will allow all queries to be equally performant. Node and disk hot spots are almost inevitable.

Even if you can get data distributed to give good performance, what happens when you want to add new nodes? How do you cope with new data sources, or new aggregations that require new disk space? These issues make design and management of a data warehouse on an MPP system considerably more difficult than on an SMP or cluster system.

> **GUIDELINE 11.1**   Design and management of a data warehouse on an MPP system is considerably more difficult than on an SMP or cluster system.

11.3.5   NEW AND EMERGING TECHNOLOGIES

Non uniform memory architecture (NUMA) machines are not a new concept. The idea has been around for some years. Recent advances in hardware technology have made machines such as the Sequent NUMA-Q a possibility. A NUMA machine is basically a tightly coupled cluster of SMP nodes, with an extremely high-speed interconnect. The interconnect needs to be sufficiently fast to give near-SMP internal speeds. The advantage of such an interconnect is that it enables the operating system to run across the whole machine as a single distributed instance, rather than the usual separate copies of the operating system running on each node. In essence it makes the distributed memory on the SMP nodes of a NUMA machine act as if it were a single shared memory.

Another new technology is the **high-speed memory interconnect**, such as the memory channel provided by Digital on its clustered UNIX systems. The memory channel allows a cluster of SMP nodes to act more as though it has one memory address space. It also removes the requirement for a shared disk to be connected to each node, because disks that are connected to one node can be shared by other nodes over the high-speed memory channel link.

Both of these new technologies overcome bottlenecks in the current cluster systems, thereby allowing much greater scalability of disk, memory and CPU on a clustered system. These technologies, and the continual improvement of disk and I/O technology, mean that the size of disk farm that cluster systems can support continues to grow. These systems are eating into the MPP size advantage, making the decision of whether to go SMP or MPP a little easier. For the development of a data warehouse the default choice currently has to be an SMP system, unless a very good reason can be given for choosing an MPP system.

11.3.6 SERVER MANAGEMENT

The systems required for data warehouse environments are generally large and complex. This, added to the changing nature of a warehouse, means that these systems require a lot of management. For systems and database administrators to manage effectively, they require the use of one or more of the increasing number of management and monitoring tools on the market.

These tools allow the automatic monitoring of most if not all the required processes and statistics. Events such as:

- running out of space on certain key disks,
- a process dying,
- a process using excessive resource (such as CPU),
- a process returning an error,
- disks exhibiting I/O bottlenecks,
- hardware failure,
- a table failing to extend because of lack of space,
- CPU usage exceeding an 80% threshold,
- excessive memory swapping,
- low buffer cache hit ratios,

can be caught and in many cases fixed automatically. This takes much of the sheer drudgery out of system management, allowing the system administrators to get on with more important, but less immediately critical, work. For a more thorough discussion of management tools see Chapter 10.

> **GUIDELINE 11.2** Management tools are required to manage a large, dynamic and complex system such as a data warehouse.

11.4 NETWORK HARDWARE

The network, although not part of the data warehouse itself, can play an important part in a data warehouse's success.

11.4.1 NETWORK ARCHITECTURE

As long as the network has sufficient bandwidth to supply the data feed and user requirements, the architecture of the network is irrelevant. It is, however, important at the design stage to consider some aspects of the network architecture. For example, if user access is going to be via a wide area network (WAN), this needs to be considered in the design of parts of the application, such as the query manager.

The main aspects of a data warehouse design that may be affected by the network architecture are:

- user access,
- source system data transfer,
- data extractions.

Each of these issues needs to be considered carefully. For example, consider the problem of getting the data from the source systems. Even if the network bandwidth is sufficient to cope with the data transfer on a daily basis, it may not get the data to the warehouse system early enough to allow it to be loaded, transformed, processed and backed up within the overnight time window. All such issues that can affect the data warehouse design need to be bottomed out very early on.

> **GUIDELINE 11.3** Ensure that the network architecture and bandwidth are capable of supporting the data transfer and any data extractions in an acceptable time. The transfer of data to be loaded must complete quickly enough to allow the rest of the overnight processing to complete.

Data extractions are any requests that cause data to be transferred out over the network. Result sets of queries that are passed to the user either directly or via a temporary table in the database are examples to data extractions. Another common data extraction is a data mart. The question that has to be answered is: Will the network bandwidth be capable of supporting the load placed on it by the identifiable or likely data extractions?

11.4.2 NETWORK MANAGEMENT

Network management is a black art. It requires specialist tools and lots of network experience. The management of the network has no direct effect on a data warehouse, except for one issue. It is important to be able to monitor network performance. The network may play a key part in data flow through a data warehouse environment. Being able to monitor this part of the data flow is necessary to enable resolution of any performance problems.

11.5 CLIENT HARDWARE

As with the network, clients are external to the data warehouse system itself. There are, however, still aspects that need to be considered during the design phase.

11.5.1 CLIENT MANAGEMENT

Management of the clients is beyond the scope of the data warehouse environment. The dependencies here are the other way around. Those responsible for client machine management will need to know the requirements for that machine to access the data warehouse system. Details such as the network protocols supported

> **GUIDELINE 11.4** Make sure those responsible for the network are fully aware of all the data warehouse network requirements, and that they can meet them.

on the server, and the server's Internet address, will need to be supplied.

If multiple access paths to the server system exist, this information needs to be relayed to those responsible for the client systems. For example, if the server is a cluster environment, during node fallover users may need to access a different machine address. All such dependencies need to be driven out and documented.

11.5.2 CLIENT TOOLS

At the design stage it may be necessary to consider what user-side tools will be used. If these tools have special requirements, such as data being summarized in certain ways, these requirements need to be catered for. Even given this requirement, it is important that the data warehouse be designed to be accessible to any tool. In fact the tool should not be allowed to affect the basic design of the warehouse itself. This protects against changing tools requirements, and is particularly important in the data warehouse arena, where requirements evolve over time.

No one tool is likely to meet all users' requirements, and it is probable that multiple tools will be used against the data warehouse. The tools should be thoroughly tested and trialed to ensure that they are suitable for the users. This testing of the tools should ideally be performed in parallel with the data warehouse design. This will allow any usability issues to be exposed, and will also help to drive out any requirements that the tool will place on the data warehouse.

> **GUIDELINE 11.5** The tools must not be allowed to affect the design of the data warehouse.

CHAPTER 12

Physical layout

12.1 PARALLEL TECHNOLOGY

12.1.1 INTRODUCTION

At the heart of any computer is the **central processing unit** (CPU). Notwithstanding I/O bottlenecks and bus and backplane capacities, the speed of the CPU is what dictates the amount of work that a computer can perform in a given time. Many techniques, such as pipelining instructions or the ability to issue multiple instructions simultaneously, are employed to try get around the limits of a single CPU. Another technique that became commercially available in the late 1980s and early 1990s was to make operating system software sophisticated enough to run across multiple CPUs at the same time. This allowed computers to scale to much greater levels of performance. Chapter 11 discusses the various hardware architectures that exploit this ability.

Clearly, having multiple CPUs in the same machine allows more than one job to be dealt with simultaneously. However, it also opens up another possibility: that of having a single job running on more than one CPU at the same time. The importance of this possibility cannot be stressed enough. It is this ability to parallelize a single job that has led to the current boom in data warehousing.

Being able to parallelize a single query has made it feasible to do work that previously, although possible, would have been uneconomic or even meaningless. As an example, let us consider a query that scans large quantities of demographic and sales data to spot trends and return a single day's sales by area and by area type. Suppose the query takes 2 days to run on a single CPU. Such a query could be useful for past analysis, where a week or two weeks' worth of data could be analyzed in detail. The query does, however, take too long to be of day-to-day value in spotting sales swings by region. Now if the same query runs across 20 CPUs, even assuming a modest scalability of 50%, the query will complete in under 5 hours.

This section discusses in detail the issues surrounding parallelism in its many forms. Parallelism has opened the data floodgates, making vast quantities of data economically available in reasonable time-frames. Naturally, the need to handle such vast quantities of data changes the rules of the data layout game. Not only have the rules changed, but the stakes have been raised, and the cost of getting the data layout wrong can run into thousands of man-days and millions of dollars.

12.1.2 PARALLEL QUERY

What is parallel query?

What exactly does it mean to parallelize a query? Before we can answer this question we need to be clear on exactly what we mean by a query. A query is a single statement that requests a certain subset of data ordered or presented in a particular way. This query will be presented to the relational database management system (RDBMS) in a language such as Structured Query Language (SQL). For example, the query

```
select customer_name, region, sum(amount_paid)
from sales
where sum(amount_paid) > 1000
and date_of_sale between '01-JAN-96' and '31- JAN-96'
group by region customer_name
order by region
```

will bring back the sales figures by region and by customer name, for all customers that have spent more than $1000 in the month of January. The where clause specifies the subset of data required from the sales table. The group by and order by clauses specify the way we want the data aggregated and presented.

The steps taken by the RDBMS to satisfy the above query are:

1 Fetch the data from the sales table.
2 Apply the restrictions from the where clause.
3 Sort the returned data.
4 Pass sorted data to requesting tool/process.

Note: no consideration is given here to the background work that the RDBMS has to do to parse the SQL and set the query up. We concentrate here on the question we originally asked. What exactly does it mean to parallelize a query? Steps 1–3 above lend themselves wholly or in part to being done in parallel. Step 4 must be done serially, as there is an implied order on the data.

How does parallel query work?

Now let us deal one by one with steps 1–4 above. Step 1 fetches the data from the `sales` table. To parallelize this process all we need is the ability to divide the table into multiple addressable parts, each part of which can be accessed and fetched by a different process. There are a number of ways of doing this, and some approaches are discussed below.

The parallelism can be implemented in the hardware, allowing intelligent disk controllers to split the requests and handle the streams of returning data. This approach can be performant, but has its restrictions. In pulling the control of the parallelism out of the RDBMS, and into the hardware, it limits the RDBMS optimizer's options. More importantly, such solutions tend to be proprietary. As these solutions require special hardware and integration to the operating system software, they also tend to be very expensive. Hardware called an **accelerator** is available that can be added to the back of an open system machine to provide such a capability. However, accelerators tend to be limited in scope and again are expensive.

The other approach is to allow the RDBMS to control the parallel access to the data. Many separate processes can be started to stream the data from disk. Again, there are a number of software architectures that can be employed. Before discussing them further it is important to define the concepts of data shipping and function shipping. In a system with many nodes and a large disk farm, it is possible that not every CPU will be directly connected to every disk. Hence processes will often be divorced from the data they are dealing with. **Data shipping** is where a process requests for the data to be shipped to the location where the process is running. **Function shipping** is where the function to be performed is moved to the locale of the data. Clearly this is more of an issue in MPP architectures than in SMP where disks are shared.

Some architectures, which are designed for shared-nothing or distributed environments, use function shipping exclusively to move the process to the data. They can achieve parallelism as long as the data is partitioned or distributed correctly. A particular query process is tied to locally available data. As the process always runs next to the data they avoid any problems with data being shipped. They are, however, limited in that ad hoc queries that do not match the partitioning strategy used cannot be effectively parallelized. This makes many queries impossible to run in meaningful time-scales.

Another approach is to have a dynamic mechanism whereby data and query process are not tied together. This method gets around the fixed partitioning problems, and always allows parallelism to be achieved, no matter what the data distribution. It can, however, lead to data shipping. This in itself is not a bad thing. For example, suppose we are running in an MPP environment and require a set of data located on a single node to be scanned in parallel. Nodes in MPP machines tend to be single CPUs and as such can support only a small number of parallel processes on each node. The exact number will depend on the power of the CPU. If we want to achieve higher degrees of parallelism we need to be able to run query processes on other nodes and ship the data.

This said, data shipping should be avoided where possible, and the RDBMS needs to have intelligence that allows it to function ship where possible, and data ship where necessary.

Step 2 above was to apply the restrictions to the fetched data. This can again be achieved in parallel. In fact, the restrictions or filters can best be applied by the scanning processes themselves. The advantage of this is that only the required data is passed back from the scanning processes, and this reduces the amount of work that needs to be done at later stages.

Step 3 was to sort the returned data. Again, there is no reason why this cannot be done in parallel. It could, as with Step 2, be applied by the same processes. This solution has its restrictions, because the sort would slow the scan, reducing the benefit of scanning in parallel. It is better to have a second sorting process that takes the filtered data from a scanning process and sorts it.

As ever, there are a number of ways this can be done. There could be a straight one-to-one matching of sort and scan processes. Each sort process would take a feed from a given scan process and sort the data. The problem with this approach is that although the data from each scan is sorted, the data overall is not, and the output from each sort process will need to be merged (Figure 12.1).

Another possibility is to divide the data amongst the sort processes by sort key. In the example, the sort keys are `region` and then `customer_name`. So each sort process could be given one or more regions to sort depending on the spread of the data. The advantage of this approach is that the resulting data will not require merging, as the separately sorted data contains no overlaps and is ordered (Figure 12.2).

Understanding how parallel query works is half the battle. It allows the layout of the data to be planned appropriately. These issues are discussed in section 12.3 below.

Some other parallel concepts

There are some other concepts, such as those listed below:

- intra-statement operations
- cost-based optimizer
- what degree of parallelism to use

that are worth discussing in connection with parallelism.

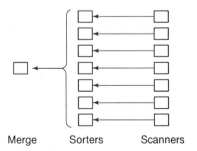

Merge   Sorters   Scanners

Figure 12.1 Scan and sort, method 1.

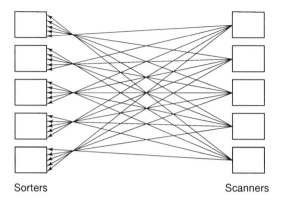

Sorters   Scanners

Figure 12.2 Scan and sort in parallel, method 2.

Intra-statement operations

Intra-statement operations are separate operations that occur within the confines of the SQL statement itself. This is contrasted with **inter-statement operations**, which take place between statements. We have covered parallel operations above in general terms. In our discussion we proposed the idea of having a set of scanning processes and a separate set of sorting processes, where the data flows from one set to another. This is a form of **pipelining**. Pipelining is where operations are carried out sequentially on a given piece of data, X. X goes through each stage in the pipe in order. However, once X has been passed on to stage 2 of the pipe, stage 1 can begin processing $X+1$ while X is still in the pipe.

Pipelining allows sequential intra-statement operations to occur simultaneously. This functionality can be extended further by allowing non-sequential intra-statement operations to happen simultaneously. For example, if we take a typical SQL statement that requires a join between three tables, let us say `sales`, `customer` and `branch_hierarchy`, with a `group by` or `order by`:

```
select     s.cust_id,
           sum(s.total_cost) total_sales,
           c.name,
           b.branch_id,
           s.account_type
           s.sales_date
from       sales s,
           customer c,
           branch_hierarchy b
where      s.cust_type='business'
and        s.cust_id=c.cust_id
and        b.branch_id=c.branch_id
group by   c.name b.branch_id s.cust_id
           s.account_type s.sales_date
order      by s.cust_id
```

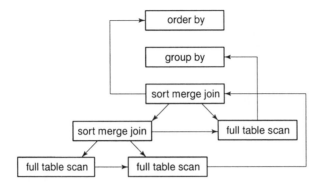

Figure 12.3 Operations tree for the data warehouse SQL statement example.

the query will decompose into a tree of operations such as depicted in Figure 12.3.

To perform the join between `sales` and `customer` both tables need to be scanned and filtered to eliminate any unwanted rows. In Figure 12.3 a `sort merge join` is being used, so the scan and sort of `sales` will be carried out simultaneously. The sort will take longer to complete than the scan, and the set of scanning processes can be moved to scan the `customer` table. Once that operation is complete the set of sort processes will have all it needs to complete the sort and merge operation. However, the set of scanning processes can be moved on to perform another operation further up the tree, and so on.

The ability to use simultaneous sets of processes to carry out non-sequential intra-statement operations gives great flexibility in the way a statement can be processed. This can lead to better statement execution plans, and ultimately gives better performance.

Cost-based optimizer
To execute each SQL statement the RDBMS uses an optimizer to calculate the best strategy for performing that statement. There are a number of different ways of calculating such a strategy, but we can categorize optimizers generically as either rule based or cost based.

A **rule-based optimizer** uses known rules to perform this function. It will have, for example, a rule that says it is preferable to use an index to access a table rather than scan the whole table. Using the predicates from the `where` clause of the SQL statement, the optimizer will search for any indexes on those columns to access the table.

A **cost-based optimizer**, on the other hand, uses stored statistics about the tables and their indexes to calculate the best strategy for executing the SQL statement. It is possible, for example, that a cost-based optimizer will ignore any indexes on a table and choose to perform a scan of the complete table to return the required rows. This is often more performant than using the index, in particular if a large number of rows is being returned. Indeed, with higher degrees of parallelism, full table scans can become extremely efficient. This means that the cutoff point of the percentage of the table being returned, at which it is quicker to scan the table rather than use an index, drops.

For a cost-based optimizer to function properly it must have up-to-date statistics on the objects being accessed. Some of the key statistics generally collected by a cost-based optimizer are:

- number of rows in the table or index,
- average row length of the data,
- number of blocks in the table or index,
- how the data is distributed,
- the cardinality of each column in a table,
- the height of an index (for b-tree indexes).

To function efficiently in a parallel environment the cost-based optimizer also requires information about the hardware environment itself. Data such as:

- number of and distribution of CPUs in the system,
- number of nodes in the system (both MPP and cluster environments),
- location of each disk that contains data,
- physical location of each part of every table or index,

are needed to allow the optimizer to calculate what it can efficiently run in parallel, and where the processes need to run. For example, it needs to know the number of nodes and the number of CPUs per node to avoid over-specifying the degree of parallelism for the statement. The data location is required to allow maximal placement of the parallel processes, and to avoid data shipping, as discussed above.

A cost-based optimizer works by assigning costs to each possible execution strategy, and then picking the strategy with the lowest cost. The most basic cost will be the number of I/Os required to return the requested data. This alone allows reasonable execution plans to be generated.

There are, however, other costs that can be considered, such as CPU overheads and memory usage. It may be possible to weight I/Os depending on the disk speed of the disk that data resides on. Other metrics, such as controller speed and system bus speed, can also be taken into account. It is also possible to weight I/Os depending on the likelihood of the requested blocks' already being cached, both on the disk caches and in the RDBMS internal buffer caches.

A cost-based optimizer is only as good as the data it has. If the cost data that the cost-based optimizer requires is not kept up to date as data changes, the

> **GUIDELINE 12.1** Ensure that object statistics are kept up to date.

execution plans that the cost-based optimizer produces will not be the most performant. Inefficient execution plans can cause an SQL statement to run anything from a few percent slower to many orders of magnitude slower. Most cost-based optimizers are not dynamic and do not automatically keep the cost data up to date, so this becomes the job of the warehouse DBA.

Degree of parallelism
The degree of parallelism is the number of processes that will be used to simultaneously perform any single operation. Getting the degree of parallelism

correct is a bit of a black art. It will of course vary from RDBMS to RDBMS. For example, the number of processes that can be used to scan a table in some RDBMSs is limited by the number of partitions that the table is spread over, as only one process can scan each partition. Other RDBMSs allow multiple processes to scan each partition, and hence the degree of parallelism can be varied.

It is not unknown for a single statement run massively in parallel to consume the entire resource of a machine. In fact the design goal of most parallel software is to scale to use the full power of any available hardware. As such it is important to consider the knock-on effects of the degree of parallelism. For instance, if multiple intra-statement operations are allowed at once, there will be multiple sets of processes. So if the degree of parallelism that is specified is say 8, and the RDBMS allows two simultaneous intra-statement operations, 16 processes will be used. Each of these processes will require memory and CPU resource to run. In particular, if any of the sets of processes is required to perform a sort, each process in the set will require more memory and probably some temporary sort space on disk.

When designing the query management environment it is important to remember that multiple SQL statements may be required to run at once. It should also be remembered that there are other activities, such as backup, data loading and data management, that will require system resource. It is impossible to isolate these operational processes completely from the query environment.

Where there are a number of simultaneous queries running, each could be running using parallel functionality, so even if you have controlled the environment to limit the amount of resource that a single statement can use, it is all too possible for a number of SQL statements to rapidly consume the entire resource of the system. Where possible, a data warehouse should be designed to batch control and stream queries. Despite the ad hoc nature of such environments this is normally possible. Given that many of the user queries will take hours if not days to run, the overhead of having a query queue for a short time is generally negligible. If this queue time becomes excessive, it is probable that the system is underpowered for the query load it is trying to handle.

As mentioned above, it is difficult if not impossible to isolate the load, management and backup processes from the query environment. Given the amount of data that is generally being dealt with on a daily basis, it is imperative that these management processes are not impeded.

> **GUIDELINE 12.2** Control is required over queries to avoid simultaneous large queries bringing the system to its knees.

12.1.3 OTHER PARALLEL PROCESSES

Parallel techniques apply to more than just queries. In the data warehouse arena there are several other important areas where parallelism applies:

- parallel load
- parallel index build

- parallel create table as select
- parallel backup and restore
- other parallel data manipulation language (DML) statements

Each of these topics is dealt with in detail in the following sections.

Parallel load

Given the sheer volume of data involved in most data warehouses, it is important to be able to load data as quickly as possible. It is not untypical to have to load several million rows of information, amounting to tens of gigabytes, on a daily basis. To achieve these sorts of loads in a reasonable time requires loading in parallel.

It helps if the RDBMS has a bulk load facility that can directly load data into a table, bypassing the normal RDBMS insert layer. This allows data blocks or pages to be completely built in memory without going through the normal row-by-row checking. These blocks can then be written to disk in large I/Os, multiple blocks at a time. This allows data to be loaded quickly, but as the RDBMS is being bypassed, it does mean that integrity checks such as constraints and triggers will also be bypassed. These will either need to be dealt with later, or the data will need to be guaranteed to be clean before loading.

It is important to remember that loading data is usually just the first step in the process of making the data available. Once loaded, it may need transformation or updating. The newly loaded data also needs to be rolled on into summaries and aggregations. This further processing can take a considerable part of any overnight window. This makes rapid loading of the data all the more important.

> **GUIDELINE 12.3**   Parallel load is normally required for data to be loaded quickly enough to enable the required postprocessing to complete within the overnight period.

Parallel index build

This is an extension of the parallel query functionality. Building an index requires scanning the entire table that is to be indexed. The data from the indexed columns needs to be extracted and sorted. As discussed above, both the scan and sort can be done in parallel.

This functionality is important, as it can radically reduce maintenance times, allowing data to be reorganized within the normal overnight window. It also makes it feasible to drop indexes before a data load and re-create them afterwards. This allows the full power of bulk data load to be used, unhindered by the requirement

> **GUIDELINE 12.4**   Parallel index build is essential to allow index maintenance within a reasonable timescale.

to update indexes as each row is added. It is generally quicker to drop the indexes, bulk load in parallel and re-create the indexes in parallel, rather than try to load the data with the indexes in place.

Parallel create table as select

Parallel create table as select (PCTAS) is a special case of parallel insert combined with parallel scanning. Because the table is being created by the statement, it is new, and as such there are no indexes and no contending statements: thus PCTAS avoids any of the usual problems of parallel insert.

In data warehouse environments it is not unusual to have to move large quantities of data on a regular basis: for example, rolling up daily data into weekly tables, and creating new aggregations. PCTAS functionality allows such operations to be parallelized, reducing the amount of time that these operations take.

Parallel backup and restore

It is imperative to the success of a data warehouse that the RDBMS supports both parallel backup and parallel restore. Backup and restore can be parallelized in many ways, and the different RDBMS systems achieve this in different ways. However, there are some basic requirements that have to be met, which are discussed below.

To parallelize backups, it must be possible to back up multiple parts of the database at the same time. Typically this will mean being able to back up at the data file level. If cold backups are being taken, this is a fairly simple problem; however, if the backup is performed while the database is open the problem becomes more complex. For a more complete discussion on backup options see Chapter 14.

Parallel restore requires the ability to restore multiple parts of the database at the same time. Again, this should be achievable at least at the data file level. Ideally, a single data file should be capable of being restored in parallel, possibly by block or page range.

There are limitations on how much the restore operation can be parallelized. Typically, the restore will require scanning a redo log file that contains all the transaction information. These logs are generally central files that are written serially in the order in which the transactions actually occurred. Thus trying to apply different parts of the redo log file in parallel may lead to the restore trying to apply changes to data that has yet to be inserted. It could also lead to updates getting applied in the wrong order. This makes the redo log files a serialization point.

Other parallel DML statements

Data manipulation language (DML) is part of the SQL language. Other parallel DML operations, such as

- parallel insert
- parallel delete
- parallel update

are the ability of a single SQL statement to perform the DML operation on a table in parallel. These DML statements are difficult to implement within a single statement while maintaining transaction consistency, and are not yet widely available in RDBMS software. While these are important abilities, they are not generally essential to data warehousing, and can in any case be simulated, if required, by breaking up the data and using multiple separate processes to perform the work.

12.2 DISK TECHNOLOGY

12.2.1 RAID TECHNOLOGY

What is RAID? Why do you need to use it? These are two questions that need to be answered and understood before the physical layout of the database can be undertaken. RAID stands for **redundant array of inexpensive disks**, and is a technology that was originally introduced in the paper *"A case for redundant arrays of inexpensive disks"* by Patterson, Gibson and Katz, of the University of California, Berkeley, in 1987. The purpose of RAID technology is to provide resilience against disk failure, so that the loss of an individual disk does not mean loss of data. Table 12.1 defines what each level of RAID means.

Striping is a technique in which data is spread across multiple disks. This allows for higher I/O performance by using the speed of several disks to satisfy a given I/O request. Note that the distinction in Table 12.1 between RAID level 1 and RAID level 0 + 1 is not really required. Striping at RAID level 1 is actually a separate process from the mirroring itself, rather than an integral part of the RAID implementation as it is at other levels. So from here on, when we refer to RAID level 1 we mean both RAID level 1 and level 0 + 1.

Parity in this context means that extra data is maintained to provide resilience. In RAID levels 2–4 this is generally achieved by having a separate parity disk that contains the parity information. This is probably best illustrated with an example.

Let us use Figure 12.4 to see how an individual byte of data is protected. Suppose that byte 1000 on disk 1 above is about to be written to disk. Before the write is performed, the RAID array needs to calculate the parity information to be stored on the parity disk. This is done by retrieving byte 1000 from each of disks 2, 3

Table 12.1 Definition of RAID levels.

RAID level	Description
0	Striping (not actually a form of RAID but has become a naming standard)
1	Full mirroring with each disk duplexed
0 + 1	Full mirroring with each disk duplexed and data striped
2	Bitwise striping of data with parity disk
3	Bytewise striping of data with parity disk
4	Blockwise striping of data with parity disk
5	Blockwise striping of data with parity information maintained across all disks

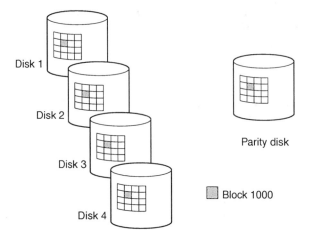

Figure 12.4 RAID 5 disk array.

and 4. The bit maps for each byte from disks 1 to 4 are compared. Suppose these bitmaps are those shown below:

```
Disk 1 - 01010101
Disk 2 - 10101010
Disk 3 - 00000000
Disk 4 - 11111111
```

Comparing the final bit in each byte we see that there are two 1s and two 0s. If we are using even parity we will want an even number of 1s across the array, so the final bit of byte 1000 of the parity disk will be set to 0. If we were using odd parity it would be set to 1. Once the parity information for the piece of data we are writing has been calculated, the I/O can be completed.

It is possible from the example above to see how the parity information is used to protect against the loss of a disk. Suppose disk 1 crashes and is damaged. The disk can be replaced, and the information that was on the disk can be rebuilt using essentially the same method used to calculate the parity information in the first case.

Experience has shown that only RAID levels 0, 1 and 5 are commercially viable and thus widely available. RAID level 3 does have some limited uses in applications that are primarily oriented toward large sequential read, and which do not require any write-intensive activity. RAID level 0 on its own is inappropriate in a data warehouse environment, because the large quantity of disks will lead to frequent disk failures.

> **GUIDELINE 12.5 RAID 5**
> suffers write performance penalties, and should be chosen only if thoroughly tested and proven to give the required performance.

Which level of resilience is best to choose for a particular data warehouse comes down to a tradeoff between the cost of RAID level 1 and the write performance restrictions of RAID level 5. It is of course possible to use a mixture of both levels of RAID. For example, RAID 5 could be used for areas that are totally read-only, while RAID 1 is used in volatile areas of the database, such as temporary spaces and sort areas.

There is a variant of RAID technology that uses large memory cache on the RAID array to enhance performance. The cache can be used in either of two ways: for read caching of blocks, or fast writes to memory. Some implementations support both read and write caching, some only read caching.

Write caching can be particularly important with RAID 5, as it can overcome many of the write performance issues. Write caching works by allowing the write to take place initially to memory rather than directly to disk, with the data being written to disk later when the I/O load is less intense. The problem with this approach is that the data written to memory has not yet reached disk, and to be useful in database environments the writes to disk must be guaranteed. To achieve this the memory must be protected against power failure, by use of technology such as battery backup, which makes it expensive.

12.2.2 SIZE AND SPEED

When designing the physical layout of your data warehouse you have to take into account the physical attributes of the hardware. Given the potential workload it is likely that on occasions each hardware element will be pushed to its limits. It is important to be aware of any potential bottlenecks. For example, it is not sufficient to know the speed of individual disks; the bandwidth of the controller that they are attached to can also become a bottleneck.

Disk technology currently supports disks up to and beyond 10 GB capacity. However, 4 GB disks are still more common on most UNIX midrange systems. They are gradually being replaced by 8 and 9 GB disks. Some vendors have even larger disks, and there are plans for 100 + GB disks, which will massively increase the capacity of each disk array.

Note, however, that larger disks are not necessarily better. In general, seek speeds and I/O rates will keep pace with the growth in disk size, so larger disks do not have to be slower. They do, however, present problems by reducing layout choices.

Let us consider an example. Suppose we have 320 GB of data and index to lay out. If we use 4 GB disks we shall have 80 separate physical disks to work with. If we use 8 GB disks we shall have 40. To support 80 disks we shall generally need more controllers, and thus will also have more controllers to work with. The downside is of course that more controllers require more bus slots, and may force you to acquire more hardware. That said, the design complexities of laying out 320 GB of physical storage are eased by having more physical devices to play with, even though it raises the management complexity somewhat.

In such a complex system there will be many data and index conflicts that need to be avoided. Sorting this problem is eased by having more smaller disks. There will also be a considerable number of small data areas that need to be placed; having smaller disks facilitates this without incurring the penalty of large, mostly empty disks or large disks crammed with lots of small, contending files.

For performance reasons, data will generally be striped across multiple disk devices. So, using the example above, let us suppose that we decide to use stripe sets of five disks. Suddenly our 40 separate 8 GB disk devices have become eight separate stripe sets, and we have to resolve all potential conflicts with only eight pools of non-conflicting disk. With 4 GB disks we have 16 areas to play with. Bearing in mind the small data areas that need to be placed, we shall in the 8 GB case have only seven disk sets to play with, as one non-striped one will need to be set aside for these small areas. In the 4 GB case we can also set aside one area, but still maintain 15 non-conflicting disk sets.

It is of course possible to take this to its – far from logical – conclusion and decide to use 1 MB disks such as floppies. Imagine what we could do with 320 000 separate devices. Clearly there is a balance to be struck, and again a mix of small and large disk technology is often the solution.

> **GUIDELINE 12.6** Ensure that you have enough disks to spread the data without clashing. It is usually better to have more, smaller disks than fewer, larger disks.

When calculating your system's I/O throughput you need to take into account the following:

- raw speed of the disks,
- speed and bandwidth of each disk channel,
- speed and bandwidth of each disk controller.

Remember that the system I/O bus or buses can become a bottleneck. Check what I/O connection technology, such as copper, fiber channel, or fiber cable, is available for the server.

The CPU bandwidth is obviously important, because processing vast quantities of data in parallel is likely to be CPU intensive. Note also that in the data warehouse environment, experience says that operations that you might not normally consider CPU intensive can become so: backups, for example. Clearly, backups are I/O hogs, in particular in systems with such large amounts of data. As technology, such as parallelism, multiple high-speed tape devices, and multiplexing, is thrown at the backup problem to speed up the performance, the CPU usage builds accordingly. It is not unknown to have a fully specified large SMP system being hit at 70–85% for several hours to complete the backups.

Clearly, the speed and capacity of hardware will vary radically from vendor to vendor, and with the configuration. Therefore Table 12.2, which gives some of the typical I/O speeds and capacities of the hardware components currently available, is shown only as a guideline. This information is useful not only for designing your database layout, but also for planning the hardware requirements. For details of hardware requirements see Chapter 11.

Table 12.2 Typical hardware characteristics.

Hardware	Speed
Tape	1–4 MB/s
Disk	3–10 MB/s
Disk controller	20–40 MB/s
I/O bus	100–150 MB/s
System bus	1–2 GB/s

12.3 DATABASE LAYOUT

12.3.1 INTRODUCTION

Once your logical database design has been completed, it needs to be converted into an actual physical layout, with each data file being mapped to a given disk or set of disks. The mapping actually needs to map a data file to a filesystem or to a raw volume. This is done by use of the system volume manager, which is used to define logical volumes. Each logical volume is an area assigned from a disk or a group of disks. A logical volume can have a filesystem defined on it or can be used as a raw device. There will probably be thousands or even tens of thousands of logical volumes to be defined. This can prove to be a management nightmare.

The key to managing such a huge number of logical volumes is to have a meaningful naming convention. This will probably be limited by the volume manager, as most volume managers only allow short logical volume names. Name lengths as low as 10 are not uncommon. Nonetheless, it is worth putting some effort into producing and documenting a naming convention.

Ideally, the naming convention should indicate where each logical volume is and what it should contain. In other words, the convention needs to tie up with both the logical database model and the physical disk layout (Table 12.3).

Note that there is a danger in naming logical volumes so specifically. If data later needs to be moved, the logical volumes will not be reusable, at least not without causing confusion by placing data in another data's namespace. This will mean re-creating or updating the logical volumes from within the volume manager.

> **GUIDELINE 12.7** Consider naming the logical volumes with names that indicate both their location and contents.

These sorts of operation should be rare, as ideally the physical data layout should not change once it has been laid down. Bearing this in mind, the management advantages gained from using a specific naming convention should far outweigh any problems.

Table 12.3   Naming convention.

Name	Description
TDM01_01	Month 1 partition of transaction detail table (data file 1)
TDM01_02i	Month 1 partition of transaction detail index (data file 2)
PI_01	Product information table (data file 1)
ACS_02	Account cheque and saving table (data file 2)
AM_01i	Account mortgage index (data file 1)

12.3.2 PHYSICAL DATABASE DESIGN

Before you can lay out the database physically, a physical database design is required. This will consist of the following:

- name and size of every tablespace in the database;
- list of every database object and which tablespace it resides in;
- name and size of every other database file/area, such as
  - journal files,
  - control files;
- name and size of every required data area external to the database.

Once the physical database design is complete, all potential data conflicts need to be identified. By data conflict we mean two sets of data that are likely to be accessed simultaneously, and are therefore required to be on separate devices. The key data conflicts that have to be avoided are:

- data and its index;
- two sets of data that are likely to be accessed simultaneously,
  - e.g. two tables that are commonly joined;
- two indexes that are likely to be accessed at the same time,
  - two indexes on the same table that are likely to be merged;
  - two indexes on different tables that are likely to be joined.

Once all the potential conflicts have been identified, they need to be prioritized. It will be impossible to avoid all conflicts, so the trick is to lay data out by starting with the major conflicts. Get that original conflicting data mapped onto separate disk sets, and move on to the next highest-priority set of conflicting data.

Another issue that needs to be considered is that of the **journal files**. These are typically small, serially accessed files. They should be physically separated from everything else, ideally on separate small mirrored and non-striped devices.

> **GUIDELINE 12.8**   Do not start laying out the database until you have a complete and finalized physical database design.

Finally, let us consider the **temporary** or **sort areas**. By temporary areas we mean the tablespaces or external areas where temporary objects are created and large data sorts to disk are carried out. As these areas are write intensive, they should not be placed on RAID 5 devices. Striping can help performance, but if striping is used then RAID 1 should be used for resilience.

12.3.3 TABLESPACE DESIGN

There are other restrictions or limitations that need to be heeded when laying out the database. These restrictions can affect the size of partition that can be used. For a full discussion on partitioning see Chapter 6.

The size of database that can be created is limited by both the size of data file that can be addressed by the operating system, and the number of data files that the RDBMS can support. Large objects will need to span multiple data files, and depending on the partitioning strategy being used, they may need to logically span multiple tablespaces. File size limits of 2 GB are common on UNIX, although this is changing, with the latest version of most hardware vendors supporting 4 GB, 8 GB or even larger files.

> **GUIDELINE 12.9** Ensure that you are aware of every hardware, operating system and database limit, before designing the database.

Another important consideration is the storage requirements for each object. There are a number of different types of object that need to be considered. The primary objects are tables and indexes, and these will be considered below. Other objects, such as rollback segments in Oracle, although important, are typically small in comparison to the rest of the database and, once isolated in their own tablespace, can be ignored as far as this discussion is concerned.

The golden rule with tables and indexes is that they should be placed in separate tablespaces. Then these tablespaces should be placed on separate disks. This avoids any contention between the access of the index and the table. Note that in some RDBMS systems the primary index will be part of the table structure itself. In this case the rule would clearly apply only to the secondary indexes.

The RDBMS is responsible for the allocation of space to objects as they grow or change. How this space is allocated can usually be specified at several different levels. Normally it is possible to specify the storage parameters for an object at the object level itself:

```
create table transaction (
txn_id        number,
cust_id       number,
cust_name     varchar2(30),
    :
    :
```

```
txn_expires date)
storage (initial 200M
    next 400M
    :
    : )
```

This can be done at creation time or later if the requirements change:

```
alter table transaction
storage (initial 200M
  next 400M
    :
    : )
```

It is usually possible to specify these parameters at the tablespace level rather than at the table level:

```
create tablespace . . .
storage (initial 200M
  next 400M
    :
    : )
```

If the storage parameters are specified at both levels, then the object level definitions will normally predominate. Finally, it may be possible to specify these parameters at the database level.

As discussed above, the larger tables will probably span multiple datafiles. Such objects should be placed by themselves in tablespaces, and the storage parameters should be set to ensure the minimum waste of space.

> **GUIDELINE 12.10** Where possible, specify storage information at the tablespace level, and let all objects within each tablespace default to those values.

Not all objects in a data warehouse will be large. Many of the reference, dimension and metadata tables will be quite small. The question is how best to place these objects.

From a logical management point of view it would be best to group these tables by function, so the reference tables would be grouped together, but separated from the metadata tables. However, there can be quite a range of table sizes in any of these groups, varying from hundreds of bytes to hundreds of megabytes. It would be a management nightmare to try and control the parameters on each of these tables directly. Therefore, ideally, all tables in a tablespace should have the same storage parameters. This allows the storage parameters to be specified at the tablespace level once, and each table will automatically pick them up.

The problem with such an approach is that it can be very wasteful of space. For example, let us suppose we specify all extent sizes for each object to be 20 MB. This is fine for objects that are 20 MB, 60 MB or even hundreds of megabytes in size. However, a reference table that contains 300 bytes of data is still going to grab a single extent of 20 MB, thereby wasting 19.7 MB of space. This space wastage can quickly add up into gigabytes if there are many objects.

To deal with this issue it is best to group tables by size. Depending on the number and size range of the tables, two or three tablespaces can be created for small and large tables, or for small, medium and large tables. Tables can then be placed where they waste least space.

> **GUIDELINE 12.11** For smaller tables, divide them into tablespaces by a mixture of function and size.

Experience shows that a combination of the above approaches works best, with tables grouped by function and then separated by size. So, for example, we could end up with a `Small_Reference` tablespace and a `Large_Reference` tablespace, and so on.

12.4 FILESYSTEMS

12.4.1 FILESYSTEMS VERSUS RAW VOLUMES

One decision that needs to be made by the warehouse designer is whether to use filesystem files or raw devices. First let us define exactly what is meant by filesystems and raw devices.

A **filesystem** in UNIX is an area of disk set aside for holding files. The filesystem will have a directory structure with a head directory. The filesystem can be mounted into a machine's directory structure by use of the `mount` command. This allows the filesystem to be mounted anywhere within the system's directory structure. All the normal file and directory commands, such as `cd`, `ls`, and `cat`, can be used on the filesystem files.

A **raw device** is a pseudo device, or area of disk that is treated as a separate named device by UNIX. The raw device can be treated as a single file, which can be read and written directly by a program. The raw device is not subject to all the normal file and directory commands, and does not appear in the system's directory structure, except as a device in the /dev directory.

The main drawback of filesystems is that they cannot be shared simultaneously across multiple systems. This is a major issue in a cluster environment. To add to the confusion, there is a concept of a shared filesystem, which can be mounted on multiple machines. However, shared filesystems can be mounted on only one machine at a time. In other words, if filesystem X is mounted on machine Node A, and it is required on Node B, X cannot be mounted on Node B until it is unmounted from Node A.

Another issue with UNIX filesystems is their lack of synchronization. Because of the way filesystems are buffered for performance, the filesystem on disk is not always consistent. When the system is shut down normally, the filesystem on disk and in buffer cache is made consistent. If the system crashes, a significant amount of work is required to resynchronize the filesystem. This is done on startup using the fsck command. It can take several minutes to re-sync each filesystem. In a large data warehouse environment, where there may be hundreds of filesystems, restarting after a system crash could take an extremely long time.

Finally, filesystems and raw devices have different performance characteristics. Different system calls are used for raw devices and for filesystems. Raw devices are accessed directly to and from disk, and their blocks do not go through the system block cache. This has the effect of making repeated access to the same block quicker in filesystems. However, for exactly the same reason, each individual access to or from disk will be quicker in raw devices. Which gives the better performance overall will depend on the pattern of access to the data. If large amounts of data are frequently scanned serially, raw devices will generally give better performance. If the same subsets of data are accessed frequently, then the memory buffering offered by filesystems will often give better performance.

The main drawback with raw devices is that they make management more difficult. As each raw device contains only a single file, a large system such as a data warehouse will require the use of many raw devices. This may be compounded by resilience issues such as mirroring, where each mirror of a raw device is itself a raw device. It is not uncommon for a data warehouse environment to consist of hundreds or even thousands of raw devices. Managing such large quantities of raw devices is a major undertaking. It places heavy demands on the volume manager software. It also requires that the database design team come up with a meaningful naming convention for these raw devices. See section 12.3.1 for a discussion on naming conventions.

In some vendor's latest versions of UNIX there is a third option, an advanced filesystem. The main feature of these advanced filesystems is that they have some form of journaling; this improves the synchronization of the filesystem, thereby protecting it against system crash. The other common feature of advanced filesystems is the ability to share the filesystem simultaneously across multiple machines. These features will lift some of the restrictions of using filesystems in large systems. However, performance is still an outstanding question.

Whether using filesystems or raw devices, but especially with raw devices, it is essential to have a volume manager that is both easy to use and functionally rich. There are a number of desirable features that a volume manager should have:

- GUI interface,
- support for striping,
- support for mirroring,
- support for reasonable-length volume names,
- ability to create volumes within and across devices.

The GUI interface should make it easier to both create the initial system and manage the system thereafter. From a creation point of view, features such as drop-down menus and point-and-click make the GUI simpler and easier to use. Volume layouts can be very complex, with volume groups spanning disks and containing many separate filesystems. Once created, the mass of volumes are easier to visualize and hence easier to manage in a GUI.

It is important that the volume manager has good support for striping. Before designing your physical layout it is necessary to understand the limits of the operating system you are using. Two questions in particular need to be dealt with:

- Does the system support striping across controllers?
- Does the system support striping across nodes?

The answers to these questions will help with the design of stripe sets. Note, however, that when using some RAID arrays these issues may be beyond your control, as typically they will be implemented as a single large stripe set. What you may be able to control is the stripe size. The size of the stripe can have a radical effect on the system's performance. Clearly, being able to stripe across nodes is only an issue on non-shared disk architectures such as MPP.

As with striping, there are a number of questions to be asked if mirroring is going to be used. It is equally as important to understand the limits of the system as far as mirroring is concerned. The main questions again are:

- Is mirroring supported in software or in hardware?
- Is mirroring supported across nodes?
- Is mirroring supported across controllers?

First, you need to establish whether the mirroring is supported in the hardware or in the software, or indeed in both. Hardware mirroring is generally more efficient but more restricted, typically being restricted to mirroring within controllers. Software mirroring will usually allow mirroring to occur across most divides. It works by intercepting each I/O and issuing multiple I/Os to the different mirrors. This approach does, however, have the performance downside of having to issue multiple I/O calls. As with striping, some disk arrays may mean you have no control over where and how mirroring is performed.

> **GUIDELINE 12.12** You need to be aware of any limitations, imposed by either the operating system or the hardware, on striping and mirroring.

Support for long volume names, and in particular for long raw device names, has been discussed in section 12.3.1. It is important to have the flexibility to name volumes meaningfully, even when there are thousands of volumes to be managed.

Finally, it is important that the volume manager allow the creation of volumes or volume groups to be flexible. It is useful to be able to create volumes or volume groups across disks. This allows volumes larger than any single disk to be created. Being able to create volumes across controller boundaries will again allow you greater flexibility. This issue is tied in with the striping issue discussed above, as being able to create volumes across controllers will generally indicate that you can stripe across controllers.

Last but not least, the volume manager must allow multiple volumes to be created within a single disk. This is a common feature, and the only question to be asked is: What overheads are required by each volume, and what if any is the minimum size of a volume? Once these limits are understood, all small data areas can be dealt with.

12.4.2 NON-UNIX SYSTEMS

In all of the discussions above we have assumed that the solution will be delivered on open-system UNIX machines. It is, however, a valid question to ask whether any of these solutions could be delivered on other systems. To answer this question it is probably easier to ask: Why are open-system UNIX machines considered to be the de facto solution?

There are a number of reasons why this is the case. UNIX systems have been around since the 1960s, but have only really gained commercial acceptance in the 1990s. This turnaround came about as the UNIX systems began to mature, and commercial software began to become available for these systems. The two main arguments for their acceptance were cost, and the fact that they were not proprietary.

The cost argument is still valid, but the battleground has changed. Where earlier UNIX systems were aimed at the workstation or low-end minicomputer market, the current systems have moved up into the enterprise arena. The cost argument is now being fought out between high-end UNIX systems and the traditional mainframe. In this area, and in particular in the data warehouse market, it is the cost performance benefits that are driving the IT decision makers toward the UNIX solution.

It is worth noting that, at the low end, UNIX is also fighting a cost battle, but here it is UNIX that is being challenged by newer solutions such as Microsoft's Windows NT. This battle has yet to play itself out. At its current stage of development and acceptance, NT is not really suitable as a large data warehouse server platform. The hardware that currently supports NT is not scalable or powerful enough to deliver the parallelism and raw power required for these large systems. It is, of course, possible that this will change over time. It is also worth remembering that NT is a likely candidate for the front-end systems that the users will use to access the warehouse and also for the datamarts.

The second argument for the move to UNIX systems was the open versus proprietary argument. Open systems were seen as more portable and standardized. The argument went that if you were unhappy with one UNIX vendor, you would just switch vendor and move the application from one UNIX system to the other. In reality this has proved more theory than practice, and it is only recently that the various versions of UNIX have really begun to converge on a common standard.

Nonetheless there were advantages of moving into the open systems arena. Despite the differences between the flavors of UNIX, they were still closer to each other than any of the proprietary systems. This had some real benefits when applications were moved from one system to another. The cost of retraining staff on a new UNIX system were minimal, as compared with retraining onto a completely new system. Any major application will require some real experience to manage and maintain. In particular, staff experienced in the operating system and hardware were vital to the successful running of such a system. Moving from one proprietary system to another often meant staff turnover, and definitely required the hiring of such experience. Such changes were avoided or at least minimized by remaining in the UNIX arena.

The upshot of the open system versus proprietary battle is that many of the older proprietary systems have all but disappeared. The main remaining real contenders are Digital's Open VMS operating system, Tandem's fault-tolerant system, and the assorted mainframe vendors. Certainly, VMS with its clustered SMP technology and Tandem with its MPP architecture are viable data warehouse solutions. It is also certain that mainframe systems have the I/O bandwidth and capacity to spin up the large amounts of disk required. However, it is valid to ask whether mainframe systems are capable of delivering the amount of raw CPU power required to support the query load and daily maintenance needed by a data warehouse. Even if the mainframe does scale to the CPU requirement, the cost of such systems is likely to be prohibitive.

It is worth noting that, even if you are implementing a data warehouse on one of these systems, most of the ideas and suggestions given in this chapter will still be valid. Clearly the system software and hardware may be very different, but the same general principles will still apply.

CHAPTER 13

Security

13.1 INTRODUCTION

A data warehouse by nature is an open, accessible system. This is not just a philosophical nicety. It is important to get to the heart of the business reasons for building the warehouse in the first place. The aim of a data warehouse is generally to make large amounts of data easily accessible to the users, thereby enabling the users to extract information about the business as a whole. Any security restrictions can be seen as obstacles to that goal, and they become constraints on the design of the warehouse.

Naturally there may be sound business reasons for any security restrictions that are applied to the data warehouse, but it is worth noting that they may lead to a potential loss of information. If analysts have restricted access to the data in the warehouse it may be impossible for them to get a complete picture of the trends within the business.

The data from each analyst can of course be summarized and passed on to management, where the different summaries can be amalgamated. However, the aggregation of the summaries does not necessarily equal the aggregation of the whole, in information terms. It is all too possible to miss important trends in the data unless someone is analyzing the data as a whole.

This is not to say that security is not important; on the contrary, security is paramount to ensuring that the data itself remains clean, consistent and integral.

This chapter discusses security from a number of aspects. It concentrates first on the requirements, discussing some of the practical, legal and other issues that need to be considered. The remainder of the chapter analyzes the impact that security has on both the performance and the design of the data warehouse.

13.2 REQUIREMENTS

It is important to establish early any security and audit requirements that will be placed on the data warehouse. Clearly, adding security will affect performance, because further checks require CPU cycles and time to perform. More importantly, and often overlooked, the security and audit requirements can severely affect the design of the data warehouse.

It is very difficult to add security restrictions after the data warehouse has gone live, so it is important to capture the ultimate security and audit requirements at the beginning. Where possible, future-proof the data warehouse against changes. During the design phase take into account what other data sources may be added later and the likely impact of these additional sources. Consider for instance:

- Will new data sources require new security and/or audit restrictions to be implemented?
- Will new users be added who have restricted access to data that is already generally available?

This task can be particularly onerous if not all the data sources and future users are known at the beginning. In this case you will have to use knowledge of the business and the purpose of the data warehouse to predict the likely requirements.

Security can affect many different parts of the data warehouse, such as:

- user access
- data load
- data movement (e.g. summary generation)
- query generation

Any audit requirements will cause all the above operations to generate overheads. Other security requirements, such as access restrictions on subsets of the data, will either require multiple copies of the data or the data will need to be restricted by the use of views. Either will cause overheads, the former needing extra disk space, the later requiring extra processing.

13.2.1 USER ACCESS

The first step in pinning down the security requirements is to classify the data. Once the data has been classified, you then need to classify the users by what data they can access.

Data classification

Data can be classified in a number of ways. The actual approach taken to data classification will depend on the level of security required. Data may be classified by its sensitivity. So, for example, highly sensitive data such as payroll information may be classified as highly restricted, while less sensitive but still commercially important data such as general customer information may be classified as company confidential. In high-security environments there will generally be a data classification hierarchy already available.

Data can also be classified by job function. This approach basically states that access to data is restricted to those users whose jobs require that access. This simple classification will cover most scenarios, but there may still be questions that need to be addressed.

To illustrate the types of issues that can still arise with this approach let us take an example. Suppose you are building a data warehouse for a bank. Suppose further that the data being stored in the data warehouse is the transaction data for all the bank's accounts. One simple question that could be asked is: Who is allowed to see the transaction data?

If this question is pursued a little deeper, we begin to get questions like:

(1) Can an analyst see data about his/her own account?
(2) Can an analyst see data about other employees' accounts?
(3) Can an analyst see data from his/her boss's account?
(4) Can an analyst see data about other members of his/her team?

and so on. Question 4 is a particularly thorny issue, as it may allow the analyst to infer information indirectly about his/her colleagues, such as their salary and the size of any pay rises.

Classifying data by function essentially simplifies the task of data classification to that of classifying the users, along with any exceptions such as those listed above.

> **GUIDELINE 13.1** Consider categorizing data access by role or job function.

User classification

As with the data, there are a number of ways that users can be classified. You can take a top-down company view, with users classified by department, section, group, and so on. Another possible classification is role based, with people grouped across departments based on their role. This approach would classify all analysts as one group, irrespective of the department they are in within the company. Once the users have been classified, you can design the users' access around that classification.

To explore these concepts further let us consider a data warehouse where the users come from two different departments, Sales and Marketing. As mentioned above, it is possible to design security by a top-down company view, with access centered around the different departments. However, it is likely that within each department there will be further restrictions placed on users at different levels. This can lead to complex nested structures of access restrictions, such as those shown in Figure 13.1.

If each department genuinely accesses different data, then it is probably better to design the security access for each department separately. You may even need to set up security at the individual level if every analyst has completely different requirements. If this is the requirement, it may be worth considering the use of

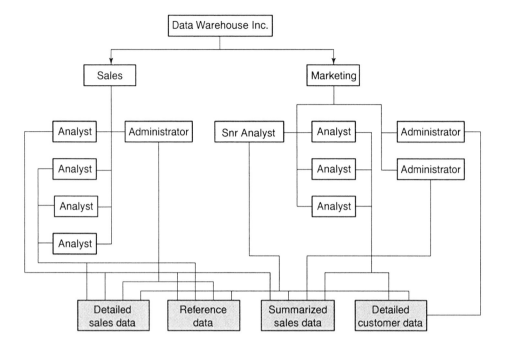

Figure 13.1 User access hierarchy.

departmental data marts (see Chapter 8). The data marts can be separated from the data warehouse, and the security restrictions can be enforced separately on each data mart. This will allow the data warehouse itself to be designed without the restrictions, which in turn will help to avoid any problems with future requirements (Figure 13.2).

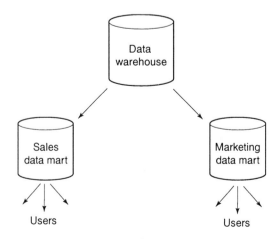

Figure 13.2 Using data marts to enforce restrictions on access to data.

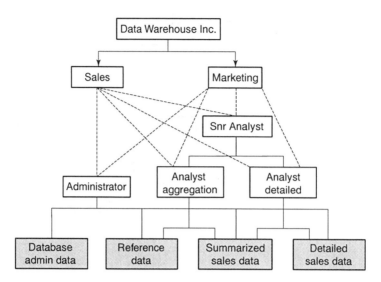

Figure 13.3 Role access hierarchy.

It is worth considering future requirements at this stage, particularly if it is likely that users will begin to access overlapping sets of data. Remember that the base data is likely to be the same for everyone, and it is only if users are completely restricted to aggregations that there is likely to be wide separation of access. If, in the future, drill-down from aggregated to detailed data is likely to be required, or a larger user community is to be added, the chances of data access requirements overlapping will increase.

If all the data is generally available and being accessed by every department, it is usually better to approach the problem from a role perspective, where roles such as analyst, manager or administrator are defined across departments. This allows security to be applied by function, with analysts having query access only, while administrators have permissions to move and possibly change data. This approach also allows access to data to be assigned to roles rather than people. Roles can then be built up from other roles, as depicted in Figure 13.3.

Which approach is better will depend on the specific set of security restrictions that need to be applied. As a guide, there are two rules of thumb:

- the tighter the security, the more person oriented the design;
- the more complex the interdependencies, the more role oriented the design.

> **GUIDELINE 13.2** The tighter the security, the more person oriented the design.

> **GUIDELINE 13.3** The more complex the interdependencies, the more role oriented the design.

Tables versus views

The standard relational approach to data access restrictions is to use views. For example, suppose you have a bank transaction table and you want to run the following query:

```
select   customer,
         account_number,
         sum(value),
         count(transaction_id)
from     txn_last_quarter
where    transaction_date
         between '01-jun-96' and '30-jun-96'
group by customer account_number
```

Let us suppose that one of the bank security rules is that no person can access the transaction data on their own accounts. To restrict users from doing this while still giving them access to the rest of the data you could create a view such as:

```
create view sales_lq as
select   customer,
         account_number,
         sum(value),
         count(transaction_id)
from     txn_last_quarter
where    transaction_date
         between '01-jun-96' and '30-jun-96'
and      account_id <> 1234567989
group by customer account_number
```

This would require the creation of a separate view for each person who has access to that table. This rapidly becomes a nightmare to maintain. It is further complicated when you take into consideration the fact that people may have multiple accounts, which would require views such as:

```
create view sales_lq as
select   customer,
         account_number,
         sum(value),
         count(transaction_id)
from     txn_last_quarter
where    transaction_date
         between '01-jun-96' and '30-jun-96'
and      account_id <> 1234567989
or       account_id <> 2468101214
group by customer account_number
```

Clearly this approach will introduce major performance overheads, and we have not even mentioned issues such as how you maintain these views as users open and close accounts.

Another approach to this problem is to place data in separate tables depending on its classification. This allows data to be accessed directly, because no view is required for each user or role to filter unauthorized data.

> **GUIDELINE 13.4** Where possible, avoid the use of views to enforce data access restrictions. They can rapidly become a nightmare to maintain.

This approach can lead to massive duplication, as there may be large overlaps in the data that roles can access. Take the example used above. To solve the problem of users' not seeing their own account data we could create a separate copy of the table with just that user's data missing for each user. The overheads in disk space and processing power would be enormous.

Another solution would be to load all non-employees' data into one table and just create separate tables as above for the employee data. This approach will not cause as much duplication, and at first glance seems a better solution, but it is still fraught with difficulties. For instance, what happens if one of the non-employees is subsequently employed by the bank as an analyst who has access to the data? In particular, how do you deal with historical data that exists in the non-employee table? Do you re-create it all without the new employee's data?

There are no easy answers to these questions, and it is important to understand the reasons for the restrictions, so that the most practical solution can be arrived at. Again, using the example above, if the rule that an employee may not see his or her own account information is based on not seeing a particular field in the records, you might ask whether it is strictly necessary to hold that field in the data warehouse. If the field is not really required, a better solution would be not to load the field in the first place. Even if the field is genuinely required, would it matter if all employee records were loaded with that field nulled out or overwritten with some fixed value?

> **GUIDELINE 13.5** Make sure you understand not just the security restrictions, but the reasons for them. This allows you to make informed decisions about how the restrictions should be applied.

13.2.2 LEGAL REQUIREMENTS

It is vital to establish any legal requirements on the data being stored. If individual customer data is being held, such as customer information for personal phones in a telco data warehouse or account details in a banking data warehouse, you may be required by law to enforce certain restrictions. The law varies from country to country, so it is impractical to enter into details, but there are certain fundamental questions that can be asked.

If the data held online is going to be used for trend analysis, and is therefore held in summarized rather than detailed form, do any legal restrictions apply? Holding data only in summarized form does of course have the downside that detailed drill-down operations are impossible.

If the customer data to be held on the data warehouse is of a minimal nature, what legal restrictions apply? It may be that the data is sufficient to identify an account but not its owner, thereby preserving anonymity. This would be sufficient to allow trending and profiling to be done blindly. If the results were to be used to put together a mailshot of a new product to identified account holders, the account ID numbers could be transferred to an operational machine where the data could be joined to customer data to cross-match account ID to customer details.

It is not just individual customer data that can be subject to restrictions. For example, if a telco rents the use of lines or switch space to other telcos, what are they legally entitled to do with the call data produced by the calls made on the other telcos' services?

Another common example of this sort of situation is flight reservations, where many airlines use a common booking system, possibly run by one of the airlines as a service. What use, if any, can the airline make of booking information for competitors' airlines? Can they even do crude analysis of call and reservation rates for capacity planning?

All these sorts of issues need to be clearly understood during the design phase of the data warehouse. In particular, they need to be considered when security requirements are being analyzed, because it may be necessary to implement auditing, or to apply restrictions to certain data. This is one reason why it is important that the design team contain at least some analysts who have specialist knowledge of the business area in which the data warehouse is being built.

> **GUIDELINE 13.6** The design team will require some analysts with knowledge and experience of the business area.

13.2.3 AUDIT REQUIREMENTS

Auditing is a specific subset of security that is often mandated by organizations. In particular, there may be legal requirements for auditing on operational systems. Given the volumes of data involved in a data warehouse, auditing can cause extremely heavy overheads on the system. To make up for these overheads, and to allow operations such as the overnight processing to still finish in time, generally requires more hardware. Thus, where possible or allowed, auditing should be switched off.

There may be many different audit requirements, but as far as the data warehouse is concerned all audit requirements can basically be categorized into the following list:

- connections
- disconnections
- data access
- data change

For each of these categories it may be necessary to audit success, failure or both. For security reasons, the auditing of failures can be particularly important, because they can highlight any attempted unauthorized or fraudulent access.

If data access is to be audited, you need to establish whether each access is to be audited separately, or whether it is sufficient to audit the fact that a user accessed a specific table during a given session. This can radically affect the audit information that needs to be held, saving both space and I/O overheads.

If changes to the data are being audited, is it sufficient to audit the fact that a change occurred, or is it required to capture the actual change that was made? Data warehouses are largely read-only environments except for the data load, and therefore data is unlikely to change once it is loaded. If the audit requirement on data change exists purely to prevent data being changed, it may be sufficient to protect the data by making it read-only, and then auditing any change from read-only to read-write.

It is imperative to restrict auditable events to a minimum. If necessary, steps may need to be taken to design the audit requirements away. This is one of the reasons why it is so important to understand not just the audit require-ments but the reason for them. It is amazing how often audit requirements exist because they are company standards and not because they are actually required on every system. These sorts of issues can usually be pushed back once the costs of implementation are demonstrated.

> **GUIDELINE 13.7** Understand the reasons for each audit require-ment. Only implement those that are genuinely required for legal, company and security reasons.

13.2.4 NETWORK REQUIREMENTS

When doing the security requirements capture it is important not to overlook issues such as network security. For instance:

- Is it necessary to encrypt data before transferring it to the data warehouse machine?
- Are there restrictions on which network routes the data can take?

These restrictions have processing implications that need to be carefully considered.

The overheads of data encryption and decryption can be very high in both time and processing power. It is also important to note that the cost of encryption is borne by the source system, and that can prove to be very expensive if the system is an already loaded system.

Network route limitation can narrow options, and may cause bottlenecks on certain sections of the network. Restricted routing also leads to greater dependency on the restricted routes, which may be disastrous if they fail.

13.2.5 DATA MOVEMENT

Each time that data is to be moved there are potential security implications. Suppose some restricted data is to be transferred as a flat file to be loaded.

When the data lands on the data warehouse machine, questions such as:

- Where is the flat file stored?
- Who has access to that disk space?

need to be answered. In addition, there are further questions raised if the flat files are required to be backed up:

- Do you back up encrypted or decrypted versions?
- Do these backups need to be made to special tapes that are stored separately?
- Who has access to these tapes?

There are other forms of data movement that also need to be considered, such as query result sets. If a temporary table is created to hold the result of a query:

- Where is that temporary table to be held?
- How do we make such tables visible?

It is important to avoid accidental or deliberate flouting of the security restrictions. If a user with access to restricted data can create generally accessible temporary tables, data can be made visible to non-authorized users. This can be overcome by having a separate temporary area for users with access to restricted data.

However, suppose that certain summarized versions of the restricted data are considered non-restricted, and are required to be made available to users who do not have access to the detailed data. Where and how are these tables made available? These processes need to be clearly understood, because they have capacity and bandwith implications.

13.2.6 DOCUMENTATION

It is important to get all the security and audit requirements clearly documented as this will be needed as part of any cost justification. This can be done as part of the SLA, but it is probably better to document the restrictions as part of a separate data warehouse security policy document.

This document should contain all the information gathered on:

- data classifications
- user classifications
- network requirements
- data movement and storage requirements
- all auditable actions

as well as any design decisions on how the security will be implemented. If roles are to be used, a detailed description of every role should also be included, along with the access rights and privileges of that role.

13.2.7 HIGH-SECURITY ENVIRONMENTS

If higher levels of security are required, it may be necessary to go to "trusted" versions of the RDBMS that have been audited to certain levels of trust. For example, the normal version of a RDBMS might conform to C2 in the NSCS's Trusted Computing System Evaluation Criteria (TCSEC or "Orange Book") in the USA and F-C2/E3 according to the European Information Technology Security Evaluation Criteria (ITSEC). This compares to a trusted version of the RDBMS, which might conform to B1 of the TCSEC and F-B1/E3 of the ITSEC.

The trusted RDBMS might contain, amongst other functionality, row labels and security clearance. Row labels allow each row of data to be classified, and therefore data of different classifications can be stored in the same table. Security clearance applies to users, and dictates which classifications of data they are allowed to see. The trusted RDBMS automatically enforces the data restrictions, allowing a user to see only data of their own clearance and below.

Trusted RDBMSs will generally run only on trusted operating systems, where the operating system itself conforms to trusted levels of security, thereby ensuring the security of the database files and everything external to the database itself. The overheads and costs of both the trusted operating system and trusted RDBMS are enormous, and are impractical for implementing a data warehouse unless these extreme levels of security are genuinely required. It is also worth noting that every aspect of the analysis, design and testing of the data warehouse will be affected by using such a system, leading to greatly expanded design and test schedules, and thereby vastly greater costs.

Covert channels

A **covert channel** is any method whereby restricted information is inadvertently given away by implication rather than by design: for example, if there are two reports, one that displays only records that the user is authorized to see, while the other displays averages based on all records. If users calculate the same averages on the data displayed in the first report, they can infer information from any data mismatch. The second report implies the existence of other records, and in fact may also give some information about the hidden records, by the difference in the averages.

It is important to avoid introducing covert channels, particularly in high-security environments. Covert channels can occur very simply during the design stage. For example, suppose your query generation screen is designed to look like that shown in Figure 13.4. If the user does not have access to Option 2 in Figure 13.4, then a screen such as Figure 13.5 is a covert channel, as it indicates that there is data that is not accessible. The answer in this case is to have a screen that in the

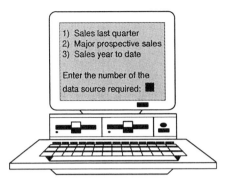

Figure 13.4   Query specification screen

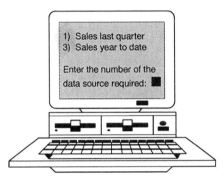

Figure 13.5   Avoiding covert channels.

background orders the option numbers consecutively, so there are no gaps that indicate missing data options.

Covert channels are not typically a problem, as the majority of data warehouses do not require such high levels of security.

> **GUIDELINE 13.8**   Avoid creating covert channels that inadvertently make information about data available.

13.3   PERFORMANCE IMPACT OF SECURITY

Security always costs. This is a statement that should be remembered at all times. Any security that is implemented will cost in terms of either processing power or disk space, or both. These costs eventually turn into monetary costs somewhere along the line.

13.3.1 VIEWS

Views are a standard RDBMS mechanism for applying restrictions to data access. In theory they are treated just like a table, but in reality a view is a stored query in its own right, and in practice there will generally be restrictions on how views are handled by the RDBMS. To understand why these restrictions apply, it is important to understand that a view may be anything from

```
select cust_id,
       sale_date,
       quantity,
       total_cost
from   sales_table
where  cust_type = 'business'
```

which is a simple restriction, to a SQL statement that contains restrictions, joins and aggregations, such as that depicted below:

```
select    s.cust_id,
          sum(s.total_cost) total_sales,
          c.zip_code,
          b.branch_id,
          s.account_type
          s.sales_date
from      sales_table s,
          customer_table c,
          branch_hierarchy_table b
where     s.cust_type = 'business'
and       s.cust_id = c.cust_id
and       b.branch_id = c.branch_id
and       c.zip_code in
          (select zip_code
          from branch_hierarchy_table
          where region = 'north west')
group by  c.zip_code b.branch_id
          s.cust_id s.account_type s.sales_date
order by  s.cust_id
```

This makes views difficult to deal with as single tables in a query. For example, what would happen if the example above was stored as a view called Sales_V, and was used in a statement such as the example below?

```
select v.cust_id,
       v.zip_code,
       v.total_sales
from   sales_v v,
       product_table p
```

```
where      p.product_id = v.account_type
and        v.sales_date > '01-jan-96'
```

How should such a statement be optimized? The view will need to be expanded and the two SQL statements merged. Is it better to take the predicates from the query and force them into the view, or to take the predicates from the view and promote them to the outer part of the query? Should aggregations and sorts be performed within the view, before it is projected, or is it better to wait until the data has been projected and maybe further restricted by the outer part of the query? These are all issues that need to be handled by the RDBMS optimizer.

Naturally, the answers to such questions will depend on the data itself as well as on the query. To take a simple example, the fact that the data is evenly distributed rather than skewed may significantly affect where it is best to apply restrictions, and to perform sorts. The RDBMS needs to be written to handle all eventualities, and like all generic code will handle certain situations inefficiently or indeed may even be unable to interpret the ensuing SQL statement unambiguously. This is why restrictions often apply to the use of views.

Some of the common restrictions that may apply to the handling of views are:

- restricted data manipulation language (DML) operations,
- lost query optimization paths,
- restrictions on parallel processing of view projections.

Inserts, updates and deletes will sometimes be restricted against more complex views, which means that complex views are basically designed to be treated as read-only.

Because of the complexity of combining views into queries, and the ambiguities that can arise, many optimizers will not consider certain optimization paths that could be applied to tables. This can result in inefficient execution of SQL statements.

The use of views to enforce security will impose a maintenance overhead. In particular, if views are used to enforce restricted access to data tables and aggregations, as these change, the views may also change. It is not untypical for data to be stored in multiple daily tables, and rolled up into a weekly table at the end of a week. This will require the creation of all the restriction views on the weekly table when it is created.

Add to this the problems of keeping track of users as they move job and as new users are added, and it soon becomes a major task just maintaining the views. This problem can be alleviated somewhat by using the role approach to security. In that case, a user moving jobs will generally require the removing of one database role and the granting of another to that user.

Another problem with using views is that they impose a parse overhead when they are accessed by an SQL statement. As well as the SQL statement itself being parsed, the underlying statement that makes up the view has to be merged into the statement and parsed. For complex views this can add seconds, or even minutes in the case of very large complex views, to the SQL statement's running time. This may not be an issue in a data warehouse, where many of the queries will be long running and take hours to perform, in which case the long parse times become irrelevant. If, however, lots of users are likely to run smaller queries frequently that use such complex views the parse times may become a major issue.

Another potential snag that is easy to overlook at the design stage is the way views may affect the performance of other features of the RDBMS. For instance, if parallel operations are being used to give the required performance, you need to ask whether there are any restrictions on the projection from a view being parallelized.

> **GUIDELINE 13.9**   Views will be necessary in any data warehouse, but they have performance overheads, and their usage should be minimized.

If projections cannot be parallelized, either generally or in certain cases, this could force the serialization of operations above them and drastically affect query performance times. This is why it is important to check what if any restrictions are imposed on views by the RDBMS you are using, and what restrictions views place on other operations.

> **GUIDELINE 13.10**   Be sure you fully understand any restrictions imposed on views. Not only can they disallow certain operations, but they may affect query optimization.

13.3.2 DATA MOVEMENT

Because of the volumes of data being handled in the data warehouse, data movement is an expensive process, in terms both of resource and of time. Any increase in the resource or time needed to move data decreases the query capacity of the data warehouse. There are a number of different ways in which bulk data movements can occur:

- data loads
- aggregation creation
- results temporary tables
- data extracts

If security checks or audits have to be applied to any of these data movements, performance overheads will apply. In particular, if the security check or audit has to be applied at the record level rather than just once on the accessing user, the performance of the operation may be radically affected.

The security requirements discussed in section 13.2 may also force the generation of extra aggregations. The effect of this needs to be fully measured, because each new aggregation to be maintained not only consumes more disk space but also places pressure on the overnight window, and can lead to increased CPU requirements. This in turn may require the purchase of more hardware.

13.3.3 AUDITING

Clearly any auditing that has to be performed will have a CPU impact, because each audited action will require some code to be run. It is important not to forget that auditing also requires disk space, because the audit output has to be stored somewhere. Given the size of the data warehouse, the audit logs are not likely to be large by comparison. Nonetheless, they may need to be held for a long time, and if heavy auditing is required they can grow quickly.

Dealing with audit logs becomes yet another operational task. It is important to be aware of any issues that surround the audit log. What happens, for instance, if the audit log fills the space allocated to it? Is all further audit information lost? Does any operation that requires auditing hang, or does it fail? This can be crucial, as the loss of a single night's processing because of audit failing can leave a data warehouse with an almost impossible task of catching up.

13.4 SECURITY IMPACT ON DESIGN

Security can also affect the design of the data warehouse. It will affect any application code that has to be written, and will also affect development time-scales.

13.4.1 APPLICATION DEVELOPMENT

Extra security code may be needed for each of the process managers:

- load manager
- warehouse manager
- query manager

The **load manager** may require checking code to filter records and place them in different locations depending on their contents. It may also need extra transformation rules to modify sensitive fields to hide certain data. Extra metadata may need to be created and maintained to handle any extra objects.

The **warehouse manager** may need code to create and maintain all the extra views and aggregations required to enforce the security. Extra checks may need to be coded into the warehouse manager to prevent it from being fooled into moving data into a location where it should not be available. For example, if performance statistics indicate the requirement for a new aggregation, the warehouse manager must be capable of checking that it is not bypassing security by creating the aggregation.

The **query manager** will certainly require changes to handle any access restrictions. It will need to be aware of all the extra views and aggregations, and will have to be able to point users at the correct versions of objects.

Note that the extra views, aggregations and tables that may be required to enforce the security will also need to be developed. Each of these and the code above will add to the development cost of the data warehouse and time will need to be built into the project plan to cope with these extra requirements. When you are calculating the extra development required for adding security to a program, procedure or form, we suggest you increase the estimate of the difficulty of the development task by one notch, making simple programs medium-complex, medium programs complex, and so on.

> **GUIDELINE 13.11** Increase the complexity estimate for any piece of software that requires security code to be added.

13.4.2 DATABASE DESIGN

If added security increases the number of database objects, such as tables and views, this will affect the database layout. Remember that each copy or version of a table can mean many more objects in the database. For example, if a table has three indexes, three constraints, and five views on it, each copy of the table will probably add not just the copy but 11 other objects to the database as well.

If enforcing the security adds to the size of the database, it automatically adds to the complexity of the database management and the backup recovery plan. This may affect your database design, particularly if you are already close to the limit of your database size, machine capacity or backup times within the overnight window.

13.4.3 TESTING

The testing of the design of a data warehouse is a complex and lengthy process. When further security is added to the task it increases the test time in two ways. First, the added complexity of the programs to be tested will increase the time required for integration and system testing. The added complexity will most likely increase the number of errors found in testing and the amount of recoding that needs to be performed.

Second, there is added functionality to be tested: this will increase the size of the test suite. This means that the testing will take longer to plan and develop, which in turn will increase the amount of time taken for testing. For more detail on testing see Chapter 19.

CHAPTER 14

Backup and recovery

14.1 INTRODUCTION

Backup is one of the most important regular operations carried out on any system. It is particularly important in the data warehouse environment because of the volumes of data involved and the complexity of the system. The aim of this section is to discuss the issues that need to be considered when designing a backup strategy, pointing out the requirements you should look for in both the hardware and software.

Backups of the operating system, application code and user directories will be required, as well as backups of the database. However, the size and overheads of these backups are small in comparison with those of the database: therefore, this chapter concentrates on the backup and recovery of the database.

There is unfortunately a tendency to put off the design of the backup strategy until the system is near completion. This is a serious mistake, and can prove to be very costly. These systems are too large and complex to bolt on backup solutions at the end. Leaving the backup until the end of the design process will often lead to the project's being forced to buy extra hardware. For instance, you may find that, because of the design of the database, the CPU requirements to perform the backup in a reasonable time-frame are far greater than the bandwidth available. CPUs are not cheap, in particular if you are forced to buy extra nodes to realize the extra CPU requirements. It is imperative that the backup strategy, the database and the application components such as the warehouse manager all be designed together.

When designing your backup strategy make it as automated as possible. The last thing you want is a backup being delayed and running into the daily user window, because an operator failed to notice the flashing light on the tape drive.

Finally, remember the reason you are taking all these backups. You need a documented recovery strategy, which covers everything from the loss of a single disk to Armageddon. It is pointless taking all those backups if you cannot use them when they are required. Recovery needs to be tried and tested.

> **GUIDELINE 14.1**   It is imperative that the backup strategy, the database and the data warehouse application all be designed together.

14.2 DEFINITIONS

Before we can discuss backup strategies in detail we need some definitions to clarify the terminology. For example, what is the difference between a cold backup and a hot or online backup? This is a question that causes a lot of confusion. The confusion is further compounded by the introduction of partial or complete backups. The definitions below should help to clarify the issue. These definitions apply to the backup of the database.

- In a **complete backup**, the entire database is backed up at the same time. This includes all database data files, the control files, and the journal files.
- **Partial backup** is any backup that is not complete.
- A **cold backup** is a backup that is taken while the database is completely shut down. In a multi-instance environment, all instances of that database must be shut down.
- **Hot backup**: any backup that is not cold is considered to be hot. The terminology comes from the fact that the database engine is up and running: hence *hot*. There are special requirements that need to be observed if the hot backup is to be valid. These will vary from RDBMS to RDBMS.
- **Online backup** is a synonym for hot backup.

Partial backups, if supported by the RDBMS, can be extremely useful in large databases. For example, partial backup allows a strategy whereby several parts of the database are backed up in a round-robin fashion on a day-by-day basis, so that the whole database is effectively backed up once a week. Clearly this approach means that you do not have a backup of the database that is consistent at a single point in time. Some RDBMSs allow different parts of the database to be at different points in time, but other RDBMSs do not. The RDBMS can always get around this issue by using the journal files to roll any older parts of the database forward in time. Note that, if parts of the database can be differently time stamped, this may cause inconsistencies in the data, which can lead to queries' returning errors or incorrect results.

Hot backups are another extremely useful feature. As mentioned above, hot backups work differently in different RDBMSs. For clarity, and to identify the issues, we shall discuss an Oracle example. In Oracle the journal files are called **redo log files**. These files are reused in a round-robin fashion, with the old data they contain being overwritten. Oracle has the concept of a database being in **archivelog** mode. This means that the redo log files are backed up before being reused. This operation can be made automatic, and becomes transparent to anyone using the database. Any form of partial backup such as a hot backup is totally useless unless the database is in archivelog mode.

In Oracle, hot backups are governed at the tablespace level. In other words, for the backup to be consistent all data files in a given tablespace must be backed up. The following sequence of commands must be followed:

(1) `Alter Tablespace <tablespace name> Begin Backup;`
(2) Back up all the data files belonging to that tablespace, using whatever backup tool you want.
(3) `Alter Tablespace <tablespace name> End Backup;`

This process must be followed for each tablespace you want to back up. The purpose of step 1 is to fix the time stamp on each data file in the tablespace at the time of that command. The time stamps on these files will not change until step 3, at which point they will be brought up to date.

If step 1 is missed out, the backup is invalid, as the tablespace will not be protected against data change during the backup. If step 3 is missed out, it can be performed later. The RDBMS will not allow you to shut the database down if there is a tablespace still in hot backup mode.

14.3 HARDWARE

14.3.1 INTRODUCTION

When you are choosing a backup strategy, one of the first decisions you will have to make is which hardware to use. This choice will place an upper bound on the speed at which a backup or restore can be processed. It does not, however, dictate the real speed at which the backup will perform, because that is affected by other things, such as how the hardware is connected, network bandwidth, backup software used, and the speed of the server's I/O subsystem and components.

The aim of this section is to outline the hardware choices that are available, and the advantages and disadvantages of each of them.

14.3.2 TAPE TECHNOLOGY

There are a large number of tape backup options on the market. There are also an equally wide range of methods of connecting these options. To simplify matters we can categorize the different technologies as follows,

- tape media
- standalone tape drives
- tape stackers
- tape silos

and deal with each of these in turn.

Table 14.1 Tape media.

Tape media	Capacity	I/O rates
DLT	40 GB	3 MB/s
3490e	1.6 GB	3 MB/s
8 mm	14 GB	1 MB/s

Tape media

There are many varieties of tape media that can be used. Table 14.1 lists the common tape media standards, their capacities and I/O throughput rates.

There are other factors that need to be considered, such as:

- reliability of tape medium
- shelf life of tape medium
- cost of tape medium per unit
- reliability of tape drive
- cost of tape drive
- scalability
- cost of upgrades to tape system

The last two points are all too frequently overlooked. It is important to be sure that your backup hardware solution will scale as you add more disk and tape drives. In other words, the I/O throughput of your system scales with added hardware. This is by no means certain, as you may begin to hit network, system bus or controller bottlenecks.

Equally important is the cost of upgrade. How much does it cost to add another tape drive? It may just be the cost of the tape drive. However, it may cost considerably more. Suppose there are no more controller slots available to connect a drive. In this case the cost of an extra controller has to be added to the upgrade cost. This takes an extra slot in the system bus of the server. If there are no slots left on the system bus, we are left with a choice of removing something to allow the tape drive to be added, or extending the server. Suddenly that single tape drive upgrade has become prohibitively expensive.

> **GUIDELINE 14.2** Your chosen tape medium must be scalable at an affordable price.

Standalone tape drives

Many of the issues that apply to tape media also apply to standalone drives. There is the added issue of connectivity. How and where is the tape drive connected? Tape drives can be connected in a number of ways:

- directly to the server;
- as a network-available device;
- remotely to another machine.

Even connecting the tape drive directly to the data warehouse server is not a straightforward issue. For example, suppose the server is a 48-node MPP machine. Which node do you connect the tape drive to? If there are multiple tape drives, how do you spread them over the server nodes to get the optimal performance with least disruption of the server and least internal I/O latency? What will be the effect of backup on the high-speed interconnect? These are not easy questions to answer, and extensive testing will probably be required to get the best balance.

Connecting the tapes as network-available devices is fine, but it does require that the network be up to the job of the huge transfer rates needed. Unless the network is extremely high bandwidth this is rarely the case. If that network bandwidth is shared with other processes, you need to ensure that sufficient bandwidth is available during the hours you require it. This in itself is a nightmare unless the network is dedicated. Even if you are guaranteed 8-hour exclusive access overnight, what happens for instance if the server has been down for several hours and the backup is running 5 hours late?

Finally, using remote tape drives is again not a problem, as long as you control the resource, and the bandwidth of the connection from server to server is sufficiently high. A common solution is to have the data warehouse sharing a dedicated backup server that is responsible for the backup of several applications. This means that the resource is shared, and you do not control it directly. Remember: it may be impossible to catch up if your backup falls behind – in particular, if you are using a system of partial backups, where only part of the database is backed up each night. Losing a night's backup in this sort of scenario can lead to several days' downtime. All it requires is that you encounter a failure before the backup is back in sync. It is always worth remembering that in these situations Murphy's Law is particularly applicable.

> **GUIDELINE 14.3** Ensure that you have control of any shared backup resource.

Stackers

Tape stackers are a method of loading multiple tapes into a single tape drive. Only one tape can be accessed at a time, but the stacker will automatically dismount the current tape when it has finished with it and load the next tape.

The prices and abilities of these devices vary, but they all have one thing in common: the ability to perform unattended backup. This means that you can back up data up to the full capacity of the stacker before having to involve an operator. This is highly desirable given the number of tapes likely to be involved in a backup, and the consequent risk of error or delay.

Some of these devices have limited intelligence and can be controlled programatically. Typically they will allow any given tape to be mounted as required.

This can help, for example, if a restore is required from a recent backup that is still in the stacker. It can also be used to control which tape files are copied to.

Some stackers will automatically label the tapes, and can use barcoding to ensure that they have the correct tape loaded. You should check for these sorts of features and compare their value versus the cost of the stacker unit.

Silos

Tape silos are large tape storage facilities, which can store and manage thousands of tapes. They are generally sealed environments with robotic arms for manipulating the tapes.

The silos will have the capacity for multiple integrated tape drives. They will also have the software and hardware to label and manage all the tapes they store. Generally they will have sophisticated tape library software, which can be accessed externally and controlled programatically.

Silos are expensive backup solutions, and it is often difficult to justify such expense for a single application. It is not untypical for silos to be shared by several applications. This can lead to the tape drives' becoming a bottleneck as applications contend for the drives at critical times. If the warehouse is sharing a silo it is imperative that the service level agreement (SLA) for use of the silo is sufficiently tight to ensure that you do not lose any backups as a result of such contention forcing overruns. For more details of the SLA see Chapter 15.

Silos can have a very large footprint, and may be difficult to place close to the data warehouse server. It will take a lot of preplanning and potential movement in your computer room to get the silo and the server connected optimally. It is common for the silo to be connected remotely over a network or a dedicated link. It is important to ensure that the bandwidth of that connection is up to the job.

> **GUIDELINE 14.4**   Ensure that the SLA for the use of the silo is sufficiently tight that you cannot lose any backups as a result of contention for its resource.

14.3.3 OTHER TECHNOLOGY

Tape is the traditional method of backup and restore, and most if not all backups eventually end up on tape. There are other media that can be and are used for backups, and in particular for near-line storage of older data. These options are discussed below.

Disk backups

There are a number of methods of using disks, such as disk-to-disk backups and mirror breaking, that are commonly used in large OLTP systems to minimize database downtime and to maximize availability. We shall examine below the applicability of these techniques to data warehousing.

Disk-to-disk backups

In disk-to-disk backup, as the name suggests, the backup is performed to disk rather than to tape. This is generally an intermediate step, and the backup will normally be backed up to tape later. There are two prime reasons for doing disk-to-disk backups: speed of the initial backup, and speed of restore.

Clearly it is quicker to do disk-to-disk backups than to back up to tape. Certainly the process is easily automated, and no operator intervention should be required. The question is: If you later have to back up to tape in any case, what do you gain? What you gain is minimum disruption of access to the data. Backup has an overhead, and its I/O demands on the data disks can make them effectively unavailable during the backup. There are other issues that need to be considered, such as backup consistency: see the discussion on hot backups in section 14.2.

Is it worth worrying about the backup overheads on the data? The answer to that question will depend on the nature of the usage profile of the warehouse. It is unlikely that users will be running online queries against the database other than during office hours. However, it is possible that 7×24 access is effectively required to support very long-running queries. These queries should be running in batch, so a temporary performance dip as the query and the backup contend for the same disks is not likely to be a major issue. All in all, unless there are urgent queries that have definite deadlines for completion, the fact that the backup may disrupt queries is not a major problem. Indeed, as discussed previously, it is more the other way around: it is vital to ensure that the queries do not affect the backup.

The other advantage of disk-to-disk backup is the fact that it gives you an online copy of the latest backup. This will speed up any restore operation that can use that backup, which in an OLTP environment is likely, because you will generally want to use the latest backup. In a data warehouse system any data loss is unlikely to be covered by the latest backup, because it will generally contain only yesterday's data. The vast majority of the data is read-only, and the required backup may have been made months ago.

Clearly, disk-to-disk backup requires more disks to be added to the server. Given the size of most data warehouses, and the consequent size of the disk farm, this is an undesirable overhead. This, coupled with the reasons mentioned above, makes disk-to-disk backups an unlikely strategy for a data warehouse.

Mirror breaking

Mirror breaking is really a variant of disk-to-disk backup. The idea is to have disks mirrored for resilience during the working day. When it is time to do the backups, one of the mirror sets can be broken out. This effectively freezes the data on that mirror set at the point in time of the break. Note: you may need to shut the database down, or use hot backup mechanisms to guarantee the consistency of the backup. This set can be backed up to tape while the other mirror set is still available for use. When the backup is complete, the mirrors can be re-synced.

This is again a common OLTP technique. It has the downside that while the mirror is broken the data is unprotected against media failure. This can be overcome by having triple mirroring, where each disk is mirrored to two other disks. This allows a single mirror set to be broken out, while still leaving the data protected against media failure by the remaining mirror. The implications of triple mirroring for a data warehouse are horrendous, in terms both of cost and of management. This tends to rule it out as a viable strategy.

The benefit gained by backup from a broken mirror set is lower impact on the running environment. As discussed above, this is not an issue in a data warehouse: in fact quite the contrary. The benefit can of course be viewed the other way around. Will breaking a mirror set help to isolate the backup from the queries? It is possible, with the right hardware setup, that this could be achieved. In which case, as triple mirroring is not feasible, the question becomes: Is the isolation of the backup worth the risk of media failure of unprotected disks? Generally the answer will be "no." Indeed, it is hard to see a set of circumstances where it would be true, short of the data warehouse having genuine 7×24 online user access, which is actually heavily utilized.

Optical jukeboxes

Optical jukeboxes are devices that allow data to be stored near-line. Write once read many (WORM) optical disks are now commonly available. Rewritable optical disks are less common but also available. Jukebox technology allows large numbers of optical disks to be managed in much the same way as a tape stacker or silo. The jukebox will have a limited number of devices where it can mount the optical disks, which means that only one or two disks can be accessed at a time.

The problem with using optical disk technology as a backup mechanism is the slow write speed of the disks. This tends to rule them out as a data warehouse backup strategy. However, when the time comes to archive data, the long life and reliability of optical media, coupled with the near-line capability of the jukebox, make them a good choice of medium for archiving.

14.4 SOFTWARE

The standard UNIX tools for performing backups, such as dd and tar, are inadequate for backup in a data warehouse environment. The software required to back up a complex environment such as a data warehouse has many aspects. There are lots of software packages on the market, each of which implements these aspects to different degrees. The aim of this section is to list and explain the elements required by the backup software to enable it to effectively manage and control the backup strategy for the data warehouse.

For completeness, Table 14.2 lists some backup software packages. It is by no means exhaustive, but is included as a guide to the most commonly used packages at the time of writing. Note, however, that the software market is constantly changing,

Table 14.2 Backup software packages.

Package name	Producer
OmnibackII	HP
ADSM	IBM
Alexandria	Sequent
Epoch	Epoch Systems
Networker	Legato

and it is advisable for you to investigate the market at the time of planning. The rest of this section is designed to help you with this process.

14.4.1 REQUIREMENTS

When considering which backup package to use it is important to check the following criteria:

1 What degree of parallelism is possible?
2 How scalable is the product as tape drives are added?
3 What is the CPU hit on the server during backup?
4 Does the package have a client–server option, or must it run on the database server itself?
5 Will it work in cluster and MPP environments?
6 What platforms are supported by the package?
7 What tape drives and tape media are supported by the package?
8 Does the package support easy access to information about tape contents?
9 Is the package database aware?

Points 1–3 are discussed in section 14.4.2. Point 4 can prove to be very important. If the package can be run in client–server mode, the data warehouse server can be treated as a client and the heavier load of the backup can sometimes be offloaded onto a separate machine.

Points 5 and 6 are to do with which machines and architectures the package supports. Clearly this is important, as there is no point having a package that will not run on your data warehouse server. Note particularly point 5, because the package may run on your server in standalone mode, but then may not support clusters or MPP explicitly. This is not an insurmountable problem, but it adds design and management complications as you try to program around the package's deficiencies.

As with server and architecture support, clearly the package must support whatever tape media and tape drives you choose to use. It is worth stressing point 7, because the tape media used by the warehouse may well change over time, as the data warehouse evolves. It is important to ensure that the package supports any of the tape standards used in-house, or any standards that are likely to be adopted. It may be sufficient to note that the package will support these media in the future, but we would advise you to get fairly definite time-scales for this support from the package manufacturer.

> **GUIDELINE 14.5** Ensure that your chosen backup software supports any media you are likely to use.

The access to information about the contents of each tape, as specified in point 8, is essential during recovery. In most recovery scenarios, it is likely that only a few tapes will be required. It is imperative that the information is available as to what data is on which tape. This is particularly important if data is parallel-streamed onto tapes. It is also essential to be able to quickly match the software tape labels against the physical tapes, particularly if the tapes need to be retrieved manually.

14.4.2 PERFORMANCE

There are a number of things that affect the performance of the backup. I/O bottlenecks are the most obvious of these. It is possible to bottleneck on both the read from disk and the write to tape. However, to achieve the sort of backup rates required, while maintaining all the information on which file is backed up to what tape, requires a lot of CPU: therefore, it is also possible for the CPU to become the bottleneck. Remember that the backup may not be isolated, and there may be other processes running, such as batch queries or the warehouse manager building aggregates.

It is possible to get different combinations of backup hardware and software that can give you anywhere from 10 GB per hour to 500 GB per hour. Whatever throughput you require, the aim with the backup is to minimize the elapsed time required for the backup, while minimizing system contention with any other running process. Remember: if you push the CPU bandwidth towards 100% usage, the CPUs will begin to spend time context-switching processes in and out of each CPU, and may end up thrashing. This has the affect of making all the contending processes run less efficiently, leading to longer elapsed times.

The way to minimize backup elapsed times is to use high degrees of parallelism. Different backup packages achieve parallelism differently, but in essence they all work by creating multiple backup streams, with each stream sucking data off disk and pushing it onto tape. Some backup packages allow you to multiplex backup streams onto a single tape. This allows parallelism to be achieved even if you have only a single tape drive. Others allow parallel backup streams, but each stream must write to different tapes, which of course requires multiple tape drives for the parallelism to be effective. For this and other reasons, such as compatibility, you should always evaluate and decide on your backup hardware and software together.

> **GUIDELINE 14.6** Evaluate and decide on your backup software and hardware together.

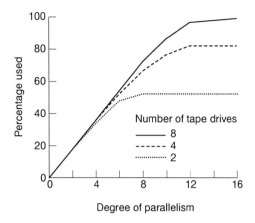

Figure 14.1 Graph of CPU usage against backup parallelism.

The downside with using parallelism is the load it puts on the server. There is a balance to be struck to maximize your throughput while minimizing your CPU usage. Whatever combination of hardware and software you pick, extensive testing will need to be performed. The tests should map CPU usage (as a percentage of total CPU) against both degree of parallelism and number of tape drives being used. The graph in Figure 14.1 shows the sort of information you need.

There are no simple rules of thumb for backup software performance, because it will depend not only on the software, but also on the speed of the disk and tape I/O subsystems. It may also depend on other less obvious factors. For example, much of the CPU overhead will be spent in maintaining information on the tape contents. Some packages keep this information in simple flat files; some store it in a database. The latter allows more sophisticated data to be stored and better front ends to be built. The result of this is that some of the benefit of the CPU overhead may not be seen until that data needs to be retrieved. However, as a guideline, it is not uncommon to see solutions in the field that use as much as 80% + of the CPU bandwidth to drive four tape drives at full I/O capacity.

Finally, the test results mapped in Figure 14.1 are also useful for determining the scalability of the tape hardware and software combination as more tape drives are added. From experience, this scalability often tails off with more than four tape drives, unless multiple instances of the backup software are being run.

14.5 BACKUP STRATEGIES

Now that we have all the definitions we need, it is time to discuss the actual backup and restore strategy.

14.5.1 EFFECT ON DATABASE DESIGN

There is a major interaction between the backup strategy and the database design. The two go hand in hand. Simple things such as the partitioning strategy chosen for the fact data can have an enormous effect on the backup requirements. Design of the database and backup have to be performed at the same time.

It is all too common to see the design of the backup strategy being done as an afterthought. This is a mistake, because it can lead to major cost and time overruns. Data warehouse systems are such large complex systems that the backup has to be an integral part of the whole system.

If the backup strategy is left until later it is more than likely that you will discover the hardware is insufficient to support the overnight window. Remember that the backup is likely to consume a considerable amount of CPU power while it is running, and it can take several hours to complete the nightly backup. As this is only part of the whole overnight processing that has to be completed, it is easy to see how you can end up in a situation where the overnight processing cannot be completed in the allowed time-frame.

To mitigate these sorts of problems you need to design the whole data warehouse system in a unified fashion. It is particularly important to manage the design of the backup, the database and the overnight processing together.

> **GUIDELINE 14.7** The design of the backup strategy and the database must be performed hand in hand.

14.5.2 DESIGN STRATEGIES

When considering the backup strategy, one of your main aims should be to reduce the amount of data that has to be backed up on a regular basis. This approach will give you the best chance of bringing down the effect of backup on the overnight processing. We shall concentrate on backup strategies that are designed around daily data loads. There are data warehouse systems that are not loaded every day, but at greater intervals. Typically these will be loaded weekly at week end or monthly at month end. These cases can be thought of as special cases of the daily load. All the same issues apply to these cases; you just have more data to load and manage, and typically a weekend rather than an overnight period to fit it in to.

Read-only tablespaces are one of the main weapons in the battle to reduce the amount of data that needs to be backed up. Having the ability to mark certain areas of the database as being read-only is vital. Making a tablespace read-only means the tablespace cannot be changed even accidentally, without bringing it back to a read–write state. Therefore, the tablespace can be backed up once and stored somewhere safe, and it does not have to be backed up again.

> **GUIDELINE 14.8** Backup read-only data twice to protect against failure in the backup media.

Actually, it is recommended that read-only tablespaces be backed up twice to protect against tape media failure. Clearly the second backup should be taken to a different tape from the first. Ideally it should also be made to a different tape device, and if possible a different controller should be used.

The use of read-only tablespaces needs to be considered in conjunction with your database design strategy. Where possible, unchanging data should be isolated in separate tablespaces so that they can be marked Read Only. When partitioning the large objects such as the fact table it is important to use a partitioning scheme that allows the bulk of the partitions to be marked as read-only.

One key decision that has to be made is the size of partition to be used. For a full discussion on how to size the partitions see Chapter 6. The size of the regular load partition affects the backup strategy, because that dictates the size of the regular backup.

Another way of reducing the regular backup requirements is to reduce the amount of journaling or redo generated. This is possible with some RDBMSs, because they allow you to turn off logging with certain operations. These options will typically be allowed only for large singular operations. For example, data load, index creation and create table as select are some of the operations that can often be performed without logging of journal information. Clearly, these operations cannot be recovered in the normal sense and therefore must be easily repeatable. This is important to ensure that these operations do not place the data warehouse at risk

Automation of backups

Given the data volumes being handled and the likely complexity of any viable backup strategy, it is important to automate as much of the backup process as possible. For example, by the use of stacker or silo technology, large backups can be accomplished without operator intervention. This minimizes the chance of error, and avoids any potential delays.

It is equally important to automate the scripts that run the regular backups. These scripts need to be sophisticated enough to report any problems and to either deal with them directly or allow the job to be restarted once the problem has been fixed.

The backup routines will be managed from the warehouse manager. The backup routines should be further integrated into the system management routines and handled by whatever system management and scheduling software is being used.

14.5.3 RECOVERY STRATEGIES

The recovery strategy will be built around the backup strategy. Any recovery situation naturally implies that some failure has occurred. The recovery action will depend on what that failure was. As such, a recovery strategy will consist of a set of failure scenarios and their resolution. The aim of this section is to categorize the main potential failures. How each failure is dealt with specifically is of course RDBMS-dependent. Whatever software you choose, the recovery steps for the failure scenarios below need to be fully documented:

- instance failure
- media failure
- loss or damage of tablespace or data file
- loss or damage of a table
- loss or damage of a redo log file
- loss or damage of archive log file
- loss or damage of control file
- failure during data movement
- other scenarios

The recovery plan for each of the scenarios should take into account the use of any operations that are not logged. For example, if a table is created with the `create table as select` statement with logging of journal information switched off, recovery of the tablespace with that table will need to take this into account. If the recovery is from a backup taken before the table was created, there will be no roll-forward information to create and repopulate the table. The operation that created the table will need to be rerun. If, on the other hand, the backup was taken after the table was created, then the table will exist and, more importantly, any changes made after the original create statement can be rolled forward using journal files.

There are a number of data movement scenarios that need to be covered. Some of the more common data movements are:

- data load into staging tables
- movement from staging to fact table
- partition roll-up into larger partitions
- creation of aggregations

A plan needs to be prepared and documented for each of these situations. The plan must include a description of the processes involved, including details of tables used, views that need to be created, and so on. This is important, because it enables anyone dealing with a failure of the process to track what has occurred. It also gives the system management and database administration teams a fighting chance of finding and fixing a problem.

Any other scenarios, such as rolling out bad data, will require DBA evaluation on a case-by-case basis. If necessary, external help, such as the hardware or RDBMS support help desks, can be called, to help resolve the problem. It is worth recording the phone numbers of these organizations in the recovery documentation.

> **GUIDELINE 14.9** Document clearly the backup strategy and any likely recovery scenarios.

14.6 TESTING THE STRATEGY

The oft-forgotten cousin of the backup recovery world is testing. All too often, backup strategies are developed and never tested. In such a complex environment as a data warehouse the tendency is to put backup testing to one side while everything else is being tested. The general outcome is that backup never gets tested, or at best is tested only minimally.

It is not sufficient simply to check that your backup scripts are backing up the intended files. All the failure scenarios identified above need to be explored, with the suggested recovery path being implemented in full. This will add at least a week to the project test plan, and possibly as much as a month, depending on the size and complexity of the data warehouse.

Testing does not end when the data warehouse goes live. Warehouses are evolving environments, and will typically start out smaller than their ultimate size. The backup and recovery tests need to be carried out on a regular basis. We suggest that the full test suite should be run twice a year, or at the very least annually. As the system itself is live, and many of the tests will be destructive, people are often wary of running these tests. The way to deal with this is to have a test and development environment that matches the live environment.

That is not to say that the test environment has to be full-scale and exactly like the live environment. It does, however, have to be large enough to allow full-scale testing to be performed. The architecture of the system should always be the same as the live system. For example, if the live system is a cluster of SMP machines, it is better for the test machine to be a cluster of smaller machines, rather than a larger standalone machine.

When running the regular backup tests, it is advisable to avoid performing the tests at busy times, such as end of year. Try to position the tests to be run at low periods in the business year. Part of the benefit of the tests is the knowledge of the system and the software being used that operational staff gain. For this reason it is important that the tests be scheduled to maximize the coverage of the systems and operations people.

> **GUIDELINE 14.10** A data warehouse is a changing environment, and you should perform regular backup testing.

14.7 DISASTER RECOVERY

What exactly constitutes a disaster? We define a disaster to be where a major site loss has taken place, usually meaning that the site has been destroyed or damaged beyond immediate repair. This means that the system will be either beyond repair in situ, or unavailable for an extended period. It calls for judgment to decide what constitutes a sufficiently long period to turn a simple outage into a disaster. It is advisable to decide on the criteria for making that judgment before any situation occurs, as attempting to make such a decision while in the middle of a crisis is likely to lead to problems.

As most data warehouses are not operational systems, let alone mission critical (see section 15.2), it is rare to have a disaster recovery plan for a warehouse. Add the cost of a disaster recovery site and the hardware required to keep such a large system running, and many companies decide not to bother with disaster planning.

The cost of not having a disaster plan can be enormous. In data warehouses with daily loads, a disaster will mean a long-term outage. If this outage is more than a few days it can mean that it is impossible to catch up with the load process. This leaves a hole in the database, and can have the effect of statistically invalidating a whole period's data. For example, the current month may become invalid, and if year-to-date aggregates are kept, or year-on-year comparisons are important, a whole year's worth of data may become effectively invalid.

For this and other reasons it is important to plan for at least minimal functionality disaster recovery. The obvious fallback plan is to use the test and development environment as a fallback server. This will require that it be positioned some distance apart from the main system.

When planning disaster recovery, identify the minimal system required. Decide which components of the data warehouse environment and application are required. It is important to check whether the chosen components of the warehouse have any dependencies on other parts. Continue with this process until the minimum set of components that both satisfy the requirements and can run independently have been identified.

Having decided to design or develop a minimal fallback system, or a full-blown disaster recovery plan, the next step is to list the requirements. Recovering from disaster requires the following:

- replacement/standby machine,
- sufficient tape and disk capacity,
- communication links to users,
- communication links to data sources,
- copies of all relevant pieces of software,
- backup of database,
- application-aware systems administration and operations staff.

As discussed above, the replacement or standby machine does not have to be as large as the main machine, but it must have sufficient capacity to run the minimal system. It must also have sufficient capacity and power to allow the recovery to take place in a meaningful time-frame.

The disaster system must have enough tape capacity to perform the recovery in a reasonable time-scale. Having sufficient disk space to run the minimum independent system is not always enough. To allow the initial recovery to happen quickly, extra disk capacity may be required. For example, it may be required to get files loaded for recovery, while accepting feed files onto the system. This will allow processing of new data to begin as soon as that part of the application is available.

If the system is to be accessible to users, clearly the communication links they need to access the machine have to be in place. It is important to ensure that any links used have sufficient bandwidth and capacity. This is particularly important if the links used are already in use by other systems. There is no point in making the disaster system available to the users if they cannot use it.

To continue the daily load process requires that the links to the source systems be in place. The same requirements apply here as to user links. These links may be as simple as a tape drive, if the feed files can be shipped on tape. Note, however, that if the delivery mechanism changes, it must be ensured that the source system can support that change. Another consideration is if a source system was also destroyed by the same disaster. Does the disaster system for the source system support what is required?

If the disaster system is not in constant standby mode, for example if it is being used for another less important system, it will need the relevant software installed. All of this software is probably available from backups. Even so, copies of the software should be available locally, ready to install just in case. Note that this may require upgrading of the operating system, if the system is not on the same release. Where possible, on the disaster system, go to a combination of versions and releases that has been tested in normal running.

The database will have to be restored from backup, and possibly rolled forward. One point to note is that, unless replication is being used, it will be impossible to bring the database right up to time. At the very least, the current online redo log file will be missing, and it is probable that a lot more will be missing. This will mean that all the missing work will need to be redone. So access to backups of the feed system data will be required. Some RDBMSs have support for hot standby databases. This allows a copy of the database to be kept in recovery mode, with archive log files being applied as they arrive on the disaster machine.

Systems administration and operations staff who are application aware will be required. Bear in mind that, during a disaster scenario, key staff may also be lost. The plan needs to cope with this, and staff at the disaster site will need to be trained in the running of the application.

Finally, test the disaster recovery plan. It would be nothing less than a miracle for a disaster recovery plan to work first time. It needs to be thoroughly tested, preferably on an ongoing basis. As with backup, recovery testing helps to familiarize staff with procedures, and will also highlight anything that has been overlooked.

CHAPTER 15

Service level agreement

15.1 INTRODUCTION

A **service level agreement** (SLA) is essential to the design process of the data warehouse. In particular, it is essential to the design of the backup strategy. You need the SLA as a guide to the rates of backup that are required, and more importantly the rate at which a restore needs to be accomplished. The SLA affects not just the backup, but also such fundamental design decisions as partitioning of the fact data.

There are many aspects to the definition of an SLA. Some of the more important topics that the SLA must cover are:

- user online access – hours of work
- user batch access
- user expected response times
  - average response times
  - maximum acceptable response times
- system availability
- planned downtime
- network access and availability
  - priority of access to network
  - priority of access to the backup hardware (silo etc.)

These topics will be explored in detail in the following sections, but first we need some definitions.

15.2 DEFINITION OF TYPES OF SYSTEM

There are a number of terms that are frequently used when talking about large systems such as data warehouses:

- operational
- mission critical
- 7×24
- $7 \times 24 \times 52$

The meaning of these terms should be clear from the names, but the terms are often loosely used – some would say even misused – so we shall define what we mean by them.

- An **operational system** is a system that has responsibilities to the operations of the business.

    In other words, the day-to-day operation of the business requires the use of this system. This means that if the system is not up and running, some people cannot easily carry out their work. If the machine was down for a day or two, it would prove to be a major inconvenience, but would not necessarily affect the business in any serious way. However, if an operational system was to be out of service for a sustained period, it would disrupt the company's ability to do business, almost definitely causing some financial loss. An example of an operational system is a system which handles the company's invoicing and shipping notices.

- A **mission critical system** is a system that the business absolutely depends on to function.

The system is critical to the mission of the business, or put another way the system is critical to the business fulfilling its function on a day-to-day basis. Any unplanned downtime of the system, in particular during the working day, means that the business becomes dysfunctional and is losing money all the time the system is out of action. An example of a mission critical system is a customer-facing application such as a dealing system, or an insurance-quoting system.

- A **7×24 system** is a system that needs to be available all day every day, except for small periods of planned downtime.

The system needs to be available either online or via batch throughout the entire 24 hours of the day. A 7×24 is not necessarily either operational or mission critical, but may be 7×24 by the very nature of its workload. An example of a 7×24 system is an application where the daily overnight processing runs from before the end of the user day to after the start of the following user day. This means that there is no time to shut the system down during a normal working day.

- A **7 × 24 × 52 system** is a true 7 × 24 system, which is required to be running all the time.

In other words, there can never be any downtime, planned or otherwise. An example of a 7 × 24 × 52 system is an application such as an air traffic control system.

15.3 IS THE DATA WAREHOUSE AN

OPERATIONAL SYSTEM OR NOT?

Having defined these system types, let us now define what type of system a data warehouse is, or more importantly what it is not. To decide this, we need to understand the business drivers that lead to the requirement for the data warehouse. For example, a retail bank may require a data warehouse for customer profile and trend analysis. A telco may require a data warehouse for the same reasons, and also for tracking the success of competitors' marketing campaigns.

Clearly, none of the above are mission critical systems. Likewise, they do not affect the running of the business on a day-to-day basis. They can of course be used to change the way the business is run in the future, but they are not operational systems. Given the ad hoc and thus unpredictable nature of data warehouses they cannot by nature be operational systems, because you cannot generally guarantee response times except in the broadest terms.

It is important to ensure that the system does not become an operational system, either directly or by implication. It is all too common to find people at an early stage thinking of the data warehouse as an operational system. This is understandable; after all, the warehouse often becomes recognized as a source of good clean data, or the best source of truth in the company's information. This perception may indeed even be true, but nonetheless the system will not have been designed to function as an operational system, and generally does not have either sufficient resilience or system support to deliver the guaranteed responses of an operational system. This is why the SLA is so important; the system will be designed to be robust enough to deliver the SLA and no more. The cost of delivering a data warehouse system to an operational SLA specification will almost certainly be prohibitive.

> **GUIDELINE 15.1** A data warehouse is not an operational system.

Note: as mentioned above, it is equally important to ensure that the system does not become an operational system indirectly. We have seen situations where it was proposed that the data warehouse become a feed system for some downstream operational systems. This by implication will place an operational responsibility on the data warehouse, as it is now on the critical path of another operational system. Note that the operational system may in turn be a feed for a downstream mission critical system, making the data warehouse a mission critical system by implication.

These sorts of situation have to be spotted early, and prevented. There are ways around such problems. For example, suppose the scenario discussed above was as shown in Figure 15.1.

This sort of problem can be circumvented by replacing the data warehouse system in Figure 15.1 with a small operational system, which cleans the data for passing on to the downstream operational system. As depicted in Figure 15.2, this new system then becomes the new source system for the data warehouse. Although

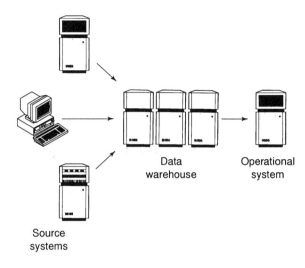

Figure 15.1 Data warehouse indirectly becomes an operational system.

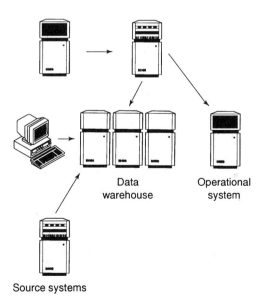

Figure 15.2 Avoiding indirect operational status.

this will require expenditure on the new operational system, it will almost certainly be more cost-effective than trying to make the data warehouse resilient enough to be operational.

> **GUIDELINE 15.2** Ensure that the data warehouse does not indirectly become an operational system.

Initially, most data warehouses will not be 7×24, but as the data grows in size and the usage profile changes, the overnight window will normally grow to fill any available time, forcing the system to become 7×24. For a full discussion of the processing of the overnight workload see Chapter 16.

15.4 DEFINING THE SLA

The topics that should be covered in the SLA were listed in section 15.1. These topics can be further divided into two categories:

- user requirements
- system requirements

User requirements are the elements that directly affect the users, such as hours of access and response times. System requirements are the needs imposed on the system by the business, such as system availability.

15.4.1 USER REQUIREMENTS

One of the key sets of requirements to capture during the analysis phase is the user requirements. Detailed information is required on the following:

- user online access – hours of work
- user batch access
- user expected response times
  - average response times
  - maximum acceptable response times

> **GUIDELINE 15.3** Ensure you gather the requirements of every group of users. Any group could have requirements that differ from the others.

The first question to be answered is: What are online user access requirements? To answer this question we need to know the answers to several other questions. For example, what are the business working hours? For each user group, what are their online working hours? It is particularly important to be able to profile the different user groups, because they may have different requirements. The overall online requirement will be a combination of all the user group requirements. This is an important baseline, because it defines the initial boundaries for your overnight window.

It is worthwhile mentioning at this stage that the initial requirements are likely to change as usage profiles change and new users are added. Where possible, these future changes should be categorized, but it is likely that the futures will not be clearly definable. This is a fact of life in the data warehouse arena. Although the futures are not clearly known, knowledge of the business and the market sector it occupies should enable you to make reasonable assumptions about future or potential use of the system. You should design the data warehouse for the definite requirements you have, but take these assumptions about the future into consideration.

The next question to be answered concerns the user batch requirements. Are the users likely to leave queries running overnight? Will they require the ability to submit large jobs to run outside the online window? These are much more difficult questions to answer, as it is likely that the users themselves will not know the answers. Most users will not have had such access to data before, and will be unsure of what they can and cannot do. A common answer to the above questions is, "Ask me again in 6 months when I've had time to play with the data."

The final user requirement that needs to be teased out is the expected response times. It is likely that, once again, the users will not really know what they want. Remember: it is unlikely that they have had access to this sort of data before. They may also have unrealistic expectations, based on a lack of understanding of the sheer size of the system involved. It is very important, when the questions are asked, that they are asked the right way around. Never ask users what they want in the way of response time. Instead ask them what they need or what they will accept. It does no harm to try to educate the users at this stage in some of the complexity and size of the data storage issues involved.

> **GUIDELINE 15.4** Always ask questions the right way around. Ask users what they need, not what they want.

When gathering users' response times, remember to ascertain both the average response times that are required and the worst response they will accept. At this stage you again need to differentiate between online response and batch response times.

With online response times the average is more important than the maximum, because this will drive the users' perception of the usability of the system. With batch response or turnaround times, users are likely to be more tolerant, and will often accept more than the declared maximum turnaround time. As long as the users perceive that they are getting fair access to the batch system, and that any important reports can be escalated or run on a priority queue if necessary, they will normally be happy. Therefore, both the average and maximum are relevant in this case, but more to the definition of the SLA than to the actual requirements.

15.4.2 SYSTEM REQUIREMENTS

The key system requirement that needs to be measured is the maximum acceptable downtime for the system. This question can be asked from the viewpoints both of user discomfort and of business damage. However, the reality is that in systems of this size and complexity you have to work to the business damage limit, not the user discomfort limit, otherwise costs and complexity soar. The SLA needs to stipulate fully any measures related to downtime. In particular, some measure of the required availability of the server is needed.

Availability can be measured in a number of different ways, but however you state it in the SLA it must be unambiguous. It is normal for availability to be measured as a required percentage of uptime. In other words:

$$D = 100 - A \qquad (15.1)$$

where D = acceptable downtime, and A is the percentage required availability.

Note that D covers both planned and unplanned downtime. This can be further broken down into acceptable online downtime (D_n), and acceptable offline downtime (D_f). These can be defined as:

$$D_n = 100 - A_n$$

$$D_f = 100 - A_f \qquad (15.2)$$

where A_n is the percentage of N for which the system is required to be available; A_f is the percentage of $(24-N)$ hours for which the system is required to be available; and N is the number of hours in the user/online day. It is of course possible to quote values for A_n and A_f of 100%, but these are unrealistic values for a data warehouse: the higher the required availability, the greater the cost of the system.

In most systems the user requirements would make $D_n < D_f$. In a data warehouse system the workload placed on the system by the overnight processing, and the time required to catch up if that processing fails, generally means that $D_n > D_f$.

These availability figures will drive the resilience requirements, and may affect the architecture. For example, if high availability is required and an SMP architecture is being used, you may want to consider a cluster solution, even if the data warehouse does not require the extra node for CPU bandwidth. The extra node can be used for automatic failover, thereby giving greater availability.

Another measure that needs to be quoted in the SLA is the permissible planned downtime. This is the maximum amount of planned time in any period that the data warehouse can be down. It is inevitable that some downtime will be required. Data warehouses are volatile environments, and changing requirements may require downtime for software upgrades, or data reorganization. This measure is important, as it will affect the design of processes such as backup, daily load and so on. These processes must be designed to allow for this planned downtime.

An issue that sometimes gets overlooked is that SLAs are not all one way. The requirements will not all be *on* the data warehouse; some of the requirements will be *by* the data warehouse. These will probably require a separate SLA or SLAs with the organization's operations, systems and network groups. The key items that need to be addressed by these SLA(s) are:

- priority of network access
- network availability guarantees

- network bandwith guarantees
- priority of access to the backup hardware

The network and the backup hardware are critical to the success of the data warehouse. SLA(s) must exist that guarantee acceptable performance of and access to both of them.

Finally, to re-emphasize the importance of having the SLA defined, remember that the SLA drives your backup recovery strategy. It stipulates your resilience criteria, and drives the architecture and database design.

> **GUIDELINE 15.5**   The SLA(s) must cover all the dependencies that the data warehouse has on the outside world.

Operating the data warehouse

16.1 INTRODUCTION

The operation of a data warehouse is a non-trivial task. The design of the operational environment is no less challenging. The design is not made any easier by the need for operations to be as automated as possible. The aim of this chapter is to cover the operational tasks, and to identify any probable issues.

16.2 DAY-TO-DAY OPERATIONS OF THE DATA
WAREHOUSE

The daily operations of the data warehouse are equally as complex as but less fraught than the overnight processing. The main purpose of the daytime usage of the machine is to service the users' queries. Nonetheless, there are other operations that can and do take place during the day, and these need to be considered carefully.

Some of the other operations that can occur during the day are:

- monitoring application daemons
- query management
  - batch
  - ad hoc
- backup/recovery
- housekeeping scripts

- data feeds
  - drip feed of load files
- data extracts
  - query results
  - data marts
- performance monitoring
- event management
- job scheduling

The warehouse application managers are likely to have a number of service or background processes running. These processes are often called **daemons**. These daemons are used to log events, act as servers and so on. The monitoring of these daemons is an operational task. Ideally, there will be a menu interface that will allow the operators to start up, halt, shut down and otherwise interface with the application daemons.

Query management is a vital part of the daily operations. Some of the monitoring and control can be automated, but there will still be a requirement for a DBA to be available to deal with any problems. This is particularly important if user profiles are not being used. The profiles can be used to control resource usage and to force-terminate a job that has exceeded its quota. If profiles are not being used, jobs will need to be killed manually if they are using excessive resource.

Backups are usually avoided during the user day, to avoid contentions with the users' queries. In addition, in a data warehouse the bulk of the data is read-only, and there is little that happens during working hours that will require backing up. It is usually only the overnight load and the update of the aggregations that require backing up. The exception will be if there are areas such as users' work areas that need saving. Sometimes these may be backed up during the day.

There are always **housekeeping** tasks that need to be run. Scripts that purge down directories, log off idle connections and so on are as much a part of a data warehouse as of any other system.

The **data feeds** may arrive at any time of the day. Having some of the data arrive during the day is not an issue unless it causes network problems. You may even be able to get it loaded into the database, or at least into a staging area, if the processing cost is not too high.

Data extracts are subsets of data that are offloaded from the server machine onto other machines. Extracts can be unscheduled user extracts of some query results, or they can be scheduled extracts such as data mart refreshes.

Extraction of user **query results** can impose a significant load on the network, and has to be controlled. Ideally, the extraction of anything larger than a few megabytes should be controlled via the schedule manager. As this may require the schedule manager to integrate with several network protocols it is not a simple task, and may require considerable programming to automate. Often the best approach is to push the extract under queue control to a file server that is on the same network segment as the user. Note: there may be security issues with this approach, and care needs to be taken not to make information available inadvertently.

Data marts are regular and, as such, more controllable data extracts. As with other extracts, they will incur network costs, unless they are transferred via some medium such as tape. These data extracts should be scheduled to avoid any conflict with data transfer from the source systems. They also need to be controlled so as not to affect any users connected by flooding the network.

Performance monitoring, **event monitoring** and **scheduling** are all ongoing and highly automated operations. They should require minimal manual input to maintain. Any manual interfacing should be via a menu system or the relevant GUI front end. These topics are discussed in more detail in section 10.3.

The operations listed at the beginning of this section are likely to affect the operation of the data warehouse on a daily basis, but there are other operational issues that can affect the operation of the system that need to be considered. Topics such as:

- security
- logins
  - user
  - administrator
- log and trace file maintenance
- startup and shutdown
  - data warehouse application
  - database
  - data warehouse server
- printing
- problem management
- upgrade management

are operations that require occasional management, but for the most part have a passive effect on the system. These tasks and services will need to be designed and developed by the data warehouse design team. **Security** is discussed in detail in Chapter 13. Any operational decisions that arise from the security analysis will need to be implemented.

Logins for each user will need to be created, maintained, and deleted. This is a task that should be menu driven to prevent accidents. Adding a user with the wrong privileges can prove to be a costly mistake. The users should all fall into easy categories or groups, allowing a template login to be created for each group. This template should have all the default accesses, profiles, roles and so on for that group. The new user can then be set up with that template as a basis and any specific requirements added.

Extra care needs to be taken with the design of privileged user accounts. The amount of damage that can be caused by the inadvertent dropping of a table or data file is enormous in a database of this size. Where possible, all privileged operations should be performed via menus that have the relevant checks in them, to prevent such accidents.

A great deal of monitoring and logging is required to keep a data warehouse system ticking over correctly. **Log files**, which log ongoing events, and **trace files**, which dump information on specific processes, will generate a vast amount of data, and can occupy a lot of disk space. Although small in comparison with the size of the database, this disk space is still significant. Scripts will be needed to maintain the logging directories. Old log files should be archived if they contain useful historical data. They should also be purged regularly, to keep space usage under control.

Some trace files will have errors or trace information from unsolved problems; others may have performance statistics from some recent test runs. If you need to keep these files they should be filed in separate named directories, where the housekeeping scripts will not find and delete them. Ideally, such files should be transferred off the live data warehouse machine onto the development machine.

Some trace information is worth keeping in its own right. For example, some RDBMSs such as Oracle generate a log file that contains all major operations run against the database. These operations include startup and shutdown, addition or deletion of data files, changes to journal files and so on. These are worth filing as a history log. The logs themselves can become too big to manage easily or browse, so they should be backed up and then cleared down.

Given the number and size of log and trace files that will be generated, it is essential to have scripts that can search these files for any errors or other important events. These scripts should be run regularly, ideally several times a day, and the process should be automated via the schedule manager.

> **GUIDELINE 16.1** Keep all log and trace information, relevant to any problems or issues still under investigation, in a separate location to avoid the information being removed by regular and automated housekeeping.

Starting up and **shutting down** of the server, database or the data warehouse application are tasks that are likely to be performed infrequently. They are, however, tasks that it is important to get right, because shutting down the machine or database incorrectly can cause problems on restart. Each will need scripted and menu-driven procedures for shutting it down, and starting it up.

The data warehouse application has daemons that need to be shut down. These should be shut down gracefully, allowing them to complete whatever work they are currently doing, not just aborted. It is useful to have options that allow a daemon to continue working, but not to accept any more work. This allows the daemons to clear their current load without taking any more on. They can then be shut down cleanly. There will be times when the daemons are required to be shut down instantly. To allow for this eventuality you must design the daemons to be restartable, picking up the threads of the tasks they were performing when they were crashed. At the very least the daemons should be able to restart any jobs they were running.

As with the application, the database will require menu-driven scripts that allow it to be shut down and started up. The database should never be forced down unless it is absolutely necessary, because this will cause it to perform recovery operations on startup, to clean up any jobs that were running when the database was shut down. This could take a long time if some large long-running jobs were aborted in the process.

One common problem with shutting down a database is getting all the users' connections logged off. It is not uncommon for users to leave connections running and forget about them. Scripts will be needed to find these connecting processes and kill them.

If the data warehouse resides on a complex configuration, such as an MPP or clustered environment, any scripts written to shut down the database will have to be able to cope with this. During a shutdown of the database, the scripts will need to know whether you are trying to shut down the database cluster-wide or just on that node.

There will also need to be scripts to shut down and start up the data warehouse server itself. As with the database, the server scripts will need to be aware of the server hardware setup. In an MPP or cluster setup the scripts will need to be capable of bringing down the system on one or more nodes at the same time.

> **GUIDELINE 16.2** Always try to shut down systems, applications or database cleanly.

Printing requirements will need to be established. From experience, printing is not a common data warehouse requirement. The result sets of most queries are too large to print meaningfully. It is most likely that the facility to print from the server will be required only by administration and operations staff. Large result sets are generally used as the base data sets for further analysis. Often these will be extracted from the server onto the user's PC for further analysis in local tools. The printing of final results from these extracts will again be done locally or on network printers.

The one requirement that does occasionally arise for printing from the server is for standard and regular reports. Even these will generally be printed on network printers closer to the user's location, or often they are mailed or copied to another machine.

Problem management is an area that needs to be clearly defined and documented. It is vital that all administration staff know who, where and when to call if problems arise. It is common to have several groups inside an organization responsible for different parts of the data warehouse. There may be a central helpdesk for application, tool or PC problems, while operations are responsible for the hardware and a separate DBA team is responsible for the database. Everyone from the users through to the developers and operators needs to know who to call.

This whole area of problem management needs to be bottomed out early in the data warehouse project. The environment and the application will be complex, and everyone involved in supporting the system or supplying a help service will need to be identified and trained.

Upgrading a data warehouse is always a problem. As the system becomes a victim of its own success, it will become harder and harder to find extended periods of time when the system can be down. This is particularly true if the server is in itself a complex environment, such as a cluster or an MPP box. Upgrading one of these systems is a major challenge in itself, even before you consider the database upgrade that this might enforce, and the code changes to the applications that may be required.

Before upgrading the data warehouse you should upgrade the test system to ensure that the upgrade goes smoothly. You should also check that the versions of the operating system, the RDBMS and any third-party software are compatible.

> **GUIDELINE 16.3** Thoroughly test any upgrades on the test system before upgrading the live system.

16.3 OVERNIGHT PROCESSING

One of the key challenges that any designer of a data warehouse has to face is the design of the overnight processing. There are a number of major issues that need to be addressed, if this is not to become a stumbling block to the success of the data warehouse.

The key issue is keeping to the time window and ensuring that you do not eat into the next business day. The sheer volume of work that has to be accomplished, and the serial nature of many of the operations, make this more difficult than it may first seem.

The tasks that need to be accomplished overnight are, in order:

1   data rollup,
2   obtaining the data,
3   data transformation,
4   daily load,
5   data cleanup,
6   index creation,
7   aggregation creation and maintenance,
8   backup,
9   data archiving,
10 data mart refresh.

Each of these tasks is discussed in detail in other chapters. Here we shall concentrate on the job of getting the whole process to run. The order shown should be fairly accurate, but there may be overlaps.

In **data rollup** older data is rolled up into aggregated form to save space. This operation is not dependent on any of the other operations in the list. Therefore, it can be performed first before the data has arrived from the source. This is important if there is a delay between the end of the user day and the arrival of the new data, because it removes part of the overnight load, avoiding some potential contention for resource later on. This step does not apply to all data warehouses.

The first real step in the overnight processing is **obtaining the data**. This in itself is probably a simple operation; the problems arise when the data is delayed or cannot be transferred. The whole process depends on this step, and cannot complete until the data becomes available.

The data transfer process should be designed, where possible, to work on subsets of the data. Any set of data that has no transformation, constraint or checking dependencies should be capable of being handled individually. The process must be designed to take this data as far through the overnight process as it can before hitting dependencies. Any time and resource saved early in the evening can be used later to speed up the process, or to catch up on lost time.

> **GUIDELINE 16.4** The data transfer and load processes need to be designed to work on subsets of the daily data, even if the data is expected to arrive as a single set.

The data transfer process is of course fraught with dangers. Data can be delayed because of late processing on the source system. This late processing can be due to system problems, increased data loads such as peak days, or a host of other reasons. Data can also be delayed because of breaks or faults on the network.

Whatever the reason, delayed data is a serious risk to the data warehouse. If a key piece of daily data does not make it to the data warehouse until the next day, how is this to be handled? If data is missing, should the available data be made visible to the users? Does that data get rolled into the aggregations, or do you wait until the rest of the data is available before updating the aggregations? These are crucial and difficult questions to answer. There are no stock answers, because the effect of missing data will depend on the business and the purpose of the data warehouse.

Even if you can answer these questions, there are a number of possible outcomes to the missing data scenario. The data may turn up a day or several days later. The data may not turn up at all. You will have to cater for all these eventualities, and in particular, procedures need to be in place to cope with the effects of data that will never arrive.

The next step is **data transformation**. This will vary from data warehouse to data warehouse, and it is possible that you will have no transformation at all to perform. If data transformation is required it will be necessary to complete the transformation before the data can be loaded, even though some of the transformation may be performed by the load process itself. This is another serialization; you cannot proceed until the transformation is complete. Again, consideration needs to be given to the design of the process, to allow some data to be transformed and made ready for load, even if other data is delayed.

The **load** step is again a potential serialization point in the overnight processing. The load itself can be parallelized, but the data cleanup cannot proceed until the data is in the database. The major consideration here is the streamlining of the load, by the use of direct load methods and parallel loading techniques. The load process is discussed in detail in Chapter 10. Again, the load needs to be designed to be capable of dealing with partial sets of the data.

The **data cleanup** processing required will again vary from data warehouse to data warehouse. There may be no data cleanup, or there could be a major match and cross-reference operation to perform, with each record being verified against other data. For example, in a call record data warehouse you may need to match each call record with the customer information to get customer ids onto the record. This whole process is again a serialization, because the index and aggregation builds probably cannot proceed until any data cleanup has completed.

The next steps, **index build** and **aggregation creation and maintenance**, cannot really proceed until all the data has arrived, and has been transformed, loaded and cleaned. If there is still data missing at this stage, and you choose to build the indexes to allow any necessary processing to continue, you may have to load the rest of the data with the index in place, or drop and re-create the indexes again.

Any aggregations that are created or updated at this point may likewise have to be updated or re-created when the missing data arrives. You have to be very careful that any aggregates you update are correct, as the aggregate of two aggregate values is not necessarily the value you want in the aggregation. You need to know the number of records over which the aggregate is generated, otherwise aggregating two aggregates may lead to skewing of the values.

For example, suppose that the average value of a transaction for a particular account is maintained on an ongoing basis. If the current value of the average is $27.50 over 1000 transactions, suppose the new records from today's load gives an average of $74.20 over two transactions. You cannot just average the averages:

$$\frac{\$27.50 + \$74.20}{2} = \$50.85 \tag{16.1}$$

because this value is badly skewed. The real average is:

$$\frac{(\$27.50 \times 1000) + (\$74.20 \times 2)}{1002} = \$27.59 \tag{16.2}$$

This is why there is a need to track the number of records involved, and not just the averages themselves.

As long as the number of records is stored in the aggregation as well as the aggregated values, then the aggregation updates can be run as often as desired. One final point worth noting on the aggregations is that as long as the creation or maintenance of the aggregates does not depend on the indexes for performance, then the aggregations can be maintained and created before the indexes are created on the new fact data. Clearly, if some aggregates do require the indexes, they will serialize behind the index creation.

The final overnight operation in most systems will be the **backup**. This has to be last, because some of the most important items that need to be backed up are the new and modified aggregations. The backup can be interleaved with other operations, because the newly loaded data can be backed up as soon as it hits the database. However, the implications of running simultaneous operations has to be taken into account. Remember: the backup will most likely have a major effect on both CPU and I/O resources. For details of the possible backup strategies see Chapter 14.

If data has to be **archived**, this process will usually get run as part of the backup. Depending on the frequency of the data archiving, this can prove to be a major overhead. For example, if data is loaded daily, but is archived monthly, this would mean backing up an extra month's worth of data overnight. This extra overhead may not fit in the overnight window. It is advisable to schedule archiving activities to run outside the overnight window, and during periods of low user activity, such as weekends.

Data marts and other data extracts – if they exist – may have to be **refreshed** on a regular basis. You need to ascertain exactly when such extracts need to be available, and how regularly they need to be refreshed. As with archiving it is advisable, if possible, to avoid making extract refresh part of the overnight window. Certainly if the **archiving** and **data mart refresh** are part of the overnight process, they need to be very tightly controlled, and their effect on the capacity of the server and the network needs to be well understood. If allowed to grow unrestricted, they will rapidly become a resource bottleneck, and will drive overnight processing into the business day.

Capacity Planning, Tuning and Testing

5

CHAPTER 17

Capacity planning

17.1 INTRODUCTION

The aim of this chapter is to cover the issues relating to the growth and performance of a data warehouse. Any data warehouse solution will grow over time, sometimes quite dramatically. It is essential that the components of the solution (hardware, software, and database) are capable of supporting the extended sizes without unacceptable performance loss, or growth of the load window to a point where it affects the use of the system.

17.2 PROCESS

The capacity plan for a data warehouse is defined within the *technical blueprint* stage of the process (Figure 17.1). The *business requirements* stage should have identified the approximate sizes for data, users, and any other issues that constrain system performance. Tuning and testing are carried out prior to the completion of each build phase, once the system and tools are built, bearing in mind that the test plan is defined at the start of the build phase.

One of the most difficult decisions you will have to make about a data warehouse is the capacity required by the hardware.

It is important to have a clear understanding of the usage profiles of all users of the data warehouse. For each user or group of users you need to know the following:

- the number of users in the group;
- whether they use ad hoc queries frequently;
- whether they use ad hoc queries occasionally at unknown intervals;

- whether they use ad hoc queries occasionally at regular and predictable times;
- the average size of query they tend to run;
- the maximum size of query they tend to run;
- the elapsed login time per day;
- the peak time of daily usage;
- the number of queries they run per peak hour;
- the number of queries they run per day.

These usage profiles will probably change over time, and need to be kept up to date. They are useful for growth predictions and capacity planning. As the number of users grows, they will allow you to make first estimates of required capacity.

The profiles in themselves are not sufficient; you also require an understanding of the business. It is useful to be able to make meaningful comparisons of workloads. So, for example, if you know that the sales analysts that are to be newly added perform a similar function to one of the groups that already exist, you can use that group's usage profile as a first estimate of the likely load that the new analysts will place on the machine.

17.3   ESTIMATING THE LOAD

When choosing the hardware for the data warehouse there are many things to consider, such as hardware architecture, resilience, and so on. One point to remember is that the data warehouse will probably grow rapidly from its initial configuration, so it is not sufficient to consider the initial size of the data warehouse. You must take into consideration the ultimate size of the data warehouse, otherwise

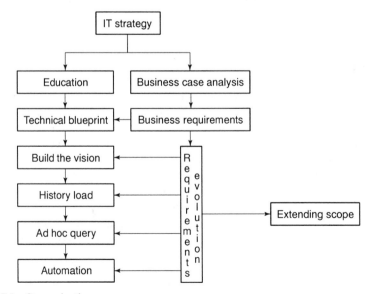

Figure 17.1   Stages in the process.

you may end up with hardware that does not scale to your requirements. It can prove extremely costly to change hardware in midstream.

There are a number of different elements that need to be considered, but the decisions all come down to how much CPU, how much memory and how much disk you will need. Some people would say "We should add how much money it will cost." However, from a capacity point of view this is irrelevant. The cost may affect your choice of hardware architecture, it may affect your choice of vendor, but it should never be allowed to affect your capacity planning.

If your sizing calls for more than the budget can afford, do not allow the required capacity to be chopped back. If that is the case, some of the functionality will need to be pared back and then the capacity can be re-estimated. This is an important point to re-emphasize, because sizing capacity to suit the budget is a common ploy. However, it is a dangerous ploy when applied to data warehousing. It is hard to overestimate the capacity requirements of a data warehouse, because there are always hidden or unexpected requirements that will add overheads. Small changes in a large system mean large changes in reality. A small growth in requirements in a data warehouse environment can mean adding enough hardware to run a full-sized operational OLTP system.

For example, we have seen a situation where adding a single byte to a field in the fact data meant adding 4 GB of storage for each year's worth of data that was kept online. There are many other similar examples that we could give. All you have to do is imagine the effect of adding some new users, or the effect of suddenly discovering that there is another data source that needs to be processed. These systems are just too big to take risks with the estimates.

> **GUIDELINE 17.1** Do not allow cost or budget considerations to affect capacity estimates.

So how *do* you go about sizing the data warehouse system? In the following pages we shall attempt to outline the rules and guidelines that we follow when sizing a system for a data warehouse. We shall deal separately with CPU, memory and disk sizing, but first let us consider in broad outline the initial configuration.

17.3.1 INITIAL CONFIGURATION

When sizing the initial configuration you will have no history information or statistics to work with, and the sizing will need to be done on the predicted load. Estimating this load is difficult, because there is an ad hoc element to it. However, if the phased approach is taken, the ad hoc element will be small to start off with, and as the functionality is phased in, the system can be grown to meet the demand.

Nonetheless, despite the lack of hard figures, an initial system will need to be specified. All you can do is estimate the configuration based on the known requirements. This is why the *business requirements* phase is so important. The documented outcome of that phase, augmented with a knowledge of the business, should be sufficient to allow a reasonable sizing to be carried out. If the requirements change later, the sizing will just need to be adjusted accordingly.

When deciding on the initial configuration you will need to allow some contingency. This is particularly important in a data warehouse project, because the requirements are often difficult to pin down accurately, and the load can quickly vary from the expected. Otherwise, the sizing exercise is the same irrespective of the phase of the data warehouse that you are trying to size. What follows, therefore, is applicable as much to the ultimate configuration as to the initial configuration.

17.3.2 HOW MUCH CPU BANDWIDTH?

To start with you need to consider the distinct loads that will be placed on the system. There are many aspects to this, such as query load, data load, backup and so on, but essentially the load can be divided into two distinct phases:

- daily processing
- overnight processing

These are discussed in detail in Part Three, but essentially they break down as follows:

- daily processing
  - user query processing

- overnight processing
  - data transformation and load
  - aggregation and index creation
  - backup

There are other operations that take place overnight and during the day, but the operations listed above are the ones that will use the most system capacity. Therefore these are the operations we shall concentrate on.

Daily processing

The daily processing is centered around the user queries. To estimate the CPU requirements you need to estimate the time that each query will take. As much of the query load will be ad hoc it is impossible to estimate the requirement of every query; therefore another approach has to be found.

The first thing to do is estimate the size of the largest likely common query. It is possible that some user will want to query across every piece of data in the data warehouse, but this will probably not be a common requirement. It is more likely that the users will want to query the most recent week or month's worth of data. The likely query period can be discerned from knowledge of the business.

Having established the likely period that will be queried, you will know the volume of data that will be involved. As you cannot assume that a relevant index will be in place, you must assume that the query will perform a full table scan of the fact data for that period. So we now have a measure of the volume of data, let us say F megabytes, that will be accessed.

To progress any further we need to know the I/O characteristics of the devices that the data will reside on. This allows us to calculate the scan rate S at which the fact data can be read. This will depend on the disk speeds and on the throughput ratings of the controllers. Clearly this also depends on the size of F itself. If F is many gigabytes then it will definitely be spread across multiple disks and probably across multiple controllers. You can now calculate S assuming a reasonable spread of the data. Remember that if the database is designed correctly and the large queries are controlled properly you should not get much contention for the disks, so you should get a reasonable throughput.

Using S and F you can calculate T, the time in seconds to perform a full table scan of the period in question:

$$T = \frac{F}{S} \tag{17.1}$$

In fact you should calculate a number of times, T_1-T_a, which depend on the degree of parallelism that you are using to perform the scan. Therefore we get

$$T_1 = \frac{F}{S_1}$$

$$\vdots \qquad \vdots \tag{17.2}$$

$$T_n = \frac{F}{S_n}$$

where S_1 is the scan speed of a single disk or striped disk set, and S_n is the scan speed of all the disks or disk sets that F is spread across. You may be able to get slightly higher throughput than S_n with higher degrees of parallelism, but you will bottleneck on I/O at degrees of parallelism much above N.

Now you can take the query response time requirements specified in the service level agreement and pick the appropriate T value, T_p say: this will give you S_p, the required scan rate, and the number of disks or disk sets you will need to spread data across. It also gives you P, the required degree of parallelism to meet query response times for a single query.

Now you need to estimate P_c, the number of parallel scanning threads that a single CPU will support. This will vary from processor to processor. The processors currently on the market will support from two to four scanners, but chip technology is moving on quickly, and this number will change over time. If possible, you should establish this by experiment. Now you can estimate your CPU requirement to support a single query with:

$$C_s = \text{Roundup}\left(\frac{2P}{P_s}\right) \tag{17.3}$$

You need to use $2P$ to allow for other query overheads, and for queries that involve sorts. To calculate the minimum number of CPUs required overall use the following formula:

$$C_t = nC_s + 1 \tag{17.4}$$

where n is the number of concurrent queries that will be allowed to run. This should not be confused with the number of concurrent users, because unless a user is running a query they are not likely to be doing anything heavier than editing. Note that the additional 1 is added to the total to allow for the operating system overheads and for all other user processing.

If users do have access to software on the data warehouse system, that allows them to use significant CPU resource even when not querying; you will need to gauge the likelihood of this activity and allow for it.

Overnight processing

The first point to note about the nightly processing is that the operations listed at the beginning of this section are, for the most part, serialized. That is, they tend to run one at a time, one after the other. This is because each operation usually relies on the previous operation's completing before it can begin.

The CPU bandwidth required for the data transformation will depend on the amount of data processing that is involved. Unless there is an enormous amount of data transformation, it is unlikely that this operation will require more CPU bandwidth than the aggregation and index creation operations.

The same applies to the backup, although you should bear in mind that backing up large quantities of data in a short period of time will cause a major kickback onto the CPU. Nonetheless, it is likely that your backup will fit into the CPU bandwidth required by the aggregation and index creation. The CPU load imposed by backup is generally due to the use of many parallel streams to speed up the backup. If the backup is spread over more hours, the amount of parallelism will come down, and its CPU bandwidth requirement will drop.

The data load is another task that can use massive parallelism to speed up its operation. As with backup, if you use fewer parallel streams it will use less CPU bandwidth and will take longer to run. Again, it is likely to fit into whatever CPU capacity is required for the aggregation and index creation. In some cases there will be postprocessing to be carried out on the loaded data. In some data warehouses this processing can be extremely heavy, and may in fact outweigh the aggregation processing. If that is the case, use the postprocessing as the baseline for the CPU required rather than the aggregation processing.

Having established what you are going to use as your baseline, you then need to estimate how much CPU capacity that operation requires to complete in the allowed time. It is not safe to assume that you will have more than 10 hours overnight to achieve all the processing, even if the user day is only 8 or 9 hours long. Delays in data arrival can cause you significant problems, and you must make sure that you can complete the overnight processing without running over into the business day. Naturally this will vary from data warehouse to data warehouse, but of the 10 hours allowed to complete the overnight processing, it is normal to have about 60% available to complete the postprocessing of the data and the aggregation and index creation. That gives about 6 hours to complete all these tasks.

As every data warehouse is different, it is impossible here to give explicit estimates for these operations. It is not even possible to give firm guidelines, because each aggregation is a different complex query and/or update plus an intensive write operation. Estimates similar to those suggested above can be carried out, but the best advice we can give you is to test each of the required aggregation, index and postprocessing operations. Beware of testing on insufficient data, because each of these tasks will probably contain operations such as sorts that do not scale linearly. When you do test them, make sure that you carry out the tests on a number of data sets of varying size. This will allow you to generate a scaling factor, which may help with sizing the full-size system.

If users are allowed to leave queries running overnight, or if queries are allowed to run for 24 hours or more, you will also need to make a separate allowance for that processing, above and beyond the calculated CPU requirement for the overnight processing.

17.3.3 HOW MUCH MEMORY?

Memory is a commodity that you can never have enough of. What you need to estimate is the minimum requirement. There are a number of things that affect the amount of memory required.

First, there are the database requirements. The database will need memory to cache data blocks as they are used; it will also need memory to cache parsed SQL statements and so on. These requirements will vary from RDBMS to RDBMS, and you will need to work them out for whatever software you are using.

You will also need memory for sort space. Each process that performs a sort will require an amount of sort area. This is usually parameterized, and can be specified by you. Remember that when you use parallel technology you may need to allow enough sort area for each sorting process. This can add up, particularly if you have multiple concurrent queries running.

Secondly, each user connected to the system will use an amount of memory: how much will depend on how they are connected to the system and what software they are running. As it is likely that the users will be connected in a client–server mode the user memory requirement may be quite small.

Finally, the operating system will require an amount of memory. This will vary with the operating system and the features and tools you are running. You can get the hardware vendor to estimate how much memory the system will use.

17.3.4 HOW MUCH DISK?

The largest calculation you will need to perform is the amount of disk space required. This can be a very tricky thing to calculate, and how successfully you do it will depend on how successfully the analysis captures the requirements.

The disk requirement can be broken down into the following categories:

- database requirements
  - administration

- fact and dimension data
- aggregations
- non-database requirements
  - operating system requirements
  - other software requirements
  - data warehouse requirements
  - user requirements

Each of these topics will be discussed below. The database will occupy the bulk of the disk space that you use, and the task of getting the sizing right is far from easy. However, the non-database requirements, although small by comparison with the database, will themselves be fairly hefty, and should not be forgotten during the sizing exercise.

You need to make allowance for any disk resilience that will be built into the system. You will almost certainly be using disk mirroring or RAID 5 extensively throughout the system. You need to calculate the overhead involved and factor it into your capacity plans.

> **GUIDELINE 17.2** Remember to allow for resilience in your disk space capacity planning. Any mirroring or RAID 5 overheads need to be counted.

Database sizing

The database will occupy most of the required disk space, and when sizing it you need to be sure you get it right. There are a number of aspects to the database sizing that need to be considered.

First, there are the **system administration requirements** of the database. There is the data dictionary and the journal files, plus any rollback space that is required. These will all be small by comparison with the temporary or sort area. It is certain that large data sorts are going to be required within the data warehouse. For example, each aggregation will require the sorting of data. Sizing the sort space is a next-to-impossible task. Unless you make the space large enough to sort the entirety of the fact and dimension data, you can never guarantee that it will be large enough. This would be a ludicrous waste of space, because no one should be allowed to run a query that would require such an action.

If you can gauge the size of the largest transaction that will realistically be run you can use this to size the temporary requirements. If not, the best you can do is tie it to the size of a partition. If you do this, make allowance for multiple queries running at a given time, and set the temporary space to

$$T = (2n + 1)P \qquad (17.5)$$

where n is the number of concurrent queries allowed, and P is the size of a partition. If you use different-sized partitions for current data and for older data, then use the largest partition size in the calculation above.

Then there is the **fact and dimension data**. This is the one piece of data that you can actually size; everything else will be sized off this. To do this sizing exercise, you will need to know the database schema. You should not even attempt to size the data until that has been finalized. All questions about the correct level of fact data, whether to denormalize tables or not, and the contents of the fact data

> **GUIDELINE 17.3** Do not attempt to size the database until the database schema is complete.

record, need to be fully answered. A change in any of these things will have an enormous effect on the sizing, and it will be impossible to size accurately until they have been bottomed out.

Clearly, when performing the original size estimates for a business case, much of this information will be missing. In this situation, the sizing will need to be based purely on original estimates of the base data size.

When sizing the fact or dimension data you will have the record definitions, with each field type and size specified. Note, however, that the size specified for a field will be the maximum size. When calculating the actual size you will need to know:

- the average size of the data in each field;
- the percentage occupancy of each field;
- the position of each data field in the table;
- the RDBMS storage format of each data type;
- any table, row and column overheads.

The average length of a data field can be very different from the maximum, and even a couple of bytes' difference between them can lead to many gigabytes' difference in the size estimate. Ideally, you should estimate the average field size by using real data. If that is not possible, you will need to use your knowledge of the business and an understanding of what each field means to calculate a meaningful average.

The percentage occupancy of each field is also important. Not every record will have every field full. If you know the percentage occupancy you can allow for this. More importantly, even empty fields can still take up space in a database record, as the RDBMS may require a marker to note that the field is empty. Some RDBMSs can leave a null or empty column out of the record provided it is at the end of the record. You need to take these database-specific tricks into account when designing and sizing the tables.

Another factor that may affect your calculations is the database block or page size. A database block will normally have some header information at the top of the block. This is space that cannot be used by data and can amount to 100+ bytes. The difference between using a 2 kB block size and using a 16 kB block size will mean something of the order of 700 bytes of extra data space in every 16 kB. In tables that span hundreds of gigabytes this can lead to significant space saving.

You will also need to estimate the size of the index space required for the fact and dimension data. Fact data should generally be only lightly indexed, with indexes occupying between 15% and 30% of the space occupied by the fact data; the cost in terms of index maintenance would be extremely heavy otherwise. Ideally, there should be only a primary key index, but you may require a concatenated foreign key index onto the dimension tables to allow star queries to work. Remember: users should rarely access the fact data; the majority of their data requirements should be met by the aggregations.

The final determinant of the ultimate size of the fact data is the amount of data that you intend to keep online. When this is known, you can decide on your partitioning strategy. This needs to be taken into account in the sizing, because it is unlikely that you will get data to load exactly into every partition. You will probably have to allow each partition to be large enough to accommodate a peak period: so each partition will generate some space wastage. You need to allow for this in your sizing.

You also need to size the **aggregations**. For the initial system you will probably be able to size the actual aggregations that are planned. All the

> **GUIDELINE 17.4** Allow for period variations when sizing partitions.

factors discussed above apply equally to the aggregations. Remember, however, that aggregations will get added as part of the tuning process. You cannot size these aggregations, because you will have no details. You need to make an allowance for these. As a rule of thumb, you should allow the same amount of space for aggregations as you will have fact data online.

You will also need to allow space for **indexes** on the aggregations. These summarized tables are likely to be heavily indexed, and it is usual to assume 100% indexation. In other words, allow as much space again for indexing as for the aggregates themselves.

So, to summarize, the space required by the database will be

$$\text{Space required} = F + F_i + D + D_i + A + A_i + T + S \qquad (17.6)$$

where F is the size of the fact data (all the fact data that will be kept online); F_i is the size of the fact data indexation; D is the size of the dimension data; D_i is the size of the dimension data indexation; A is the size of the aggregations; A_i is the size of the aggregations indexation; T is the size of the database temporary or sort area; and S is the database system administration overhead.

If you want to get a quick upper bound on the database size, Equation 17.6 can be reduced as follows:

$$
\begin{aligned}
\text{Space required} \quad &= F + F_i + D + D_i + A + A_i + T + S \\
&= 3F + F_i + D + D_i + T + S && \text{as } A = A_i = F \\
&< 3.3F + D + D_i + T + S && \text{as } F_i \leqslant 30\% \ F \\
&< 3.5F + T + S && \text{as } D \leqslant 10\% \ F \text{ and } D \approx D_i \\
&\leqslant 3.5F + T && \text{as } S \ll T \text{ and } S \ll F \quad (17.7)
\end{aligned}
$$

If F is sized accurately this formula will give a reasonable estimate of the ultimate system size. To show a worked example, suppose the fact data is calculated to be

36 GB of data per year, and 4 years' worth of data are to be kept online. This means that F would be 144 GB. Then using Equation 17.7 we get

$$
\begin{aligned}
\text{Space required} &= 3.5F + T \\
&= (3.5 \times 144) + T \qquad\qquad \textbf{(17.8)} \\
&= 504 + T \text{ GB}
\end{aligned}
$$

Now suppose the data is to be partitioned by month; that would give a partition size P of 3 GB. If four concurrent queries are to be allowed, using Equation 17.5 we can now estimate the size of temporary space T:

$$
\begin{aligned}
T &= (2n + 1)P \\
T &= [(2 \times 4) + 1]3 \qquad\qquad \textbf{(17.9)} \\
T &= 27
\end{aligned}
$$

This gives a total database size of 531 GB for the full-sized system.

Care needs to be taken when using this formula to size the initial system, as to begin with the dimension data could actually be larger than the fact data. Remember that F in the above formulae is the ultimate size of the fact data: that is, it corresponds to the ultimate size of the fact data that will be kept online. Once the ultimate size of the system has been calculated, it can be scaled back accordingly. For example, if it is intended to keep 3 years' worth of data online, the formula above will represent the size of the database after 3 years' worth of data has been loaded. To size the initial system for 6 months' worth of data you can say

$$
\text{Initial space} = \frac{3.5F + T}{[(n \times 12)/6] + 1} \qquad\qquad \textbf{(17.10)}
$$

where n is the number of years' of data you intend to keep online (in this case 3). Note the $+1$ under the line: this will account for the dimension data's being a bigger percentage of the fact initially. This means that Equation 17.10 reduces to

$$
\text{Initial space} = \frac{3.5F + T}{7} \qquad\qquad \textbf{(17.11)}
$$

which is your initial sizing. One final word: remember that every data warehouse is different. These figures are only guidelines.

> **GUIDELINE 17.5**   Use the formulae in this section carefully. They are intended as guidelines, not as a panacea.

Non-database sizing

When calculating the amount of non-database disk space required, remember to take the server environment into account. If you are running in a cluster or MPP environment, you may need to allow space on each node for many of the things discussed below. For example, the operating system will need to be installed on each node. So should each of the tools, but it is sometimes possible to save space by making things available through facilities such as the network file system (NFS). There is a downside to this approach in that if you lose the node that has the actual software, you will lose all access to that software. You need to be careful not to introduce single points of failure into the system.

The operating system will require its own space. It may not be huge in the scheme of things but you need to make allowance for it. The operating system itself will typically require between 500 MB and 1 GB. However, you will also need to make allowance for swap space, and leave enough room for system crash dumps, both of which could be large, as you will be using a considerable amount of memory.

There will be other software that has disk space requirements. The RDBMS software will need to be installed. Any other third-party tools you use will have their own requirements. Make sure you leave lots of room for the log and trace files these tools will produce; this is particularly important for the monitoring tools.

The data warehouse application will require space for all the code and tools. It will also require log and trace space for each of the managers: load, warehouse, and query. The load manager will also need disk space allocated for the source files that need to be loaded. This load area can be large, and you may want to allow room for several days' worth of load files to cover any eventualities.

The users will require disk space, even if they are connected in client–server mode from a PC or other system. It is certain that users will want to create data extracts that they can download to their machine, or reports that they will want to print. Space needs to be available to allow them to do this. If directly connecting to the data warehouse system users may also want directories to save SQL queries and other work.

CHAPTER 18

Tuning the data warehouse

18.1 INTRODUCTION

Tuning a data warehouse is more difficult than tuning an OLTP environment because of the ad hoc and unpredictable nature of the load. A data warehouse, of its very nature, evolves over time. As a result, many aspects of the warehouse environment will change as the profile and the usage of the data change.

Change in user profiles and data access patterns clearly means changes in the queries that are being run. These changes can also have knock-on effects on the aggregations that need to be generated or maintained, perhaps even affecting what data needs to be loaded, and how long data needs to be maintained.

It is all too possible in a data warehouse environment for a single query to monopolize all of a system's resources, particularly if it is running with high degrees of parallelism. Often the correct tuning choice for such eventualities will be to allow an infrequently used index or aggregation to exist to catch just those sorts of query. To create those sorts of indexes or aggregations, you must have an understanding that such queries are likely to be run. Ultimately, to tune a data warehouse you must have an understanding of the business.

18.2 ASSESSING PERFORMANCE

Before you can tune the data warehouse you must have some objective measures of performance to work with. Measures such as

- average query response times,
- scan rates,
- I/O throughput rates,
- time used per query,
- memory usage per process,

are needed to give you some feeling for the working of the system. You also need a clear idea of the target measures that you want to achieve. These measures should be specified in the service level agreement (SLA). After all, there is no point in trying to tune average response times if they are already better than those required. In fact, tuning beyond requirements can prove counterproductive. If the users get used to faster responses, they will not be best pleased when the response times fall back to the previous levels as more users are added to the data warehouse.

When assessing performance it is essential that you have realistic expectations. It is equally important that the users also have reasonable expectations. You could specify any measure or performance requirement in an SLA, but writing it down does not make it affordable or even possible.

The size and complexity of a data warehouse, as well as the ad hoc nature of the queries, make expectations difficult to set. Most users will have no real concept of the scale of the system or the data it contains. As with many things in life, people will most likely see only what is relevant to them, and they will naturally tend to think that is all there is. Indeed, a large amount of effort goes into designing the data warehouse so that appears to be the case. Views and aggregations are used to hide much of the complexity from the users.

It is unreasonable to expect all queries to complete in less than 3 minutes. In fact it is unreasonable to expect all queries to complete in any given time-scale. As it is possible to run any ad hoc query, in practice a user could always write a query you had not tuned for. This would mean that the query would have to go to the fact data directly, and not to some aggregation.

A reasonable expectation, and thus a reasonable tuning goal, would be some statement like "90% of all queries against recent data to complete in under 5 minutes." Clearly the actual time quoted must relate to the amount of recent data that exists. The time will be different, for example, if there is an order of magnitude difference in the data size.

> **GUIDELINE 18.1** Ensure that everyone, from the data warehouse designers to the users and senior management, has reasonable performance expectations.

Given the ad hoc nature of a data warehouse, there is limited tuning that can actually be done. Unlike a large OLTP system there is little that can be done in the way of tweaking of parameters or changes to the application that are likely to have a lasting effect. What tuning can be achieved is discussed in the sections below.

One solution that is available is to throw hardware at the problem. This can be an effective solution, in particular as the number of users and the size of the data scale up. One point to note, however, is that hardware is not a panacea. Adding more CPU bandwidth will not solve all problems. If the problem is an I/O bottleneck, adding CPU makes the problem worse rather than better, because it will allow more users and more concurrent queries to stress the same I/O bandwidth. See Chapter 17 for more details on sizing and adding hardware.

Scaling of queries can be addressed by hardware as data size increases. Using more disks will spread the I/O load, but there will always be an ultimate I/O bottleneck that will require significant changes to address. If you exceed the disk controller bandwidth you will need to add controllers. If you exceed the I/O bus bandwidth you will need to add nodes, and so on.

You can also add extra hardware to support extra users running the same sort of load. This will also be subject to the same sort of scaling restrictions as mentioned above.

One thing you can do is ask for certain hardware guarantees. You should be able to get hardware guarantees for I/O throughput, scan rates, and processing capacity. Software performance guarantees are much more difficult to get. There are generally too many factors that can affect the performance of a piece of software for meaningful guarantees to be given.

18.3 TUNING THE DATA LOAD

Because the data load is the entry point into the system, it provides the first opportunity to improve performance. This is a crucial part of the overnight processing, because it is likely that nothing else can run until the data load is complete. Any problems in transferring the data, or delays in its arrival, can have a major effect on the successful processing of that night's data. Therefore, anything that can be done to improve the data load performance is likely to be of benefit.

Database-loading software can work in a number of different ways. The more normal way is for the data to be inserted into the database using the SQL layer. This approach means that all the checks and constraints of a normal insert have to be performed. For example, all records inserted into a table will cause code to be run to find space in the table to put the record. If not enough room is available there, more space may have to be allocated to the table and so on. These checks take time to perform and they are costly in CPU. The purpose of these checks is to try to make maximal use of the space, packing the data as tightly as possible.

Some data load programs allow many of these checks to be bypassed, and the data to be placed directly into preformatted blocks, which are then written to the database. As this direct approach bypasses much of the normal code paths, it may be significantly quicker. The downside is that it can work only in whole blocks of data, and partially empty blocks of data cannot be used. This can lead to some space wastage. The space wasted is usually quite small, but the time gain can be quite significant.

A better way of phrasing this is: Can you afford not to take the gain in performance? Remember that the effect of failing to get an overnight's processing complete can be catastrophic. It could cost you anything from a day's processing lost to the users, to a whole period's worth of data being effectively useless.

Another costly part of any data load is the maintenance of any indexes on that data. This is particularly important if you are loading into a table that already contains some data. The options are either to maintain the indexes as the data is being loaded, or to drop the indexes and re-create them when the load is complete. Experience shows that the latter option is likely to be quicker, particularly if the RDBMS supports the re-creation of the indexes in parallel. There is of course a cut-off point at which this approach is no longer more efficient. The position of this point depends on how much data is already loaded, and how many indexes and constraints need to be rebuilt.

For example, let us suppose that the data is partitioned into monthly tables. At the beginning of any month the current monthly table will be empty, and the indexes will be non-existent. In this case it will definitely be better to load first and create indexes later. At the end of the month, the table and indexes will have 29 to 30 days' of data already loaded, and indexed. You have to load the last day's worth of data for that month. It is no longer clear cut which approach will be quicker. We now have to trade off the cost of index maintenance against that of index rebuild. Which is more efficient can depend on many things. Primarily it will depend on the size of the data already in the partition, and the number of indexes on that partition.

It is also worth noting that even if the approach of dropping the indexes, loading the data, and re-creating the indexes is slower as a whole than loading with the indexes active, this will mean that the data will load to the table quicker. This can be important, because it might allow the next stage of the overnight processing to begin earlier.

Any integrity checking that needs to be performed will make a significant difference to the performance of the load. The level to which the rules must be enforced will depend on the purpose of the data warehouse. If complex business rules need to be enforced, the processing required to ensure that the rules are observed can be heavy. It is best to try and limit this checking as much as possible on the data warehouse system. That is not to say that the integrity issues should be ignored; they need to be addressed if the data warehouse is to give maximal benefit. If possible, these integrity checks should be applied on the source systems.

If the data warehouse is to be used for trend analysis, where data is examined in aggregated form and rarely if ever examined in detail, there may be scope for allowing variance from the business rules. It is likely that any errors in the data will be damped out in the aggregation. The clear gain from enforcing the rules is that you will be sure that your individual items of data are correct, but if data is not accessed at that level, and any variances from the business rules get lost in aggregation, it will be of no value to spend money on the rule enforcement. There are obvious dangers with this approach, and it should only ever be used if it is certain that the detail data will never be used, and that the aggregations do indeed damp out any variances in the quality of the data. Ideally, if this approach is going to be used, the business should be prepared to throw away the detailed data once the aggregations have been calculated.

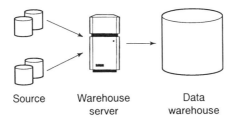

Source   Warehouse   Data
              server   warehouse

Figure 18.1   Data flow through the data warehouse.

There are a number of ways in which the integrity issues can be handled. These issues are discussed in Part Two: Data Warehouse Architecture. Essentially the flow of data is as depicted in Figure 18.1.

As shown in Figure 18.2, there are opportunities to transform the data at every stage of this data flow. If all data transformation or integrity checks occur before the data arrives at the data warehouse system, all you need to know is the expected time of arrival. If the checks are performed on the data warehouse system, either before or after the data is loaded, or indeed a combination of both, they will have a direct effect on the capacity and performance of the system. Any tuning of the integrity checks will depend on what form they take.

It is not uncommon to apply rudimentary checks to the data being loaded. For example, if the data is telephone call records, you may want to check that each call has a valid customer identifier. If the data is retail information, you may want to check whether the commodity being sold has a valid product identifier. One point to note is that just because some of the loading data fails such a check it does not necessarily mean that the data is invalid. For the call records, it could easily be that the data is correct and that the customer information is not up to date. This can happen when a new customer is added as a service

> **GUIDELINE 18.2**   Limit, to the absolute minimum required, the number of integrity checks that need to be applied on the data warehouse. Where possible, integrity checks should be performed on the source systems.

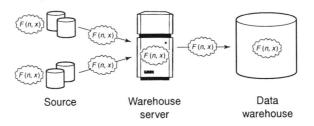

Source   Warehouse   Data
              server   warehouse

Figure 18.2   Where data can be transformed.

subscriber. They will probably use the phone immediately the service is connected, but it may take several days for the customer information to trickle through to the data warehouse from the customer systems.

There is little that can be done to tune any business rules enforced by constraints. If the rules are enforced by using SQL or by trigger code, that code needs to be tuned to maximal efficiency.

Loading large quantities of data, as well as being a heavy I/O operation, can be CPU intensive, especially if there are a lot of checks and transformations to be applied to each record. As mentioned above, the load speed can be improved by using direct load techniques. The load can also be improved by using parallelism. Multiple processes can be used to speed the load. This helps to spread the CPU load amongst any available CPUs.

If using multiple loads, care is needed to avoid introducing I/O bottlenecks. Ensure that the source data file does not become a source of contention. Ideally, the source data should be split into multiple files so that each load process can have its own source file. The source files should also be spread over multiple disks to avoid contention on a single disk or I/O controller.

The load destination can also become a bottleneck, particularly if a large number of load processes are being used. This needs to be considered as part of the original database design. Each table to be loaded should be spread over multiple spindles. This can be done by striping the database files across multiple disks, or by spreading the table to be loaded over multiple database files.

> **GUIDELINE 18.3**   Spread the load source files and the load destination files to avoid any I/O bottlenecks.

18.4   TUNING QUERIES

The data warehouse will contain two types of query. There will be fixed queries that are clearly defined and well understood, such as regular reports, canned queries and common aggregations. There will also be ad hoc queries that are unpredictable, both in quantity and frequency. Both types of query need to be tuned, but they require different techniques for dealing with them.

18.4.1   FIXED QUERIES

Tuning the fixed queries is no different than the traditional tuning of a relational database. They have predictable resource requirements, and because you have the query it can be tested to find the best execution plan. The only real variables with these queries are the size of the data being queried and the data skew. Even these variables can be dealt with, because the query can be tested as often as desired.

When testing fixed queries, you should record and store the most successful execution plan for each query. This will allow you to spot changing data size and data skew, as these will cause the execution plans to change. On most RDBMSs the execution plan can be obtained without actually running the query. This can be important for long-running queries that are heavy users of resources, because a changing execution plan will indicate that something has changed. Having advance notice of the change will allow you to test the query on the test system.

> **GUIDELINE 18.4** Store the expected execution plans for known queries.

Not a lot can be done to the fact data to improve performance. However, when dealing with the dimension data or the aggregations, the usual collection of SQL tweaking, storage mechanisms and access methods can be used to tune these queries. New aggregations can be created, or extra indexes added to the dimension data, b-tree indexes or bit-mapped indexes if the database supports them. Different storage mechanisms, such as clustered tables, hash clusters or index-only tables, could be used.

Care must be taken to ensure that any tuning done does not adversely affect the performance of ad hoc queries.

18.4.2 AD HOC QUERIES

The number of users of the data warehouse will have a profound effect on the performance, in particular if they are ad hoc users. It is important to have a clear understanding of the usage profiles of all your users. For each user or group of users you need to know the following:

- the number of users in the group;
- whether they use ad hoc queries frequently;
- whether they use ad hoc queries occasionally at unknown intervals;
- whether they use ad hoc queries occasionally at regular and predictable times;
- the average size of query they tend to run;
- the maximum size of query they tend to run;
- the elapsed login time per day;
- the peak time of daily usage;
- the number of queries they run per peak hour;
- whether they require drill-down access to the base data.

The more unpredictable the load, the larger the queries, or the greater the number of users the bigger the tuning task. These usage profiles need to be tracked over time, because it is likely that they will change. They will not help directly with tuning, but are useful for growth predictions and capacity planning.

A typical data warehouse will have somewhere between 10 and 50 users, although the first signs of data warehouses with large user populations have started to appear. It will not be long before the hardware and software will be able to support hundreds of concurrent users on a data warehouse.

The more ad hoc the nature of the query mix, the more difficult the job of tuning the data warehouse. Clearly, it is important to identify any queries that are regularly run, and to ensure that any tuning performed does not affect the performance of these bread and butter jobs.

The trick with tuning this sort of environment is to move the query mix from ad hoc to predictable. To do this, it is necessary to identify any similar ad hoc queries that are frequently run. If such queries exist, the database can be changed to make their running more efficient. New indexes can be added, or new aggregations created and maintained specifically for those queries.

> **GUIDELINE 18.5**   You need to turn an unpredictable query mix into a predictable query mix.

The way to turn an unpredictable query load into a predictable load is to control the queries via batch queues. This allows you to control throughput and use the full power of the machine on a single query. This is precisely the ability that is driving the data warehouse revolution. The fact that large queries that were once impossible to run can now be completed in a sensible time-frame is what gives you business advantage and makes the data warehouse so worthwhile.

No user should be able to submit a query directly, and all queries should be controlled via the query manager or some front-end tool that limits what they can see. When a user submits a query the query manager will place it on a query queue, and the query will run when it reaches the top of the queue.

Note that queuing may not be as relevant if the data warehouse is being used only for browsing summaries and for drill down. In that case, the query management could be controlled via the front-end/browsing tool.

Once you accept the fact that the major data warehouse queries need to be queue controlled, the next question is: how many queues to create? This will depend on the number of concurrent queries that you want running during the day, and on the number of queries that you want to leave running overnight. Remember that anything running overnight will potentially clash with the overnight processing.

This sort of query management is necessary, if the system is not to descend rapidly into chaos. Any large query is likely to be capable of monopolizing the entire resource of the box. If two such queries are allowed to run at the same time, you will end up with problems such as CPUs thrashing, and everyone suffers.

If all queries run by the users are large, the above approach will probably go unnoticed. As each query will take a substantial amount of time to run, the fact that it has to sit in a queue for a while will probably not be all that relevant. As long as the users can get some form of predictable performance they will generally be happy. Many people will say the phrase "happy users" is a contradiction in terms, but experience shows that proper handling of user expectations is required. This is particularly important in a data warehouse, where the users may often have no clear idea of the implications of what to them seems to be a simple query.

It must be remembered that the reason for the use of query queues is not a throw-back to the mainframe mentality, where every CPU cycle is sacred and has to be accounted for. The data warehouse is there for the users to query, and some of those queries are expected to be from the nether regions, even if not actually from Hell. This is not Big Brother in action; the queues are to allow the system to be used maximally without flooding the system so heavily that it either sticks its legs in the air and dies, or hides in the corner until the nasty queries have gone away. What is important is that the users get results back in a timely manner, even if that means days.

It is equally important that no query can monopolize the system. Such queries should be detected and killed. The user will need to be asked to modify the query so that it runs in a meaningful time-frame, with reasonable resources. This may mean creating aggregations especially for that query so that it can be run without hitting fact data, and aggregating it on the fly.

If there is a mix of small and large queries to be run, then allowance will need to be made for the smaller queries. Multiple queues can be used, with a separate queue for smaller queries. This queue can be monitored, and resource quotas enforced. If a query submitted to the small queue exceeds its quotas it should be killed and resubmitted to the large queue. This last point is important, and the resubmission should be seamless. However, the user should be informed that the query has been re-queued; you may even want to implement a system whereby the user is alerted that the query has failed and is given the choice to let the query run on the large queue or not. This all depends on how sophisticated you want to make the query manager.

As well as small and large queries there is the question of priority queries. If there are users or particular queries that are to have priority access, you will need to use queue prioritization. It is possible to have separate priority queues that require privilege to access, but that approach could become very messy if a large query is started on the priority queue, and there is already a heavy query running on a non-priority queue. A better approach is to have a priority query skip to the head of the queue it should run on. If necessary, any running query can be halted and restarted to allow the priority query to run immediately. This should be possible, because the query details can be captured by the query manager when the query is submitted.

Restartable queries are a function of the query manager. The query manager will be required to capture information about each query submitted. Ideally, it should capture the query itself, and the execution plan it will use, plus the information on the resource that the query used.

Note that some care needs to be exercised in using this functionality. It is unlikely that the RDBMS will support a truly restartable query, by which we mean a query that, if restarted, picks up from where it left off when it was stopped. Therefore resubmitting it to the queue means that the query will start from scratch again. There are a number of issues with this. One issue is that you may not want to restart queries that have already been running for a long time. Another issue is that a restarted query may not see the same data as when it originally ran.

If a query has been running for 3 days and has 5 minutes to run, you probably do not want to stop and restart it. The problem, of course, is that you generally do not know exactly when the query will finish. You will, however, know how long it has been running. You will also know whether there are any limits on the amount of time a query is allowed to run. Using this information, you can make an informed decision as to whether to kill the query, and reschedule it, or not.

The other problem is that the restarted query may not see the same data as when it originally ran. This is possible if the query contains concepts such as *today*, *yesterday*, *last month* or *last quarter*. It can also happen if views are used instead of direct table names. As views onto the fact tables are likely to be re-created frequently, often nightly, and any query directed to the fact tables is likely to use views, this could happen quite frequently. Any of the situations above will cause the data queried to be different from what the user requested, and possibly different from what they intended.

The aim of the data warehouse designer is to get queries to run against the aggregated data rather than against the raw fact data. This will speed up the queries by avoiding sorts and scanning a smaller set of data. In fact, creating an appropriate aggregation is the main tuning tool that can be applied to speed up ad hoc queries. This is far more likely to be effective than tuning database parameters.

> **GUIDELINE 18.6** Get queries to run against aggregations rather than against the base data itself.

In a truly ad hoc environment, any such gains will be short lived as queries fall out of use. Any aggregations or indexes created for a query can then be dropped, but be aware that those indexes or aggregations may now be being used by other queries. To measure usage profiles for each index and aggregation, you will need answers to questions such as:

- How many different queries run against an aggregation table?
- How often does each of these queries run?
- What indexes on an object are used most frequently?
- What queries use each index, and how would they be affected if the index did not exist?

The answers to these questions will guide your decisions on what indexes and aggregations to keep, and which of them can be deleted. Naturally, there is not likely to be a neat answer, as it is almost inevitable that there will be more indexes and aggregations required than you have room for on the system. You must also take into consideration the fact that the maintenance of each aggregation or index will place overheads on the overnight processing.

The key to choosing the right aggregations is knowledge. You must have a clear idea of what queries are running. You also need to know what data fields each query is accessing, and at what level of aggregation.

One of the query manager's jobs is to collect that information. The query manager should grab and maintain the following data:

- query syntax
- query execution plan
- CPU resource used
- memory resource used
- I/O resource used
- query elapsed time
- how frequently query is run

For a more detailed discussion see Chapter 10.

Another important function of the query manager is to transform any queries submitted through it. The query manager needs to be aggregate aware. It can use its own metadata and the metadata collected by the warehouse manager to redirect queries to aggregations and the correct views.

As in all tuning exercises, there is a balance to be struck. For example, suppose we are tuning the aggregations. There may be aggregations that are used only occasionally by single, infrequently run queries. However, if those queries are important, and the business requires that they complete in a certain time, those aggregations may prove to be critical.

CHAPTER 19

Testing the data warehouse

19.1 INTRODUCTION

As with any development project, a data warehouse will need testing, only more so. The complexity and size of data warehouse systems make comprehensive testing both more difficult and more necessary. The fact that queries that take minutes to run on small data sets may take hours or even days to complete on a full-size data set means that small-scale testing is not sufficient. It is necessary to establish that queries scale with the data. The upshot is that comprehensive testing of a data warehouse takes a long time. This makes predicting test schedules difficult.

There are three basic levels of testing:

- unit testing
- integration testing
- system testing

In **unit testing**, each development unit is tested on its own. Each module – that is, program, procedure, SQL script, UNIX shell script and so on – will normally be tested by its own developer. All unit testing should be complete before any test plan is enacted. A module will undergo frequent testing during its life cycle, and each change to the module will require the unit to be re-tested.

In **integration testing**, the separate development units that make up a component of the data warehouse application are tested to ensure that they work together. There is likely to be a limit to any integration testing that can be performed before testing of the entire suite of units that make up that component of the data warehouse application. Therefore, it is not unusual for integration testing to take place quite late in the development cycle. Where possible, integration testing should have been completed at least once for each component before enacting the test plan.

In **system testing**, the whole data warehouse application is tested together. The components are tested to ensure that they work properly together, that they do not cause system resource bottlenecks, and so on. Again, because of the size of a data warehouse system, it is usually possible to perform only minimal system testing before the test plan proper can be enacted. So any pre-plan system testing is normally carried out on a radically cut down version of the system environment. Such tests are useful only in highlighting inconsistencies in the data warehouse components, and will give no real indication of performance or resource issues.

System testing should not be confused with **user acceptance testing**, which will also tend to be a complete test of the data warehouse application. In user acceptance, as the name implies, the users conduct their own tests on the system. The user acceptance testing for a data warehouse is no different from that for any other application, and is not discussed further.

System testing is the first time where bought-in products such as management and query tools are tested in the full system environment. This will often be the first real indication of both the usefulness and in particular the overheads of such tools. Isolated testing of these products generally gives no indication of their effects on a system.

> **GUIDELINE 19.1** Sufficient testing needs to be performed to establish that queries scale with the data.

Full-scale system testing requires a comprehensive test plan, and the aim of this chapter is to discuss in detail the development of such a plan.

> **GUIDELINE 19.2** Full-scale testing requires a comprehensive test plan.

19.2 DEVELOPING THE TEST PLAN

19.2.1 TEST SCHEDULE

One of the first tasks in developing a test plan is to come up with a test schedule. Most product development methodologies contain metrics for producing time estimates for testing as well as development. From experience, these metrics fall well short of the requirements for testing a data warehouse application.

The shortcomings of these metrics are due to the size and complexity of data warehouse systems. For example, a simple problem with a large query can cause it to run inefficiently. However, because of the size of the query it may take a day to show that it is not going to complete in the desired time-scales. By the time the query has been tuned and re-run several times, many days of testing time may have been lost.

Hardware failure, such as losing a disk, or human error such as accidentally deleting or overwriting a large table, can cause hours or even days of delay. The bottom line is that the data warehouse environment is just too new and too complex to allow rapid testing to a rigid schedule.

As a rule of thumb we suggest that you apply your normal metrics for estimating the amount of time required for testing, and then double it. Note that this doubling should take place after any adjustment for contingency normally added, and after any other percentage adjustment normally made. So if the normal metrics throw up the figure of 50 person-days of testing, and experience says to add 50% contingency, bringing the total to 75 person-days, our advice would be to double this final figure, making 150 person-days.

This may seem a lot, and indeed in some cases will be close to or even exceed the development times allocated, but it is vital to allow enough testing time if the data warehouse is to work. If insufficient time is allowed for testing before going live, you will effectively end up performing system tests on the live system itself. This is not a comfortable place to be, especially with irate users and rapidly disillusioned management breathing down your neck.

> **GUIDELINE 19.3**   Double the amount of time you would normally allow for testing.

19.2.2 DATA LOAD

One question that needs to be answered early is: Where is the test data going to come from? Is real user data going to be used, or will the data be generated? Either approach is valid, but there are a number of pitfalls and issues with each.

Using historic data has the advantage that it is real data, and as such will probably have the same data skews and biases as the data that the data warehouse has to capture. The problem is how to capture the real data in the first place. As the mechanisms that the data warehouse will use to capture the source data are unlikely to be working yet, one-off methods may have to be developed to get the data required.

For example, suppose the source data requires modification on the source system before being transferred to the data warehouse system. It is possible that the changes will not have been made on the source system in time for the system test. This could mean that the data you get will be in a different form from the data that the data warehouse will normally receive. This will require transformation programs to be written just to perform the system test.

During testing you will need to test the ultimate system that is likely to be used. However, phased growth of the data warehouse machine is fairly common, with the data warehouse having no data and only a few users when the system goes live. The machine will grow, with data being added daily and users phased in. This often means that the original hardware bought will support the initial data warehouse but not a full-scale system test. It is therefore not uncommon for system testing to take place on the hardware vendor's site, in one of its benchmark suites.

Performing the system test off site can cause other problems with data. Many organizations, such as banks, will not allow real data off site for legal and competitive reasons. This may mean having to either modify some real data to make it fact free but still representative, or generate random data.

Even if the real data is available to you, there is the problem of how it will be loaded. In a 1 TB system, a system test of at least a 10–20% system is required. This means that 100–200 GB of data needs to be loaded. This is a non-trivial task, which may involve large quantities of tapes, and the data can often take several days to extract and load.

If data has to be generated, a number of issues need to be considered, such as:

- How will the data be generated?
- Where will the data be generated?
- How will the generated data be loaded?
- Will the data be correctly skewed?

There are many different ways in which the required data could be generated. Bespoke data generation programs could be written. A data generation package could be purchased. Use could be made of already available software, such as that supplied by the TPC Council for the TPC benchmarks, to generate the data.

There are other questions: How is the generated data stored? Can it be generated straight into the database, or does it need to be staged somewhere on disk? Is it possible to use something like a UNIX pipe to pump the data from the generation program into a database load program? If the data in the database is partitioned and the data generator used generates the data randomly across partitions rather than randomly within partitions, the database load program will need to filter the data as it loads. This will slow down the data load considerably.

Whatever method is chosen to generate the data, it is important to ensure that the generated data is correctly structured and distributed. If the generated data has a normal distribution and the real data does not, any query performance tests will be useless. It is also important to ensure that the generated data has the same table-to-table ratios. So, for example, in a banking data warehouse application, ensure that there is the right ratio of transactions to account, and the correct ratio of accounts to customers. If these ratios are not correct the query execution plans are likely to be different from those in the live system, and so any query performance testing may prove to be of no use.

> **GUIDELINE 19.4**   If the test data is generated, ensure the data has the correct balance and skew. Make sure the ratio of fact to dimension is correct and so on.

19.3 TESTING BACKUP RECOVERY

Clearly, testing the backup recovery strategy will be one of the key tests. Each of the scenarios indicated below needs to be catered for:

- instance failure
- media failure
- loss or damage of tablespace or data file
- loss or damage of a table
- loss or damage of a redo log file
- loss or damage of archive log file
- loss or damage of control file
- failure during data movement
- any other scenarios

It is imperative that the tests be carried out completely, not just on paper. So, for example, to test the recovery of a lost data file, a data file should actually be deleted and recovered from backup. It is not sufficient to check that a particular data file has been backed up, and to therefore assume that it can be recovered. For these reasons, the backup tests should be conducted throughout the whole of the system testing, but the recovery tests should all be scheduled for the end of the system testing.

> **GUIDELINE 19.5** Schedule the recovery tests last, because a failed test can cause considerable delays.

Any backup management software to be used should also be fully tested. It is important to test that each backup issued does what it was requested to do, and that the backup can actually be recovered. Check any scripts used during the backup. Double check that they are picking up all the files they should be, and ensure that each backup gets all the file types it should, such as database data files, redo files and so on, as well as any flat files required to be backed up. Ensure that these scripts are dynamic, and pick up new files as they are added. Add a data file to test this. Then delete a file or files from the database, and check that the scripts do not still look for it.

Check that the backup database is working correctly, and actually tracks what has been backed up and where it has been backed up to. If that works then check that the information can be retrieved. Check that all the backup hardware is working: tapes, tape drives, controllers and so on.

> **GUIDELINE 19.6** Every backup test should be verified by performing recovery using the backed up data.

19.4 TESTING THE OPERATIONAL ENVIRONMENT

Testing of the data warehouse operational environment is another key set of tests that will have to be performed. There are a number of aspects that need to be tested:

- security
- disk configuration

- scheduler
- management tools
- database management

Security is difficult to test unless you have clearly documented what is not allowed. If, as suggested in Chapter 13, there is a separate data warehouse security document, testing should be a relatively straightforward matter of extracting the list of disallowed operations, and devising a test for each. This set of tests should be run several times during system testing to ensure that newly added data, aggregations and so on do not cause security breaches. Note that the relevant subset of tests should also be carried out after each recovery operation, to ensure that the data remains secure.

During the system testing the **disk configuration** should be tested thoroughly to identify any potential I/O bottlenecks. This is where decisions on stripe widths and versions of RAID technology will be tested, and any problems with the chosen configuration will be highlighted. For a detailed discussion of disk configuration options see Chapter 12. From a testing point of view it will be necessary to test each configuration both for bulk operations, such as restoring a data file, and for daily operations, such as data load and querying.

We recommend that each test be performed multiple times with different settings. For example, if striped disks are being used for a particular part of the data warehouse, the battery of tests carried out on those disks should be repeated for different stripe widths. It is important to ensure that the tests include all likely operations, including a complete restore of those disks, any daily operations and any bulk data operations, such as data rollup and aggregation. This will allow you to pick the best compromise stripe width for that part of the system as a whole, and not just the best stripe width for daily operations.

> **GUIDELINE 19.7** Test I/O operations for different stripe widths.

Where possible, these tests should be carried out on different-sized data sets. This will allow you to gauge the scalability of the solution as the data warehouse grows. This is particularly important if RAID 5 technology is being used, as the overheads of RAID 5 may be bearable with small data quantities, but can rapidly become unacceptable once the data grows to fill the disks.

To control the daily operations of the data warehouse requires some sort of **scheduling software**, and this needs to be thoroughly tested during the system testing. In particular, the scheduling software will need to interface with the warehouse manager, which will need the scheduler to control the overnight processing and the management of the aggregations. Given the possibility for many of the processes in the data warehouse to swamp the system resources if allowed to run at the wrong time, scheduling control of these processes is essential to the success of the data warehouse.

It is crucial to be able to strictly control the sequencing of certain processes. For example, the overnight aggregation maintenance processes cannot be allowed to run until the daily data load has completed. If it did run at the wrong time, clearly some data would be missing from the aggregations. Unwinding such a problem could take a long time, and in certain cases may be effectively impossible. This makes it imperative that the scheduling software be capable of handling flow control between processes, and this needs to be thoroughly tested.

> **GUIDELINE 19.8** Test scheduling software and processes thoroughly.

During the system testing use the opportunity to test all of the **management tools** that are going to be used to operate the data warehouse. Tools such as

- event manager,
- system manager,
- configuration manager,
- backup recovery manager,
- database manager,

can be tested as the database is built, loaded, backed up, and queried.

It is important to take the opportunity to check that the event manager actually does track and report the events that are required. Events such as

- running out of space on certain key disks,
- a process dying,
- a process using excessive resource (such as CPU),
- a process returning an error,
- disks exhibiting I/O bottlenecks,
- hardware failures,

need to be reliably tracked and reported, if the system is to be automated.

The backup recovery manager and the database manager are discussed elsewhere in this chapter, but it is worth remembering that these tools are probably best tested by their usage in configuring and operating the test and development systems.

This also holds true for the system manager and the configuration manager. The test system should be configured and managed throughout the test period by the operations and management staff who will ultimately have to do the job for the live system. This is important for genuine evaluation and for skills transfer.

> **GUIDELINE 19.9** Many of the tools, such as the system manager and the backup recovery manager, are best tested by their use during the system tests.

19.5 TESTING THE DATABASE

The testing of the database can be broken down into three separate sets of tests:

- testing the database manager and monitoring tools
- testing database features
- testing database performance

19.5.1 TESTING DATABASE MANAGER AND MONITORING TOOLS

As with the other management tools, the best way to test the database manager and monitoring tools is to use them in the creation, running and management of the test database. These tasks should be carried out by the DBAs who will be running the live system.

19.5.2 TESTING DATABASE FEATURES

To test the RDBMS software first make a list of the features that you want to test. The main features you will need to test are those specific to data warehousing. Features such as

- querying in parallel
- create index in parallel
- data load in parallel

need specific attention. One of the main aims is to gauge the scalability of these operations on the real data.

19.5.3 TESTING DATABASE PERFORMANCE

Query performance is one of the most difficult things to measure in a data warehouse, not least because of the ad hoc nature of the queries that will be run. There will probably be a set of fixed queries that have to be run regularly, and they should be tested. To measure the ad hoc queries, the best that can be done is to use the documented user requirements along with knowledge of the business to generate some queries that are meaningful to the business, and test those.

Try to test the most complex and awkward queries that you can dream up, as long as they are genuine queries that the business is likely to ask. Any simpler queries that are likely to be run by the users should also be tested. Remember that some of the more awkward queries are likely to take some time to run – perhaps even a couple of days. This means that to test them thoroughly could take a week or more of elapsed time.

Nonetheless, the time should be taken to test these queries with different aggregations, different index strategies and different degrees of parallelism. The resource usage profiles gathered while running these tests could prove very useful later on as predictors of resource usage of similar queries.

> **GUIDELINE 19.10** Take the time to test the most complex and awkward queries that the business is likely to ask against different index and aggregation strategies.

The queries should also be tested against different-sized data sets. As the amount of data grows it is likely that the query execution plans will change. It is important to note the point at which they change, and what the resource usage implications are. This can be particularly useful with queries that have sort operations. A sort will not scale linearly, and it will be useful to know how sorts on the different-sized data sets do actually scale.

Index build times are an important operational measurement to gather. The tests should check, in particular, the effects of using differing degrees of parallelism. This can prove to be very important in keeping the overnight processing within the limits required. In a data warehouse, indexes are often required to be re-created because, for data loads and other bulk data movements, it is generally quicker to drop indexes, perform the data movement and create a new index, than to perform the data move with indexes in place.

Aggregations can be classified into two types: identified and ad hoc. Identified aggregations are those that you already have stated requirements for. Ad hoc aggregations are those that are created to solve particular performance problems. These will be created and deleted as necessary, and are impossible to test.

Each identified aggregation should be tested thoroughly. There are often a number of ways in which a given aggregation can be created or maintained. Each method should be checked and the best compromise of performance and resource usage chosen. These tests are important, because they will often show up the fact that a particular aggregation is impractical.

Note that it may be possible and quicker to build some aggregations from other aggregations rather than from the base data. These options should also be explored in testing.

19.6 TESTING THE APPLICATION

Testing the load, warehouse and query managers is just traditional testing of developed code. The main thing is to test that all the managers integrate correctly, and to ensure that the end-to-end load, index, aggregate and query works as expected.

Ensure that each function of each manager works correctly. For example, with the load manager, tests will be needed to ensure that each data field is transformed correctly, that the data load scales in parallel, and that the correct data ends up in the specified location within the data warehouse.

It is important to test the application over all period boundaries. If there are week-end and month-end tasks that need to be performed, these need to be tested as well. End-to-end tests from load to query should be performed for several daily cycles. This repetitive testing will catch any dependency errors on moving from daily processing to overnight processing to daily processing again. It also allows for testing of the loading of data into tables that already contain data.

To test the query manager thoroughly will require user access to the system. User access times need to be strictly controlled, because user queries could invalidate test statistics for other tests. The user tests should focus on the use and integration of the front-end tools rather than on queries, which can be tested separately under controlled conditions. It is important that the tools and the query manager work together, and that the query manager can successfully gather query statistics.

19.7 LOGISTICS OF THE TEST

One of the key questions to answer about the system test is: How big a system should you test on? To answer this question you have to ask yourself what you are really testing. This is a more difficult question to answer than it might first seem.

The simple answer to the second question is that you are testing a suite of data warehouse application code. This answer is true, but it is not complete. The aim of the system test is to test all of the following areas:

- data warehouse application code
- day-to-day operational procedures
- overnight processing
- backup recovery strategy
- query performance
- management and monitoring tools
- scheduling software

There is one other point that needs consideration, and that is scalability. Many of the operations in a data warehouse do not scale linearly, and so the results of tests made on smaller systems may not be valid on the live system. Failure to test to the full scale of the data warehouse may leave you with a design that simply does not work when the system grows. This can prove to be very costly in hardware or redesign time to put it right.

> **GUIDELINE 19.11** Ensure that the data warehouse design scales as the data scales.

Remember also that many data warehouses start off empty, and it is not untypical to start off with a machine sized for the first 6–9 months of growth. If the plan is to keep 3 years' worth of data online, the starting system constitutes only one sixth to one quarter of the final system. Any system testing done on such a box will possibly be invalid on the larger system.

The upshot of this is that the system testing must be aimed at testing the final system where possible. Naturally it makes no commercial sense to purchase the complete system at the start, so it is unlikely that full-scale testing can be performed on the data warehouse hardware itself. It may be possible to loan or lease enough hardware to perform the test, but the more practical solution is to use the hardware vendor's benchmarking facilities to perform the scalability tests. This means that a smaller-scale full system test can be carried out on the initial configuration, and then the scalability tests can be performed on the larger benchmark system.

Even if you are forced to test on a smaller system, make sure to test for the larger system. For example, suppose the plan is to have base data partitioned by month. This means eventually having 36 monthly partitions of 10 GB, say. If 250 GB of usable disk space is all that is available, a full-scale test cannot be performed. It is, however, possible to test that the queries and operations work correctly across 36 1 GB partitions. When these tests are complete, data can be reloaded or regenerated to do scalability tests. Starting with one 10 GB partition, scalability can be tested as partitions are added. The combination of these tests may give some indication of how the full system will run.

So, to summarize, the aim of the system testing is to test all aspects of the data warehouse at its ultimate size.

As with any new system, there will be bedding-in problems on the machine. This leads to another commonly asked question: Do you back up the test system during the tests? There will be backups performed as part of the tests, but they will be specially aimed at the individual tests being performed and not at actually securing the test system. Given the size of the system, backups can become a major overhead, and can prolong the system test elapsed times.

It comes down to a risk calculation. If all the disks are mirrored, then testing is less likely to be affected by media failure than if the disks are running unprotected. Nevertheless, this is no guarantee against loss of data, in particular as the hardware being used is probably new and still in the infant failure zone. New hardware is more likely to fail in the first few days and weeks of being used. This should be taken into consideration when deciding what – if anything – to back up during the tests. If possible, time should be allowed for the hardware to bed in. A suite of tests could be built to exercise all the disks, controllers, memory, and CPUs.

One thing to ensure is that backups of the test results are done on a daily basis, or even more frequently. They are not likely to be large, and the backup overhead will be small.

Monitoring tools are extremely important during the system testing. These tools can be classified as either passive monitoring tools or active monitoring tools. A **passive monitoring** tool works by taking snapshots of statistics at various stages. Typically, a snapshot would be performed just before a test, and again immediately after a test. An **active monitoring** tool gathers data continuously. These tools are in fact also interval or snapshot driven, but will typically take snapshots every few seconds or minutes. Active tools normally have graphical displays that allow tests to be visually monitored. Be careful not to make the snapshot interval too small, or the monitors will begin to have a measurable effect on the system.

Where possible, test everything twice. This will help avoid situations like the following. Someone tested that an uninterruptible power supply (UPS) was working by pulling the power from the system. The UPS worked fine, and was put into live running. Some days later there was a power failure. The system crashed badly, and when the UPS was investigated, a fault was found in the battery connections that meant they were not recharging correctly.

> **GUIDELINE 19.12** Test everything twice.

Futures

CHAPTER 20

Data warehouse futures

The last few years have seen database sizes in the open systems arena grow by a couple of orders of magnitude. As this book goes to publication, 1–2 TB systems are becoming more common, and work has begun on 10+ TB systems. By the end of the century we will be on the brink of the petabyte system (1 PB = 1024 TB).

These order of magnitude changes are of major significance. With each multiple of 10 the techniques required to architect, design, build and manage large systems have to be revisited, and more often than not have to be replaced with completely new techniques.

As the size of databases grows, the estimate of what constitutes a very large database (VLDB) continues to grow. The acronym VLDB has become so stretched in the range that it covers that a new acronym is required to distinguish these future systems from what has happened to date. We define an extremely large database (ELDB) to be 100+ TB.

Restrictions in the currently available hardware and software are forcing organizations to limit the amount of data they can keep online. For example, a telco call record data warehouse may require as much as a 1 TB database to keep just a single month of data online and easily queried. It is not hard to envision the requirement to store a year or more of data online. When you add marketing, sales and customer profiling information to the data warehouse, a 100 TB ELDB becomes a possibility.

What is hard to envision, however, is how such a system would ever reach a petabyte in size. Telco systems tend to generate more data for a given period than, say, banking or retail systems. They therefore generally require the most space for a given period, and either will be bigger systems or will store data for shorter periods. Taking this into account, and considering the example above, the question has to be asked: Will there ever be a business requirement for a 1+ PB system?

To answer this question, it is important to note that all the data in the telco example above is textual data. This is the normal "letters and numbers" type of data typically stored in relational databases. However, the world of business is increasingly making use of other forms of data. Multimedia, video and document data have been around for a long time, but this data cannot be so easily manipulated as text data. For example, searching photographic data for all photographs of men with beards is not a simple task. The equivalent textual task of searching a table or tables for all rows that contain a certain value in one of the columns is, however, easily managed by the relational database software available today.

The software that allows the integration and manipulation of non-textual and textual data is really only just becoming available. It is this non-textual data that will bring about the business requirements for 1+ PB databases.

Size is not the only determinant of the complexity of the task involved in planning, building and running ever-larger data warehouse systems. As more and wider-ranging data is added to these systems, their usefulness increases. More users will want access to this data. Indeed, the competitive advantage of having extremely large integrated data systems will increasingly depend on the bulk of an organization's employees being able quickly and easily to access that data. Adding large numbers of concurrent users to the ELDB equation will require radically different architectures and designs.

As the Internet continues to grow, and in particular as the number of Web-enabled applications grows, so will the requirement for customers to access data online. This again adds to the user base of these ELDB systems.

The future shape of data warehouses will be very different from that of the data warehouses that are being created today. The requirement to handle vast quantities of multiformat data, while satisfying a user base of thousands, will drive solutions toward distributed databases and three-tier architectures.

Distributed databases will be required to avoid the shipping and replication of enormous quantities of local multiformat data. The sheer quantity of the data in an ELDB will make it necessary to spread the data over multiple separate databases for management purposes.

Distributed databases exist today, but they can suffer from severe performance problems as database boundaries are crossed. Problems such as query optimization across database boundaries will need to be solved. Cross-database integrity can be guaranteed by currently available database software, but the performance implications for even a medium-size database can be extreme. In the realm of ELDBs the performance implications would be crippling.

Data warehouses currently being built tend to be two-tier client–server architectures. The future will require the use of middleware. To handle the different user requirements of a large user population, multiple applications will have to be built on top of the data warehouse. The size of the user population itself will drive data warehouse architects toward three-tier hardware and software architectures.

The increasing popularity of the Web paradigm, with the consequent uptake by business of intranets to allow users access to integrated data, automatically introduces multiple tiers into the organization's data architecture. Any data warehouse that forms part of that data architecture will need to be multi-tiered.

The data-mart concept that exists today is a simple example of a three-tier distributed architecture. Note, however, that data marts as built today are generally designed to allow a single integral data store to be created, and smaller departmental data sets to be extracted from the central system. Such a system would not be suitable for an ELDB with a large user population. As discussed above, the ELDB may itself need to be distributed for management and other reasons. With a large user population it is unlikely that local data marts will be capable of answering all queries. This is particularly true where users of a given data set are not localized in one area.

It will be some years before 1+ PB open-systems data warehouses become a reality. The current challenge is data warehouses of the order of 10+ TB, two orders of magnitude short of a petabyte. How the market develops depends on the ever-changing hardware and software technologies. It is dangerous to predict anything in the IT marketplace, but this chapter has given a brief glimpse of where we think the data warehouse is going to be early in the new millennium. One thing is for sure: whatever happens in the data warehouse marketplace in the next few years, it will continue to be leading edge, and it will be challenging.

Appendices

APPENDIX A

Methodology

INTRODUCTION

The objective of this section is to describe the methodology for the delivery of a client–server data warehouse. This plan builds on the delivery process covered within Part One: Introduction, and assumes that you are familiar with the basic data warehouse architecture concepts in section Part Two: Data Warehouse Architecture. After reading this appendix, you should be able to define a realistic project plan for the delivery of a data warehouse.

The template project plan described in this section represents a realistic view of the activities that need to take place to deliver a data warehouse. Clearly, business drivers vary between projects, so the precise makeup of the project plan will be unique to a specific project; however, you should treat this project plan as a good starting point. Put another way, if you do not plan to carry out all the activities described in this section, check that your requirement *is* different, and that the project is not exposed to unnecessary risks.

OVERVIEW

Within a data-warehousing project, we have to deliver the following components:

- a business case study (optional, although strongly recommended),
- a prototype (optional),
- a business requirements study,
- a technical blueprint,

and then the three build components of a full data warehouse:

- an extract and load process,
- a warehouse management process,
- a query management process.

The definitions of these components can be found Part Two: Data Warehouse Architecture. Each of these components is incrementally built as we progress through the delivery process. For example, in the first build phase, we would focus on delivering the bulk of the load manager; the second build phase would focus on delivering the bulk of the warehouse manager; and so on.

In order to provide an accurate indication of the project style and effort, we shall cover the tasks and deliverables for delivery of the first build phase. Our experience has been that subsequent phases are either variations on the theme (when more data sources are added), or very specific to each organization, so are not covered within this document.

BUSINESS CASE, BUSINESS REQUIREMENTS AND TECHNICAL

BLUEPRINT

Each of these studies is essentially an intellectual exercise that is required prior to starting the build of part of the data warehouse. All these activities require senior business analysts who are well versed in the business issues and understand the market sector, and senior technical architects who understand the technical and design issues of decision support systems and data warehouses.

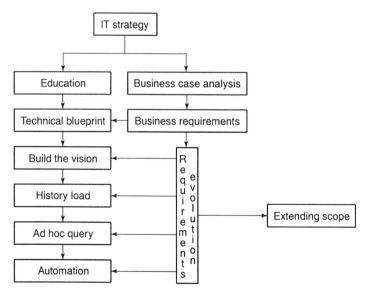

Figure A.1 Data warehouse delivery process.

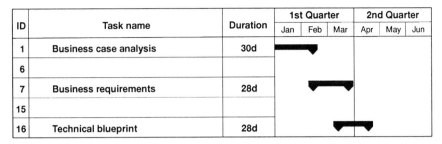

ID	Task name	Duration	1st Quarter			2nd Quarter		
			Jan	Feb	Mar	Apr	May	Jun
1	Business case analysis	30d						
6								
7	Business requirements	28d						
15								
16	Technical blueprint	28d						

Figure A.2   Gantt chart of the first three phases within the delivery process.

We would advise you not to skimp on these activities. If any of the conclusions produced from these studies is suspect, they will carry the risk of adding a substantial cost penalty to the project when you address those issues in the future. In practice, it can be very cost-effective to make sure that the information requirements (as opposed to reports) are fully understood prior to designing and building the data warehouse.

Dependencies between the phases are simple. The *business case* precedes the *business requirements* and *technical blueprint* phases, and the *business requirements* must be partially completed before the *technical blueprint* can start. This is necessary so that we can first understand the overall user requirements for data analysis, which are then used to architect a solution that can evolve in incremental phases to address all the business requirements.

The Gantt chart in Figure A.2 is included to illustrate the point. The effort estimates provided are fairly indicative of the elapsed time that these activities take. In some cases, it may be possible to reduce the elapsed time by the addition of extra resources. For the purposes of clarity, we shall assume that each activity is carried out by a single resource.

PROTOTYPING

Any prototyping activity should focus on proving the concept planned to be addressed within the main build. In most cases, prototypes should attempt to use a small subset of data from a realistic data source, and one of the proposed user access tools.

Access to a realistic data source should highlight what the data cleanup issues may be like, and whether a copy management tool is appropriate. You should also end up with a better understanding of the strengths and weaknesses of the proposed user access tool, and how suitable it is for your specific requirements (so don't buy anything yet).

We recommend that the prototype is not focused to deliver business benefits, because that will limit your ability to experiment with the new tools and concepts. Rather, you should set the expectation that business benefits may be derived (as a bonus), but the main purpose of the exercise is to clarify user requirements by allowing them to "play" with the concept of decision support data.

Project plans for a prototyping activity are fairly simplistic:

- Configure copy management tool (optional).
- Extract data subset from source.
- Apply minimal data cleanup activities.
- Configure user access tool
- Create a number of reports.

In our experience, the parameters for these activities vary widely between projects, and so they will not be covered here. We recommend that any prototyping activity is timeboxed to a 6 week period. If this is not achievable, consider delivering the *build the vision* stage with a smaller scope, which will deliver production quality results in an 8 week period.

BUILD THE VISION

This phase builds the three system processes that are required to create a data warehouse. For the purposes of clarity, we shall first discuss the overall project structure prior to discussing the detail task definitions.

The build phase is broken down into a set of activities that design and build the three system components (load, warehouse, and query managers), produce a limited number of reports and canned queries, test the solution and finally, support the transition to production. Project management and technical management are assumed to occur throughout the project (Figure A.3).

Load manager design and build

As discussed in Chapter 4 the load manager implements the extract and load process. For the *build the vision* phase, this is the component that we must focus on building first, because it enables us to extract the data from the source systems and populate the data warehouse.

The effort estimate for this system will vary depending on the number and complexity of the source systems being loaded. Our advice is that you attempt to

ID	Task name	Duration	2nd Quarter			3rd Quarter			4th
			Apr	May	Jun	Jul	Aug	Sep	Oct
23	**Build the vision**	118d							
24	Load manager design and build	53d							
43	Warehouse manager design and build	63d							
68	Query manager design and build	10d							
70	End user report	20d							
76	Testing	108d							
85	Transition to production	35d							
93	Project and technical management	90d							

Figure A.3 Top level breakdown of the *build the vision* phase.

scale back the user requirements in order to minimize the number of source systems that need to be extracted within the first phase.

Warehouse manager design and build

The warehouse manager is the system component that converts the structure of the source data into a form suitable for analysis. Also, this component manages the creation of aggregations, user views and database indexes, and automates backup/recovery and archiving. In later stages, the warehouse manager can be expanded to determine the most appropriate aggregations, by automatically monitoring the types of query being made (query profiles).

To a very large extent, the purpose in this phase is to automate the facilities necessary to run a production data warehouse. Any facility that is, strictly speaking, not required in the short term is delayed till later stages. We would advise you to determine what elements of the warehouse manager are required within your particular project, and amend the template plan as necessary. We have assumed that automation of data access control and user management is deferred till later phases.

Query manager design and build

The query manager is the component that directs user queries to the most appropriate source, and manages the use of the available processing power to avoid the "query from hell." In later stages, the query manager can be expanded to monitor query profiles automatically, so that the warehouse manager can determine the most appropriate aggregations.

In most cases, significant components of this system manager are provided by the user access tool, so the work required in this phase is minimal. We suggest you allow a small amount of time to create an outline infrastructure for the query manager, so that the hooks are there to allow you to expand its functionality in future.

End-user reporting

User access tools in themselves may not provide all the functional interfaces required by the end users. Typically, we would expect that a number of reports and canned queries would be built as part of this build phase. Clearly, the precise number required will vary between projects, so the effort estimates for this task will vary accordingly.

As an indication of the effort required, we would recommend that you allow an average of 4 days to design, build and test a query or report. This figure should be substantially reduced if groups of queries or reports are essentially the same query with different parameters. We suggest that you allow a total of 5 days per report or screen that is parameter driven: that is, the user can decide at runtime which parameters drive the query.

Testing

As with all systems development, substantial effort is spent in testing the system components. The testing is broken down into a number of areas:

- integration testing each major component;
- system testing that all the components work together;
- volume testing that the data warehouse processes can cope with the planned data volumes;
- acceptance testing prior to transition and project completion.

As far as possible, the testing is automated to cover the areas identified; however, there is an additional test that is normally executed manually. **Reconciliation testing** sanity-checks the data content of the data warehouse to ensure that it makes sense, and that the process of data cleanup and integration has not produced spurious results.

This type of testing is very difficult to automate. In our experience, the most effective way to perform this activity is by scheduling effort from a number of business users to sanity-check query results against their expectation of what they should look like.

Transition

This activity turns the data warehouse into an operational environment, and additionally tunes performance and performs the initial data load to kick-start the data warehouse. In most cases, the initial data load is relatively small: for example, 3 months' history, as opposed to 2 years' history.

If at all possible, the initial load should be carried out as a set of loads performed in sequence (at the expected frequency of operation, e.g. daily). That is, the extract and load process is repeated as many time as necessary to extract the data from the source systems at the standard interval. This will keep checking that the load process is functioning correctly, and that the data cleanup facilities are operating on the basis on which they were designed.

For example, let us consider a case where we are seeking to backload 3 months' worth of retail sales history, where the load manager is designed to operate on a daily basis. We suggest you load the data a day at a time, rather than loading everything in one go.

Because the load process is unlikely to take more than a few hours, these daily loads can be stacked end to end in order to complete in a reasonable elapsed time (90 iterations, for example). This process will check that the repetitive loading of data functions correctly, and can supplement the planned integration tests.

Management and QA

Management activities within a data warehousing project should incorporate project and technical management. We recommend that the technical architect who has performed the *technical blueprint* phase is retained on a part-time basis throughout this build phase, to ensure that the work being carried out fits within the bounds of the technical architecture.

In addition, we recommend that a quality assurance role is performed by experts in decision support and data warehousing. In our experience, it is best performed by two people: a senior business analyst, who is expert on how decision support information is exploited within the business, and a senior technical architect/project director, who has delivered many data warehousing solutions.

TASKS AND DELIVERABLES

Within this section, we shall identify the tasks and steps required to deliver the first four phases of a data warehouse: that is, up to and including *building the vision*. Subsequent phases vary substantially between projects, and are variations on the themes described here.

All estimates are provided in person-days, and an indication of durations is included in the Gantt charts that identify dependencies between steps. For clarity, we have assumed that *a single resource is allocated to each task*. In practice, we would expect an average of two resources working on each task.

The tasks that we shall cover are (one each) for *business case analysis*, *business requirements analysis*, *technical blueprint study*, and all the tasks within the *building the vision* phase.

TASKS

- Business case analysis
- Business requirements analysis
- Technical blueprint study
- Building the vision
- Load manager design and build
  - The major tasks within the load manager activity are:
    (1) Extract and load the data (for each major source system)
    (2) Design and build the load manager process
    These tasks will deliver the source data in the transient storage area, ready for clean up and transformation into the data warehouse starflake schema.
- Warehouse manager design and build
  - The major tasks within the warehouse manager activity are:
    (1) Design and build database structures.
    (2) Validate and clean the data
    (3) Design and build operational infrastructure.
    (4) Design and build warehouse manager process.
    These tasks will deliver the source data converted into a starflake schema, ready for analysis. In addition, user views, synonyms, indexes and aggregations are also created.
- Query manager design
- End-user reporting
- Testing
- Transition to production
- Project and technical management

TASK 1:   BUSINESS CASE ANALYSIS

DESCRIPTION

This task determines the business case for investing in a data warehouse. It identifies the projected returns from the information content of the data warehouse over a 3–5 year period.
  Examples of returns are:

- Reduce the marketing spend by $5 million per annum.
- Convert 15% of secondary shoppers into primary shoppers.
- Increase market penetration by 25% over three years.

In other words, all the returns are measurable, quantifiable, and significant.

STEPS

1 Identify and prioritize all unmet business needs for decision support information.
2 Calculate the projected returns from each type of information.
3 Calculate the capital expenditure and operational expenditure for delivering and running a data warehouse. Consider other options.
4 Document and present the business case.

ESTIMATING

Effort varies depending on the complexity of the solution, and the clarity of the vision within the organization. In most cases, we recommend that the effort is limited to approximately 40-person days' duration, in order to force the decision-making processes to take place.

RISKS

Minimal. Do not be surprised if the conclusions are that a data warehouse is inappropriate; it is far more important to make sure that you are building a data warehouse for the right reasons.

Step	Effort
Identify and prioritize requirements for information	10
Calculate projected returns	8
Calculate capital expenditure and operating expenditure for the data warehouse	10
Document and present	12

TASK I: DELIVERABLES

PREREQUISITES

A corporate IT strategy, documented or not, which includes the use of decision support information.

TOOLS

None specific.

DELIVERABLES

A business case document and a presentation to senior executives.

DEPENDENCIES BETWEEN STEPS

ID	Task name	Duration	rter	1st Quarter			2nd Qua	
			Dec	Jan	Feb	Mar	Apr	May
1	Business case analysis	30d						
2	Identify and prioritize requirements for info	10d						
3	Calculate projected returns	8d						
4	Calculate capital expenditure and operational expenditure for the data	10d						
5	Document and present	12d						

TASK 2:   REQUIREMENTS ANALYSIS

DESCRIPTION

This task identifies the information requirements for the short and medium term: specifically, the logical model for the data warehouse, and the kinds of query that need to be supported after the first build phase. This task also identifies the source systems that will be providing the information for the data warehouse, and the business rules that need to be applied to the data.

You should allow 80% of the task effort to focus on the immediate requirements. The remaining 20% of the effort should be spent trying to understand what the information requirements for the future look like.

We recommend that you increase this effort (that is, the overall task duration) if the medium-term requirements are not well understood. Errors at this point could prejudice the ability of the architecture to evolve to satisfy the longer-term requirement.

STEPS

1 Interview key users.
2 Produce the logical model for the data warehouse. This should be based on the corporate enterprise data model: that is, the logical model of the data warehouse is a subset of the information used by the organization.
3 Produce the initial query profile. Expect it to change on an ongoing basis.
4 Identify business rules that are applied to the data, in order to ensure accurate and consistent data within the data warehouse.
5 Identify source systems and mapping rules.
6 Identify longer-term scope.
7 Identify initial sizing estimates (used in the technical blueprint phase to architect a solution for the whole scope).

ESTIMATING

A logical model of approximately 30 entities produces a data warehouse of medium complexity. This will be expected to translate into much higher numbers of source tables, and an unspecified number of source systems. Estimates are provided for complex, simple, and medium-complexity projects.

RISKS

Because the data warehouse requirements are never fully understood, beware of a tendency to extend this task. A common comment is "We still don't fully understand the requirements."

We strongly recommend that this activity is monitored closely and timeboxed, because the requirements will almost certainly be impossible to define completely.

Within this task, focus on designing flexibility into the data warehouse. Failure to do so at this point may lead to substantial cost penalties in the future.

In addition, an enterprise data model may not exist; in that case, we suggest you spend some time trying to brainstorm what a potential one might look like.

Step	Complex	Medium	Simple
Interview key users	10	8	5
Produce the logical model for the data warehouse	15	10	7
Produce the initial query profile	13	8	5
Identify business rules	12	7	4
Identify source systems and mapping rules	15	10	5
Identify longer-term scope	15	11	5
Identify longer-term sizing estimates	3	2	1

TASK 1:   DELIVERABLES

TASK 2: DELIVERABLES

PREREQUISITES

1 A documented business case, which identifies the areas of focus for the business requirements.

2 An enterprise data model, which identifies all the significant items of information used by the business.

3 A definition of the business processes that will be supported by the data warehouse. It is used to understand how to structure data to support those processes.

DELIVERABLES

1 A logical model for the whole data warehouse, and identification of the subset being implemented in the first build phase. Includes attribute and relationship definitions, although any modeling technique may be appropriate (e.g. dimensional modeling, ERD, object oriented).

2 Query profiles for the first production deliverable. Typically contain a set of required reports and canned queries, and identify the number and location of the users. Query performance expectations and query complexity are also identified.

3 Business rules definitions to be applied to the extracted data.

4 Source system mappings at the logical level: that is, entity in source system(s) to entity(s) in data warehouse, including conversion of attributes and relationships.

5 Data sizing estimates for the whole data warehouse, and an indication of which subsets or aggregation levels may be appropriate initially.

TOOLS

Requirements and data modeling tools, such as Bachman tools.

DEPENDENCIES BETWEEN STEPS

ID	Task name	Duration	rter	1st Quarter			2nd Quar	
			Dec	Jan	Feb	Mar	Apr	May
7	**Business requirements**	28d						
8	Interview key users	8d						
9	Produce the logical model for the DW	10d						
10	Produce the initial query profile	8d						
11	Identify business rules	7d						
12	Identify source systems and mapping rules	10d						
13	Identify longer-term scope	11d						
14	Identify initial sizing estimates	2d						

TASK 3:   TECHNICAL BLUEPRINT

DESCRIPTION

This task will define the technical architecture for the whole data warehouse, not just the first deliverable. It determines the overall solution, including:

- technical architecture of solution (database architecture, system architecture, and infrastructure);
- database sizings and query performance expectations;
- identification of the mechanisms for data transfer and load;
- recommendations for the sizes and configuration of hardware;
- access control, backup and recovery guidelines.

STEPS

1 Interview IT decision makers. Used to understand the existing IT infrastructure, and identify any hardware preferences.
2 Determine overall architecture. Produces the initial conclusions; which are then fed back prior to refining and documenting.
3 Feed back initial conclusions. Expect major revisions as the result of this step, because this is where the true size and cost of the data warehouse are clearly identified.
4 Refine and rework initial conclusions.
5 Document and present.

ESTIMATING

This task is typically timeboxed, because it has a tendency to keep growing. If the effort being expended is much greater than the guideline figures, the task is probably going into too much detail.

RISKS

If the midpoint feedback from the right people does not take place, the initial decisions may be suspect or risky, and further work on them may be inappropriate.

There is a tendency for preoccupation with the hardware architecture (Is it MPP or SMP? Which manufacturer has the best offering? etc.). Typically, this is a red herring, and should be put to one side till the end of this task. In most cases, the capacity headroom issues will indicate the appropriate shortlist of hardware vendors.

Step	Complex	Medium	Simple
Interview IT decision makers	5	3	1
Determine overall architecture	10	8	6
Feed back initial conclusions	1	1	1
Refine and rework initial conclusions	15	10	5
Document and present	6	6	4

TASK 3:   DELIVERABLES

PREREQUISITES

1 Overall scope definition for the data warehouse, not just for the first build phase.
2 The data sizings and query profiles with performance expectations.
3 Documented IT infrastructure.

DELIVERABLES

A document identifying:

- database architecture,
- system and hardware architecture,
- infrastructure architecture,
- backup and recovery guidelines,
- data partitioning strategy,
- data sizings and performance guidelines based on hardware sizings,
- hardware sizings and capacity headroom projections,
- access control guidelines,
- mechanisms for data transfer and load.

TOOLS

None specific.

DEPENDENCIES BETWEEN STEPS

ID	Task name	Duration	rter	1st Quarter			2nd Quar	
			Dec	Jan	Feb	Mar	Apr	May
16	**Technical blueprint**	**28d**						
17	Interview IT decision makers	3d						
18	Determine overall architecture	8d						
19	Feedback initial conclusions	1d						
20	Refine and rework initial conclusions	10d						
21	Document and present	6d						

TASK 4: EXTRACT AND LOAD THE DATA

DESCRIPTION

This task will extract the source data from the source system, and load it into the temporary area of the data warehouse. Other tasks will then clean up and convert the data into appropriate structures (that is, starflake schemas: see Chapter 5).

The extraction can be performed by:

- bespoke programs running on the native environment, e.g. RPG, producing flat files, etc.;
- database extracts from the source database, e.g. DB2, into flat files;
- a copy management tool being configured to perform the extraction and load directly.

Flat files are moved to the data warehouse hardware environment, and loaded into the database using database-specific fast-load facilities.

This task is repeated for each source system or subject area.

STEPS

1 Design and build extract from source system:
- Using flat files: takes the data from the source system and generates an ASCII file.
- Using a copy management tool: defines the mappings between source tables and destination tables, in order to generate the conversion programs.
2 Design and build transfer to new hardware.
3 Design and build load into temporary area.

ESTIMATING

Effort varies, depending on the complexity of the source system and the number of entities being extracted. By and large, you should allow reasonable effort to build the extract for a single physical entity. This figure will be on average one day per physical entity (in the source system) using a copy management tool, and can be somewhat higher if the extract is handwritten.

Once the first "infrastructure" facilities are created for a source system (that is, to automatically transfer the data to the hardware environment running the data warehouse), subsequent feeds from other subject areas in the same source systems will be much easier; estimates can be reduced accordingly.

Data loads are unique for each subject area, so the steps need to be repeated each time: that is, effort estimates are not reduced as the number of loads increase. If the extraction is complex (for example, if all of the data is not readily available at the same time), all estimates should be increased accordingly. Medium-complexity estimates are provided based on the extraction and load of up to 10 major entities.

Because a medium-sized data warehouse contains approximately 30 entities, expect the *total* effort to extract and load to be a multiple of the effort estimates provided.

RISKS

Very common for the complexity of the extract to be underestimated.

Step	Complex	Medium	Simple
Design extract from source system	6	4	3
Build extract from source system	15	12	10
Design transfer to new hardware	5	3	1
Build transfer to new hardware	15	8	3
Design load into temporary area	3	2	1
Build load into temporary area	7	5	3
Commission the copy management tool	3	3	3
Specify the mappings for the copy management tool	15	10	6

TASK 4:   DELIVERABLES

PREREQUISITES

Completed business requirements and techni-cal blueprint documents, although some activity can start prior to the completion of those documents. Investigate this point on a case-by-case basis.

DELIVERABLES

For each source system:

1   programs that extract the data into flat files;
2   programs or scripts that transfer flat files to the data warehouse hardware;

3   fast-load scripts that load the files into the staging area in the data warehouse database; or
4   copy management tool configurations that perform the transfer and load.

TOOLS

Specialist copy management tools or programming languages native to the source environment. In addition, will require use of the fast-load database facilities.

DEPENDENCIES BETWEEN STEPS

ID	Task name	Duration	rter	2nd Quarter			3rd
			Mar	Apr	May	Jun	Jul
25	**Extract and load (for each major source**	43d					
26	Design extract from source system	6d					
27	Build extract from source system	15d					
28	Design transfer to new hardware	5d					
29	Build transfer to new hardware	15d					
30	Design load into temporary area	3d					
31	Build load into temporary area	7d					
32	Commision the copy management tool	3d					
33	Specify the mappings for the copy manag	15d					

TASK 5: DESIGN AND BUILD LOAD MANAGER PROCESS

DESCRIPTION

This task will deliver an automated system process that will initiate and carry out the extracts on all the required source systems. This system process will then load the data into the temporary staging area within the data warehouse.

STEPS

1 Design and build load manager on data warehouse platform. Delivers the system process on the hardware that is running the data warehouse.

2 Design and build process controller on source system. The controller must be capable of being automatically initiated either by the load manager, or by a significant event that identifies that the data is ready for transfer. This step is repeated for each source system.

ESTIMATING

Once the first process controller facilities are created for a source system (that is, to automatically transfer the data to the hardware environment running the data warehouse), subsequent feeds from other subject areas in the same source systems will be much easier; estimates can be reduced accordingly.

RISKS

It can be very difficult to determine exactly when the extract should be initiated. This should be clearly identified prior to the start of this task.

Step	Effort
Design load manager on data warehouse platform	4
Build load manager on data warehouse platform	10
(For each source system)	
Design process controller on source system	3
Build process controller on source system	7

TASK 5:   DELIVERABLES

PREREQUISITES

This task cannot be completed until the programs that perform the source system extractions are built. Otherwise, testing the process controllers would be unrealistic.

DELIVERABLES

1   For each source system, a set of scripts or programs that control the extraction process.

2   An overall controller on the data warehouse system, using either programs or shell scripts.

TOOLS

Specialist copy management tools or programming languages native to the source environment. Also, source system job control language, and UNIX shell scripts.

DEPENDENCIES BETWEEN STEPS

ID	Task name	Duration	rter	2nd Quarter			3rd Quar	
			Mar	Apr	May	Jun	Jul	Aug
34	**Design and build load manager process**	**53d**						
35	Design load manager on DW platform	4d						
36	Build load manager on DW platform	10d						
37	(For each source system)	1d						
38	Design process controller on source syste	3d						
39	Build process controller on source system	7d						

TASK 6: DESIGN AND BUILD DATABASE STRUCTURES

DESCRIPTION

This task will deliver all the programs and database scripts that populate the data warehouse with the source data in the transient area. All user views, indexes, synonyms and aggregations are also created. This task can be complex, because the transformations to the data warehouse database structures may be involved.

STEPS

1 Design physical database. Converts the logical model to a detailed database design, within the overall architectural structures defined in the technical blueprint.

2 Create physical database. Physically creates the database, and partitions the tablespaces and disks etc. Disk striping is performed within this activity.

3 Design and build transform into the data warehouse schema. Converts the source data in the transient area into the starflake schema within the data warehouse.

4 Design and build scripts to generate indexes.

5 Design and build scripts to generate summary tables. These scripts can be designed to generate the aggregations from metadata definitions in the data warehouse. The metadata interface is delivered by the task *design and build warehouse manager*.

6 Design and build scripts to create business views.

ESTIMATING

The main estimation variable within this task is the extent to which the generation of summary tables is automated. If the desire is to data-drive the production of summary tables, significant effort will be expended in providing this facility.

The alternative is to provide a system that can be extended easily to incorporate additional scripts to create additional aggregations. This is much easier, and forms the basis for the medium-complexity estimates.

The effort required for the database design activity will vary according to the number of entities being included, and the complexity of the transformations. Don't forget: the previous activity to define the mappings from source system to the data warehouse operated only at the *logical*, not the *physical* level: that is, it did not map into a starflake schema.

RISKS

It is critical that a correct balance is achieved between queries accessing the starflake schema and aggregations. The step to generate the summary tables tends to continually grow in response to new user requirements.

Step	Complex	Medium	Simple
Design physical database	30	20	10
Create physical database	8	5	4
Design transform into DW schema	12	5	3
Build transform into DW schema	25	10	7
Design scripts to generate indexes	7	4	2
Build scripts to generate indexes	20	10	4
Design scripts to generate summary tables	20	10	5
Build scripts to generate summary tables	50	30	10
Design scripts to create business views	10	7	3
Build scripts to create business views	20	15	5

TASK 6: DELIVERABLES

PREREQUISITES

1 Data warehouse logical model, defined in the business requirements.
2 Source data in the transient storage area, in order to test the transformation programs.

DELIVERABLES

1 Physical database design, ideally in a CASE tool.
2 A physical database instance on the data warehouse hardware.
3 Scripts or programs to transform the source data in the transient area into the starflake schema.

4 Scripts or programs to generate indexes, views and synonyms.
5 Programs to generate summary tables, possibly driven by metadata definitions.

TOOLS

CASE tools for the design activities, particularly so that the database DDL can be generated directly from those definitions. Also, consider using programming tools such as C or C++ with embedded SQL, stored procedures, and SQL scripts.

DEPENDENCIES BETWEEN STEPS

ID	Task name	Duration	rter	2nd Quarter			3rd Quar	
			Mar	Apr	May	Jun	Jul	Aug
44	**Design and build database structure**	**63d**						
45	Design physical database	20d						
46	Create physical database	5d						
47	Design transform into DW schema	5d						
48	Build transform into DW schema	10d						
49	Design scripts to generate indexes	4d						
50	Build scripts to generate indexes	10d						
51	Design scripts to generate summary table	10d						
52	Build scripts to generate summary tables	30d						
53	Design scripts to generate business views	7d						
54	Build scripts to generate business views	15d						

TASK 7:   VALIDATE AND CLEAN DATA

DESCRIPTION

This task will clean the data in the transient storage area of the data warehouse, and make sure that it is fully consistent.

STEPS

1 Design and build data validation functions. This is typically done using stored procedures or programs with embedded SQL.

ESTIMATING

Estimating this task can be very difficult, because it assumes knowledge of the degree of data cleanliness within the existing source systems. Unless an activity has taken place that has addressed this point, start off with these estimates and expect them to rise substantially. For this reason, it is good practice to allow significant contingency for this task.

The medium-complexity estimates represent the effort required to validate and clean 30 relatively clean entities. Increase this figure if there are more than 30 entities, and/or the data is dirty.

RISKS

Very common for the cleanliness of the data to be substantially underestimated.

Step	Complex	Medium	Simple
Design data validation functions	20	10	6
Build data validation functions	50	25	15

TASK 7: DELIVERABLES

PREREQUISITES

1 Source data loaded into the data warehouse staging area.
2 Business rules identified within the *business requirements* phase.

DELIVERABLES

A suite of functions and/or programs that check the data against itself and other data sources, and against the information already in the data warehouse.

TOOLS

Specialist copy management tools or programming languages native to the source environment. In addition, will require use of the fast-load database facilities.

DEPENDENCIES BETWEEN STEPS

ID	Task name	Duration	rter	2nd Quarter			3rd Quar	
			Mar	Apr	May	Jun	Jul	Aug
40	**Validate and clean data**	**35d**						
41	Design data validation functions	10d						
42	Build data validation functions	25d						

TASK 8: DESIGN AND BUILD OPERATIONAL INFRASTRUCTURE

DESCRIPTION

This task delivers the programs and scripts that provide the backup/recovery, access control, and archiving facilities.

STEPS

1 Design and build backup/recovery mechanisms. They vary according to the size of the data warehouse, but should never be underestimated.

2 Design and build archiving mechanisms. These mechanisms automatically archive aged data off the data warehouse into longer-term storage media.

3 Design and build access control mechanisms. These mechanisms enforce any data privacy regulations or insider-trading firewalls.

4 Set up systems software for backup/recovery. Necessary in most cases where the size of the data warehouse is too large to utilize standard UNIX backup mechanisms.

ESTIMATING

Typically, relatively little effort is expended on the activities within this phase, because the bulk of the work is deferred to later phases. With the exception of backup/recovery, the mechanisms developed are the bare minimum necessary.

RISKS

Access control facilities can be notoriously complex, so the elapsed time on those steps could increase quite substantially.

Step	Complex	Medium	Simple
Design backup/recovery mechanisms	8	5	3
Build backup/recovery mechanisms	15	10	7
Design archiving mechanisms	2	1	1
Build archiving mechanisms	5	2	2
Design access control mechanisms	10	2	1
Build access control mechanisms	30	5	3
Set up systems software for backup/recovery	9	6	4

TASK 8:   DELIVERABLES

PREREQUISITES

None of the deliverables can be built until the source data is in the data warehouse starflake schema: that is, ready to back up, archive and apply access control. These mechanisms can in theory work against table definitions, but are difficult to test in practice.

DELIVERABLES

1   A configured specialist backup/recovery tool.

2   Programs and scripts that implement backup recovery.
3   Programs and scripts that provide hooks for future archiving and access control facilities.

TOOLS

UNIX programming languages and scripts, together with a specialist backup/recovery tool.

DEPENDENCIES BETWEEN STEPS

ID	Task name	Duration	rter	2nd Quarter			3rd Quar	
			Mar	Apr	May	Jun	Jul	Aug
55	**Design and build operational infrastructu**	**35d**						
56	Design backup/recovery mechanisms	5d						
57	Build backup/recovery mechanisms	10d						
58	Design archiving mechanisms	1d						
59	Build archiving mechanisms	2d						
60	Design access control mechanisms	2d						
61	Build access control mechanisms	5d						
62	Set up systems software for backup recov	6d						

TASK 9: DESIGN AND BUILD WAREHOUSE MANAGER

DESCRIPTION

This task will deliver the system process that performs all the required activities of the warehouse manager. All the database and infrastructure operations are packaged into a system process that can be fully automated. These facilities must be capable of recovering in the event of failure, and of restarting without or with minimal human intervention.

STEPS

1 Design and build the warehouse manager. For this phase, the focus of the task is on the database operations rather than the operational management facilities, which are deferred till later phases.

2 Design and build metadata tables and interfaces. This is done in order to prime the data warehouse with information on which summary tables are required. The interfaces are typically database forms, Visual C++, or Visual Basic, because minimal programming logic is required. This step can be deferred to a later phase.

ESTIMATING

The medium-complexity effort guidelines quoted here apply to a warehouse manager that does not have the ability to generate aggregations from metadata definitions. If that is the requirement, use the effort estimates in the *complex* column.

RISKS

Step	Complex	Medium	Simple
Design warehouse manager process	12	8	4
Build warehouse manager process	30	20	12
Design metadata interfaces	7	0	0
Build metadata interfaces	18	0	0

TASK 9:   DELIVERABLES

PREREQUISITES

As before, all the facilities that perform the database and operational transformations must be in place prior to commencing the building of these components.

DELIVERABLES

1   Programs and scripts that implement the warehouse manager process.

2   Screens and reports that provide interfaces to the metadata definitions.
3   Database design for metadata and the associated physical tables.

TOOLS

Any of the following: C, C++, Visual C++, Visual Basic, and UNIX shell scripts.

DEPENDENCIES BETWEEN STEPS

ID	Task name	Duration	rter	2nd Quarter			3rd Quar	
			Mar	Apr	May	Jun	Jul	Aug
63	**Design and build warehouse manager**	**28d**						
64	Design warehouse manager process	8d						
65	Build warehouse manager process	20d						
66	Design metadata tables and interfaces	7d						
67	Build metadata tables and interfaces	18d						

TASK 10:   QUERY MANAGER DESIGN

DESCRIPTION

This task will design the query manager required to support the full data warehouse. Nothing is physically built within this phase; that is, it is typically deferred to a later phase, because the need to have a query manager can be bypassed by creating queries that access the required tables directly.

As the complexity of the data warehouse and/or the number of users increases, query management becomes more significant in order to optimize the use of system resources.

STEPS

Design the query manager process.

ESTIMATING

This effort is timeboxed to 10 days in order to ensure that only the outline design is put in place, taking into account the facilities within user access tools. If any activities are required now to prepare the ground for the future, they would have to be added to this activity.

Avoid work on this component if at all possible, because the focus of this phase is the accurate extraction of source data.

RISKS

There is a tendency to spend additional time on this activity. Avoid if possible.

Step	Effort
Design query management process	10

TASK 10: DELIVERABLES

PREREQUISITES

Technical blueprint document, and decisions on which user access tools will be used.

DELIVERABLES

A design statement on the way forward to implement a query manager in the future.

DEPENDENCIES BETWEEN STEPS

None.

TOOLS

None specified.

TASK 11:   END-USER REPORTING

DESCRIPTION

This task will produce the canned queries and reports, and configure the user access tool to access the data in the data warehouse.

STEPS

1 Design and build end-user canned queries.
2 Design and build end-user reports.
3 Configure the user access tool metadata. This step populates the metadata structures within the user access tool, in order to allow it to generate SQL against the structures in the starflake schema.

ESTIMATING

The effort estimates will vary directly with the number of reports and screens that are required. A good guideline is to allow 4 days per style of report or screen: that is, if a screen is parameterized, it allows us to produce a number of different queries out of the same screen. The data values applied to each dimension may be different, but the style of the query is the same (for example, top 10 selling products in a product group over a specified time period). In the estimates quoted, we have allowed for five screens and five reports.

The effort to configure a user access tool can vary substantially. Figures quoted here are based on configuring a multidimensional analysis tool, while data dippers can be configured in substantially less time. If required, create additional steps to configure multiple user access tools.

RISKS

Although the user access tool may be configured quickly, it can take a significant amount of time to coax it into generating performant queries. Allow sufficient contingency for that activity, and consider delaying the use of a complex tool till a later phase.

Step	Effort
Design end-user canned queries	5
Build end-user canned queries	15
Design end-user reports	5
Build end-user reports	15
Configure the user access tool metadata	15

TASK II: DELIVERABLES

PREREQUISITES

1   Physical database for the data warehouse.
2   Query profiles as defined in the *business requirements*.

DELIVERABLES

1   Screens and reports that access data within the data warehouse.

2   A user access tool that is configured to operate against the data warehouse database design.

TOOLS

Any database reporting and access tool, such as Visual Basic, or database forms, or a user access tool, such as Business Objects, Decision Suite, or DSS Agent.

DEPENDENCIES BETWEEN STEPS

ID	Task name	Duration	rter	2nd Quarter			3rd
			Mar	Apr	May	Jun	Jul
70	**End-user reporting**	20d			▼▼▼		
71	Design end-user canned queries	5d			▯		
72	Build end-user canned queries	15d			▨		
73	Design end-user reports	5d			▯		
74	Build end-user reports	15d			▨		
75	Configure the user access tool metadata	15d			▨		

TASK 12:   TESTING

DESCRIPTION

This task will specify and perform all the system, integration, volume and acceptance tests of the data warehouse.

STEPS

1   Specify and perform integration tests. These tests check that each component system is functioning correctly.

2   Specify and perform system and volume tests. These tests check that all the systems are operating together correctly, and that they can handle the required data volumes.

3   Specify and perform reconciliation tests. These tests are executed manually to sanity-check the content of the data warehouse.

4   Specify and perform acceptance tests. This includes performance testing.

ESTIMATING

Effort for these activities must allow for the recovery time once a failure is encountered. We would advise against reducing these figures.

RISKS

Step	Effort
Specify integration tests	15
Perform integration tests	20
Specify system and volume tests	8
Perform system and volume tests	20
Specify reconciliation tests	8
Perform reconciliation tests	10
Specify acceptance tests	15
Perform acceptance tests	10

TASK 12: DELIVERABLES

PREREQUISITES

All the system and database components must be in place prior to the start of performing the integration tests. All specifications should be produced at the start of the project, and system tests should be performed as soon as each major component is built.

DELIVERABLES

A set of repeatable system, integration, volume and acceptance tests, and a set of repeatable, manual reconciliation tests.

TOOLS

None specified.

DEPENDENCIES BETWEEN STEPS

ID	Task name	Duration	rter	2nd Quarter			3rd Quarter			4th
			Mar	Apr	May	Jun	Jul	Aug	Sep	Oct
76	**Testing**	108d								
77	Specify integration tests	15d								
78	Perform integration tests	20d								
79	Specify system and volume tests	8d								
80	Perform system and volume tests	20d								
81	Specify reconciliation tests	8d								
82	Perform reconciliation tests	10d								
83	Specify acceptance tests	15d								
84	Perform acceptance tests	10d								

TASK 13: TRANSITION TO PRODUCTION

DESCRIPTION

This task transitions the data warehouse into a production environment. The initial set of data is preloaded, and the data warehouse is performance-tuned if necessary.

STEPS

1 Tune operating system. This step is critical; most data warehouses require a degree of tuning of the operating system and database (see next step) in order for them to achieve the expected performance levels.
2 Tune database.
3 Tune queries. Only necessary if a set of canned queries or reports have been produced as part of this build phase.
4 Tune user access tool.
5 Perform initial data load. This step will backload the initial set of history into the data warehouse, and is assumed not to be too large.
6 Production support.

ESTIMATING

Effort estimates will vary depending on the volume of data being loaded as part of the initial data load. We have assumed that no more than 50 GB of history is being used to start up the data warehouse. If there is a requirement for greater data volumes, increase effort estimates accordingly.

RISKS

If the system does not achieve expected performance levels, allow substantially more time to tune the various components. It is good practice to allow sufficient contingency on this point.

Step	Effort
Tune operating system	3
Tune database	5
Tune queries	10
Tune user access tool	5
Perform initial data load	15
Production support	10

TASK 13:   DELIVERABLES

PREREQUISITES

The tuning activities will typically take place during integration testing. The initial data load should not take place till after integration tests, although they can be performed in parallel if necessary.

DELIVERABLES

A production-quality data warehouse that has been seeded with an initial set of data.

TOOLS

None specific.

DEPENDENCIES BETWEEN STEPS

ID	Task name	Duration	rter	3rd Quarter			4th Quar	
			Jun	Jul	Aug	Sep	Oct	Nov
85	**Transition to production**	**35d**						
86	Tune operating system	3d						
87	Tune database	5d						
88	Tune queries	10d						
89	Tune user access tool	5d						
90	Perform initial data load	15d						
91	Production support	10d						
92	Data warehouse delivered	0d						30/10/97

TASK 14: PROJECT AND TECHNICAL MANAGEMENT

DESCRIPTION

This is an ongoing task, which performs project and technical management of the data warehousing project as a whole. It begins at the very start of the build phase, and continues until the data warehouse is delivered (that is, the end of the *building the vision* phase).

STEPS

1 Project management.

2 Technical management and quality assurance. This step provides involvement of the technical architect all the way through to project delivery. This is necessary to ensure that the component systems comply with the architectural guidelines within the technical blueprint.

3 Decision support systems quality assurance. This step is assumed to be performed by an expert in decision support systems. It is critical to the success of the project, because it provides an expert view on the use of data within the business.

4 Data warehousing quality assurance. This step is assumed to be performed by an expert in data warehousing solutions. It is critical to the success of the project, because it provides a real-world view of the pitfalls within this process, and ensures that the data warehouse is capable of evolving in the future.

ESTIMATING

Effort estimates are guidelines only, and should be modified depending on the expertise of the people involved.

RISKS

In complex solutions, it may be necessary to assign the project manager and technical architect full time to the project.

Step	Effort
Project management	3–4 days per week
Technical management and quality assurance	2–3 days per week
DSS top cover and quality assurance	2–3 days per month
Data warehousing top cover and quality assurance	2–3 days per month

TASK 14:   DELIVERABLES

PREREQUISITES

None.

DELIVERABLES

None.

DEPENDENCIES BETWEEN STEPS

None.

TOOLS

Project tracking and change management tools.

Accessing the data warehouse

The data warehouse is there to be accessed by users. The whole purpose of building the data warehouse is to give an identified set of users access to a particular set of data.

The whole area of access to the data is a minefield. There are a host of tools that can be used, each with its own advantages and disadvantages. There is a battle raging in the industry over relational versus multidimensional tools. New terms such as OLAP, MOLAP and ROLAP are being bandied around. This makes the choice of tools an interesting challenge if not an impossible task. The aim of this appendix is to aid you with this task by discussing all of the major issues.

CHOOSING AN ACCESS TOOL

There are a couple of golden rules relating to tools that need to be adhered to when designing the data warehouse:

1 Never design the data warehouse to suit a specific tool.
2 Make no assumptions about the type of tool that will be used.

Rule 1 is the cardinal rule. Never make the mistake of designing the data warehouse around a particular tool. Even if a specific tool has been chosen as a company standard, there is no guarantee that some users with specific needs may not use different tools, or that the standard will not change. The tools marketplace is constantly changing, and any choices made today may be invalid in a few months' time.

Remember that the data warehouse will evolve over time; new users added later may have different requirements, and different tools. It is an extremely costly and painful task to reorganize a data warehouse after the fact.

Unfortunately, designing the data warehouse around a specific tool is one of the common mistakes made. It is impossible to stress strongly enough how costly this can prove. If the data warehouse is structured around a specific tool and that tool is later found to be inadequate, or other tools are required for specialist operations, it is unlikely that these tools will work efficiently. The data may be structured in just the wrong order, or too few or too many tables or views may be involved. Experience shows that the effect of the data warehouse's being designed around one tool on the performance of a second tool can be anywhere between 30 and 300%.

Once rule 1 has been accepted, rule 2 follows logically. If you cannot predict the tools or types of tools that will be used, it makes no sense to design the data warehouse for a specific type of tool. The data warehouse should be designed for efficiency of query access, and ease of management. Clearly the design has to be centred on some basis. Primarily it will be based on the understanding of the business requirements, and the types of query that are likely to be asked. This is discussed in detail in Part 3: Design.

> **GUIDELINE B.1** Do not design the data warehouse around a specific tool or tool type.

TYPES OF TOOL

There are as many different tools as there are people to use them. Each tool has its own strengths and weaknesses, but also each tool is generally designed for a specific purpose. No one tool will do everything; certainly it will not do everything well. To help this discussion we can classify the usage of tools against a data warehouse into three broad categories.

- data dipping
- data mining
- data analysis

Each of these tool types is discussed below.

Data dipping tools

Data dipping tools are the basic business tools. They allow generation of standard business reports. They can perform basic analysis, answering standard business questions, such as: What were the sales last month? How many new customers have been added in the last week?

As these tools are relational they can also be used as data browsers, and generally have reasonable drill-down capabilities. Most of the tools will use metadata to isolate the user from the complexities of the data warehouse and present a business friendly schema.

Data mining tools

Data mining tools are specialist tools designed for finding trends and patterns in the underlying data. These tools use techniques such as artificial intelligence and neural networks to mine the data and find connections that may not be immediately obvious.

A data mining tool could be used to find common behavioral trends in a business's customers, or to root out market segments by grouping customers with common attributes. Users of these tools will generally be analysts who already have a deep understanding of the business data.

The analysis thrown up by the data mining tool can be used to design new products and promotions, and to help improve customer loyalty.

Data analysis tools

Data analysis tools are used to perform complex analysis of data. They will normally have a rich set of analytic functions, which allow sophisticated analysis of the data. These tools are designed for business analysis, and will generally understand the common business metrics, such as market share, churn and profitability.

Data analysis tools can again be subdivided into two categories, MOLAP tools and ROLAP tools. MOLAP and ROLAP are terms that sprang up to distinguish two different approaches to analyzing data. They came into existence because the term OLAP has become an industry buzzword. To understand the difference between them, first one has to know three things:

- What is OLAP?
- What does relational mean?
- What is multidimensional analysis?

Let us take these questions one at a time. First, what is OLAP? The term OLAP is an acronym for online analytical processing. Much has been written about the subject in the computer literature, and for a detailed discussion you should consult some of that work. For our purposes it is sufficient to have a basic understanding of the term.

OLAP is primarily all about being able to access live data online and analyze it. It is about the methods, structures and tools required to perform this analysis. OLAP is about rapid access to and analysis of data. OLAP tools are designed to allow reasonably large quantities of data to be analyzed online. An OLAP tool will allow a user to quickly perform standard analytical functions on the data and to represent both data and results graphically. The idea is to allow the user to easily manipulate and visualize the data.

Relational technology has been around for many years, and is fairly well understood these days. Again, there is a large body of literature on the subject. For our purposes it is sufficient to say that basically the relational model works by allowing data to be normalized into relations, usually referred to as tables. This normalization minimizes data duplication, making the data more manageable, while still allowing data to be efficiently manipulated. The power of relational technology is in the relational operations that allow data to be joined, unioned, intersected and so on. This, along with the standardization on a common SQL language, has made relational databases the norm in the marketplace today.

Multidimensional analysis is a technique whereby data can be analyzed in many dimensions at once. The term *dimension* in this context means an attribute such as cost, duration, or name. These attributes will generally be equivalent to a column in a relational table. The idea is that instead of analyzing the data in a two-dimensional table, the data is loaded into a multidimensional hypercube to be analyzed.

Using matrix arithmetic and sparse matrix optimizations this allows the data to be stored space-efficiently and analyzed very rapidly by the loaded dimensions. Some tools also allow the use of multiple separate but related hypercubes; this reduces the sparsity of the matrices and makes the dimension calculations more efficient.

The acronyms MOLAP and ROLAP stand for multidimensional OLAP and relational OLAP respectively. They are terms that have come into use to differentiate multidimensional tools from relational tools. The distinction is somewhat artificial, because many of the MOLAP tools have an SQL interface that allows them to extract data from a relational database. This said, the SQL interface is automatic, in that it generates the SQL automatically, but the SQL generated is not necessarily efficient.

The advantage of using a multidimensional tool is that on a predefined set of data it gives user-friendly, fast access to powerful analytical and statistical functions. Multidimensional tools suffer a heavy performance hit when uploading a cube, but once the data is in memory they can carry out certain operations on that data far more efficiently than a relational tool can. Operations such as time series analysis and top-ten bottom-ten selection can be performed extremely efficiently. These operations, while possible in a relational tool, are difficult to program in SQL, and will not perform efficiently. The other thing that multidimensional tools do very well is dimensional slicing. If data has been loaded into the cube dimensioned by office, region, sales_quantity, sales_value and product, the tool will be able to switch almost instantly from displaying data by region to displaying data by product or by sales_value.

MOLAP tools are good to use for analyzing aggregated data in conjunction with its dimension data. They are not so good if you need to drill down to detailed data at the fact level, or if you need to query very large quantities of base data. If you are going to use a MOLAP tool against the data warehouse it will be better to help the SQL performance by creating aggregations that will allow the commonly accessed cubes to be quickly built, or even prebuilt. This will allow the MOLAP tool to get up and running very quickly. It will also prevent inefficient generated SQL from trying to build data sets at the correct aggregated level for the desired cube. In effect, these aggregations are data marts designed specifically for the MOLAP tool.

ROLAP tools are the traditional SQL-oriented tools that have tight integration to the relational model. These tools have been around a long time, but are changing all the time. The current generation of ROLAP tools are powerful and easy to use. They use metadata to isolate the user from the underlying complexities of the data warehouse, and to present a business perspective of the data.

ROLAP tools can be distinguished from the data dippers by their range and depth of analytical functionality. As with the MOLAP tools these are business-aware tools that understand business terminology. Being relational they can be used as data browsers, and will have good drill-down capability from aggregation to detailed data.

Future tools

The future heralds ever more powerful tools that are data warehouse aware – tools that are designed for and are capable of dealing with very large databases. Some of the features that will appear in tools in the near future are:

- optimizer-aware tools
- accurate query time prediction
- accurate resource usage prediction
- improved summary management
- improved integration of data generation, visualization and browsing

In the longer term, tools will arrive that can perform fully the roles of the query manager and the warehouse manager.

ANALYZING THE USER QUERY REQUIREMENTS

One of the key steps in the analysis stage is ascertaining the user query requirements. Before the data warehouse layout can be designed you need a clear understanding of the queries that are likely to be run. Although there will probably be some canned queries or standard reports that can be identified, it is unlikely that the users will have a clear definition of everything they want.

Even if the users are unusually forthcoming, and can give chapter and verse on their requirements, it is unlikely that this will be the whole story. There may be other users who are to be added later, and there is no guarantee that their queries will be the same as those of the current users.

As the users get used to the data warehouse and its abilities, they may begin to explore data in different ways. Remember: it is the ad hoc nature of a data warehouse that makes it what it is. As the users' requirements change over time, the data warehouse will evolve, but the database design needs to remain constant. So, when performing the analysis requirements capture, it is vital to gain an understanding of the business, and the business sector it occupies. This is the one constant: even if the business changes, it is unlikely that it will change so radically that it moves business sector. A telco is not likely to become a bank, and an airline is unlikely to become a retail chain. In the unlikely event that such a change does occur, the data warehouse will probably need to be designed again from scratch in any case.

> **GUIDELINE B.2** To fully understand the user requirements and round them out, you must gain an understanding of the business.

Knowing the business means knowing the nitty gritty of the business calendar as well as the day-to-day running of the business. You need to have a general understanding of all aspects of the business, including:

- key periods
- business dates
- business times
- meaningful levels of data detail
- important summary fields

The key periods are the important reporting and financial periods. Does the business have special processing each week, each month, each quarter and so on? Some businesses are not interested in information in the short term, such as daily, and will tend to analyze data over weekly or larger periods. This may be because a given day's business takes several days to process through the operational systems, with the data becoming available to the data warehouse over the period of a week or longer. It could be that the business does not do daily analysis because it never had the processing power to do it. You need to understand the reasons and the requirements. Just because they do not analyze daily data now, possibly because they have not been able to, it does not mean they will never want to analyze data on a daily basis.

Key business dates need to be documented. The start of the company's business year, the start of the local tax year and so on are key dates, and will have effects on the processing load on the data warehouse. Some companies have standard business holidays when the business closes down for a number of days or weeks.

Another set of requirements that need to be established is the times of business or business working hours. Questions such as:

- What are the business's weekday working hours?
- What are the weekend working practices?
- On which day does the business week start?
- Are there any days when the business closes early?

need to be asked and the answers documented as part of the requirements document.

Remember to capture all the time, period and business date information by department, as different parts of a business may have different dates and times. This information is crucial to the data warehouse design, because it can for example radically affect your weekend processing if some parts of the business have their week begin on Sunday and others have their week start on Monday.

> **GUIDELINE B.3** Make sure that period information is captured by department, group and any other organizational divisions.

Part of analyzing and understanding the business is getting to grips with the key business indicators, and the data dimensions that are important. What dimensions or data fields will the users want to summarize and query on? These fields will form the basis of all your aggregations, and this information – in conjunction with the date and period information discussed above – will allow you to define the base set of aggregations that will be required.

As part of the analysis you also need to drive out the meaningful levels of data detail. For example, if the business is a food retailer, does it need to keep detailed records down to the sale of each individual tin of baked beans, or is it sufficient to summarize sales of baked beans by tin size by brand by day? The questions:

- How much detailed information is required on each key dimension?
- What level of detail does that data need to go to?

need to be asked, and the answers have to be very clearly documented. It is not sufficient just to answer the questions above; you must understand and document the reasons for the answers. In most cases the business will not be interested in individual sales of an item. It will usually want to look at sales by product at a daily summarized level. However, if the business ultimately wants the capability to do basket analysis, data may need to be kept at a much more detailed level.

It is vital that you get this right, because the decision on what constitutes the fact data for the data warehouse will depend on these answers. This is one of the most important decisions you will make in the whole project. If you get the level of detail wrong for the fact data you may ultimately have to scrap the whole data warehouse and start again. Just to reinforce this statement, and to ensure that it is not taken as a throwaway comment, if you get the level of detail wrong for the fact data you will probably have to scrap the whole data warehouse and start again. The whole design, the sizing, the capacity planning and so on will be based on this decision. If the level of detail is incorrect, the hardware will be the wrong size, the database design and layout will be incorrect, and any partitioning you are using will be wrong. You will need to start over.

If you are aware that, as in the example above, the level of detail will increase later, you can design with that in mind, and ensure that any design you put in place now should not hamper that change later.

> **GUIDELINE B.4**   It is imperative to get the level of detail at which data must be stored correct. If this decision is made incorrectly, the data warehouse will need to be completely reorganized at some future date.

Having an understanding of these details will allow you to round out the query requirements. It allows the user requirements to be rationalized, and a reasonable estimate of the sorts of queries that are possible in the future to be calculated.

The queries themselves will fall into several categories:

- batch reports
- canned queries
- ad hoc queries

Each category requires its own analysis, and will place its own considerations and constraints on the design.

The batch reports are generally a well-understood requirement. Initially, the reports are likely to be a set of existing reports that are currently run on other systems. As they are well understood, these reports are often used as part of any pilot scheme. Note, however, that if these reports are written in a programming language on a different system, it may take some time to port them to SQL on the data warehouse. Finally, as they are batch reports, they can be run offline, and scheduled around any daily access and the overnight processing.

With proper scheduling these reports can be run extremely quickly using high degrees of parallelism. This allows the full power of the machine to be brought to bear on these reports, and the batch reports can be finished quickly.

The canned queries are also predefined queries, but they differ from reports in that there is a requirement to run them online. Canned queries also differ from reports in that they are often parameterized, and hence the data set they visit can vary radically in size. As with the batch reports these queries are a good starting point for testing and development. You can measure the resource requirements of these queries, and the results can be used for capacity planning and for database design.

The canned queries are again good candidates for use on a pilot system, or for early delivery in a phased development.

Ad hoc queries, as the name suggests, are the unpredictable element of a data warehouse. They are also generally the main reason for developing the data warehouse in the first place. It is exactly that ability to run any query when desired and expect a reasonable response that makes the data warehouse worthwhile, and makes the design such a significant challenge.

The ad hoc query profile will be difficult if not impossible to predict. The best that can be done is to develop an understanding of the queries that are likely to be run. This will come from an understanding of the business and from the requirements capture. This information can then be used in the design of the database to meet those requirements.

DESIGNING TO THE QUERY REQUIREMENTS

To address the challenge of designing the data warehouse to be query efficient even for ad hoc access, techniques such as star schemas, denormalization, query parallelism and data partitioning are used to make the data warehouse as query efficient as possible. These techniques are explained elsewhere in this book.

The aim is to design and lay out the fact data to make it as accessible and query efficient as it can be. The partitioning, while used primarily for ease of management, should also be designed for performance, with data partitioned in business meaningful chunks. Data is denormalized to avoid costly joins between huge tables. The fact data and its dimension data are organized into some variant of a star schema to allow star query access between the dimensions and the fact table. Finally, queries are parallelized to allow them to process such vast quantities of data in a realistic time-scale.

The data layout is then designed to take all this into account. The fact and dimension data are placed on disk to minimize the possibilities of any I/O bottlenecks and to maximize parallel access to the fact data. The irony is that, having gone to such great lengths to make the fact data maximally accessible, the next step is to ensure that the users never access it. You should aim to have 90% or more of all queries answered by access to aggregations. A query that runs against an aggregation will avoid the sort and aggregation work that it would have to do if it was run against the fact data. As sort is one of the most costly operations, and one that does not scale linearly as the data grows, the savings made by avoiding sorts are significant.

The data warehouse will evolve over time and the query usage profile will change. As it changes, the history data captured by the query manager will be required to predict the resource usage of the new query profile. The data can also be used to predict what new aggregations would be useful, and if current aggregations are being used.

The query manager will also be needed in its query generation role to point queries at the best location for the data they are trying to access. It will use the metadata created and maintained by the warehouse manager to achieve this.

AVOIDING THE "QUERY FROM HELL"

The "query from hell" is the DBA's nightmare. It is a query that occupies the entire resource of a machine and effectively runs for ever, never finishing in any time-scale that is meaningful. Naturally, it is a query to be avoided.

Given the vast quantity of data in a data warehouse, such queries are all too possible to generate. The problem is that it may be impossible to tell the difference between an acceptable query that takes up to 48 hours to run and one that will run for much longer and effectively never finishes.

Unless it is possible to measure exactly how far a query has progressed and how much more processing it has left to do, it will be impossible to predict when a query will end. The only way of preventing such queries is by controlling exactly how much resource a query can have. This can be done in two ways.

First, profiles can be used to limit the amount of resource a user process can use. When that amount is exceeded, the query will be terminated automatically. This will not prevent a query running, but it will stop it running for ever using vast amounts of resources. The advantages of profiles are that they are automatic, and they require no external control. The disadvantage is that they kick in only after a lot of resource has already been wasted.

Second, queuing of queries can be used to control their resource usage. If all queries must be submitted via the query manager, then the degree of parallelism and other resources of the query can be controlled. Any query that is likely to run for extended periods of time can be limited in what resource it will use. This will mean that the query will take longer to run, but it will stop a single query interfering with the other processing necessary to maintain and run the data warehouse.

Summary of all Guidelines

3 DATA WAREHOUSE ARCHITECTURE

GUIDELINE 3.1 Start extracting data from data sources, when it represents the same snapshot of time as all the other data sources.

GUIDELINE 3.2 Do not execute consistency checks until all the data sources have been loaded into the temporary data store.

GUIDELINE 3.3 Expect the effort required to clean up the source systems to increase exponentially with the number of overlapping data sources.

GUIDELINE 3.4 Always assume that the amount of effort required to clean up data sources is substantially greater than you would expect.

4 PROCESS ARCHITECTURE

GUIDELINE 4.1 Do not load data directly into the data warehouse tables until it has been cleaned up. That is, use temporary tables that emulate the structures within the data warehouse.

GUIDELINE 4.2 Consider partitioning the fact table on the basis of the refresh cycle. For example, if data is loaded on a weekly basis, consider using weekly partitions. Small partitions can be amalgamated into larger partitions on a regular basis: at month end, for example.

GUIDELINE 4.3   Consider dropping all indexes against the fact table partition subject to the load, prior to inserting data into the table. Create the indexes in parallel once data has been loaded.

GUIDELINE 4.4   Do not create views which combine large numbers of fact table partitions, since the impact on query performance is substantial.

GUIDELINE 4.5   Determine what business activities require detailed transaction information, in order to determine the level at which to retain detailed information in the data warehouse.

GUIDELINE 4.6   If detailed information is being stored offline to minimize the disk storage requirements, make sure that the data has been extracted, cleaned up, and transformed into a starflake schema prior to archiving it.

GUIDELINE 4.7   Ensure that the fact table definitions are accurate prior to starting the bulk population of these tables.

GUIDELINE 4.8   Expect dimension information to change on a regular basis, and structure the data warehouse to minimize the cost of change. Specifically, isolate dimension from fact data, and carefully select foreign keys for fact tables.

GUIDELINE 4.9   Consider partitioning the large fact tables on the basis of time periods relevant to the business.

GUIDELINE 4.10   Avoid a design solution which requires greater than 500 tables in total, unless the business is prepared to accept a much higher operational management cost.

GUIDELINE 4.11   Mark all inactive partitions read-only, and then back up twice. Further backups are not required since the data will not change.

GUIDELINE 4.12   Avoid creating a solution which requires more than (approximately) 200 centralized summary tables on an ongoing basis.

GUIDELINE 4.13   Inform users that summary tables accessed infrequently will be dropped on an on-going basis.

GUIDELINE 4.14   Allow space in all sizing calculations for a reasonable number of specific aggregations owned by each user, and impose these user limits within the database.

GUIDELINE 4.15 Populate data marts via an enterprise data warehouse in order to clean up the data and ensure consistency.

GUIDELINE 4.16 When using data marts, always design the data warehouse for full data retention, and consider storing data in archive until a requirement to analyse all the detailed data exists.

5 DATABASE SCHEMA

GUIDELINE 5.1 Avoid embedding reference data into the fact table, because that will protect the fact data from restructuring when the reference data changes.

GUIDELINE 5.2 Always determine the factual transactions being used by the business processes. Don't assume that the reported transactions within an operational system are fact data.

GUIDELINE 5.3 Structure key dimensions to represent the key focal points of analysis of factual transactions. Use the relationships to the fact table within the logical model as a starting point, but restructure where necessary to ensure you can apply the most suitable foreign keys.

GUIDELINE 5.4 Look for denormalized dimensions within candidate fact tables. It may be the case that the candidate fact table is a dimension containing repeating groups of factual attributes.

GUIDELINE 5.5 Design fact tables to store rows that will not vary over time. If the entity appears to vary over time, consider creating a fact table which represents events which change the status of that entity.

GUIDELINE 5.6 Identify the historical period significant to decision making processes, and the degree of detail required. This could substantially reduce the volume of data required within the fact table.

GUIDELINE 5.7 If the business requirement does not require all the detailed fact data, consider storing samples and aggregate the rest.

GUIDELINE 5.8 Do not store aggregated columns within fact tables. It is usually cheaper to aggregate the columns on the fly.

GUIDELINE 5.9 Ensure that every byte in the column definitions within a large fact table is needed. Savings here will have a substantial effect on the size and complexity of the fact table.

GUIDELINE 5.10 Use non-intelligent keys in fact tables, unless you are certain that identifiers will not change during the lifetime of the data warehouse.

GUIDELINE 5.11 Use physical dates in fact tables, rather than foreign keys that reference rows in a *time* dimension table.

GUIDELINE 5.12 Consider using date offsets from the implied start date of a fact table partition. If date offsets are used, create a view which looks like the logical table, by adding the offset to the start date.

GUIDELINE 5.13 Consider the use of date ranges in fact tables, where the access tool can cope directly with the structure. If used, make sure that no on-the-fly data expansion is occurring within the access tool.

GUIDELINE 5.14 Denormalize entities accessed often into the star dimension table. All other entities should remain in the snowflake structure.

GUIDELINE 5.15 If data in a dimension is networked, denormalize the most commonly accessed hierarchy into the star dimension. If the query profile changes in the future, add columns that denormalize the new (commonly accessed) hierarchy.

GUIDELINE 5.16 If a dimension table grows to a size similar to a fact table partition, or scanning a dimension table absorbs a significant percentage of the available query time, consider partitioning the table horizontally and creating a combinatory view.

GUIDELINE 5.17 Expect outlying entities in the starflake schema to change substantially over time. Don't spend too much time trying to pin down the user requirements in those areas.

6 PARTITIONING STRATEGY

GUIDELINE 6.1 Consider the use of different sized partitions where the business requires a mix of data dipping recent history, and data mining aged history.

GUIDELINE 6.2 Consider partitioning on a dimension other than time, if the user functions lend themselves to that.

GUIDELINE 6.3 Do not partition on a dimensional grouping which is likely to change within the life of the data warehouse.

GUIDELINE 6.4 Structure horizontal partitions to round-robin. Remember that the size of each partition may vary.

GUIDELINE 6.5 Normalizing data in a data warehouse can lead to large inefficient join operations. Such operations should be avoided.

GUIDELINE 6.6 Consider row splitting a fact table if some columns are accessed infrequently.

GUIDELINE 6.7 Consider striping fact data across nodes where the total, concurrent data to be shipped is well below the throughput on the interconnect. If latency issues are apparent, horizontal partition the fact data across the nodes, and make use of node affinity features.

GUIDELINE 6.8 A number of good solutions horizontally partition data to a level meaningful to the business monthly segments, for example and then stripe each partition across the nodes.

7   AGGREGATIONS

GUIDELINE 7.1 Design summary tables along similar lines as fact tables, making use of existing dimension structures.

GUIDELINE 7.2 If common queries use more than one aggregated value on the same dimension, aggregate the required values into a set of columns within the same summary table.

GUIDELINE 7.3 Consider amalgamating a number of related facts into the same summary table.

GUIDELINE 7.4 Consider aggregating at the level below the level required for known common queries.

GUIDELINE 7.5 Always use intelligent keys in a summary table.

GUIDELINE 7.6 Consider denormalizing the dimension into the summary table, in order to speed up queries by removing the need to join tables. Don't use this technique if there are large numbers of rows in the summary.

GUIDELINE 7.7 Always store physical dates within summary tables.

GUIDELINE 7.8 Date offsets are probably inappropriate within a summary table.

GUIDELINE 7.9 Avoid the use of date ranges within summary tables, unless the user access tools can operate effectively with them.

GUIDELINE 7.10 Consider using a high level of indexation on the summary tables.

8 DATA MARTING

GUIDELINE 8.1 You should not have more than a handful of data marts for a data warehouse with an overnight load process, because the processing time is likely to exceed the load window.

GUIDELINE 8.2 Populate multiple data marts from an enterprise data warehouse. This will ensure data

GUIDELINE 8.3 Avoid using data marts as an alternative to aggregation. Costs will be higher, without providing the overview capability of aggregations.

9 METADATA

GUIDELINE 9.1 Adopt a common notation to describe source and destination data. Ideally this notation should be a superset of the destination data types.

GUIDELINE 9.2 The more data sources that need to be mapped, the more valuable a transformation and mapping tool becomes.

GUIDELINE 9.3 To choose the correct source for a query you need to be able to track all occurrences of each data field through every aggregation, index and table.

GUIDELINE 9.4 Gathering of resource statistics can cause overheads. Where possible statistics should be gathered passively.

GUIDELINE 9.5 Most required data can be extracted from the SQL syntax and the execution plan. This means the analysis can be performed any time at your convenience.

10 SYSTEM AND DATA WAREHOUSE PROCESS MANAGERS

GUIDELINE 10.1 Because of the size and complexity of the system, tools will be required to manage the data warehouse efficiently.

GUIDELINE 10.2 If the data warehouse is running on a cluster or MPP architecture, the schedule manager must be capable of running across that architecture.

GUIDELINE 10.3 An event manager is required to track the myriad of things that can go wrong on such a large and volatile system.

GUIDELINE 10.4 Ensure that the backup software you use is database aware and integrates with your RDBMS.

GUIDELINE 10.5 Make sure that there are control checks to ensure that all data gets loaded, and no data gets loaded twice.

GUIDELINE 10.6 Associate a creation procedure with each aggregation. This allows aggregation creation to be tailored without changing the warehouse manager software. If the procedure does not exist the aggregation can be created directly using the relevant SQL.

GUIDELINE 10.7 Design and test the archiving process into the data warehouse from the beginning, even if it will not be employed for some time. This will avoid any nasty shocks down the line.

GUIDELINE 10.8 Ideally all query access to the data warehouse should go via the query manager.

11 HARDWARE ARCHITECTURE

GUIDELINE 11.1 Design and management of a data warehouse on a MPP system is considerably more difficult than on an SMP or cluster system.

GUIDELINE 11.2 Management tools are required to manage a large, dynamic and complex system such as a data warehouse.

GUIDELINE 11.3 Ensure the network architecture and bandwidth is capable of supporting the data transfer and any data extractions in an acceptable time. The transfer of data to be loaded must complete quickly enough to allow the rest of the overnight processing to complete.

GUIDELINE 11.4 Make sure those responsible for the network are fully aware of all the data warehouse network requirements, and that they can meet them.

GUIDELINE 11.5 The tools must not be allowed to affect the design of the data warehouse.

12   PHYSICAL LAYOUT

GUIDELINE 12.1   Ensure that object statistics are kept up to date.

GUIDELINE 12.2   Control is required over queries to avoid simultaneous large queries bringing the system to its knees.

GUIDELINE 12.3   Parallel load is normally required for data to be loaded quickly enough to enable the required postprocessing to complete within the overnight period.

GUIDELINE 12.4   Parallel index build is essential to enable index maintenance within a reasonable timescale.

GUIDELINE 12.5   RAID 5 suffers write performance penalties, and should be chosen only if thoroughly tested and proven to give the required performance.

GUIDELINE 12.6   Ensure you have enough disks to spread the data without clashing. It is usually better to have more smaller disks than fewer larger disks.

GUIDELINE 12.7   Consider naming the logical volumes with names that indicate both their location and contents.

GUIDELINE 12.8   Do not start laying out the database until you have a complete and finalized physical database design.

GUIDELINE 12.9   Ensure you are aware of every hardware, operating system and database limit, before designing the database.

GUIDELINE 12.10 Where possible specify storage information at the tablespace level, and let all objects within each tablespace default to those values.

GUIDELINE 12.11 For smaller tables divide them into tablespaces by a mixture of function and size.

GUIDELINE 12.12 You need to be aware of any limitations, imposed by either the operating system or the hardware, on striping and mirroring.

13   SECURITY

GUIDELINE 13.1   Consider categorising data access by role or job function.

GUIDELINE 13.2   The tighter the security the more person oriented the design.

GUIDELINE 13.3 The more complex the interdependencies the more role oriented the design.

GUIDELINE 13.4 Where possible avoid the use of views to enforce data access restrictions. They can rapidly become a nightmare to maintain.

GUIDELINE 13.5 Make sure you understand not just the security restrictions, but the reasons for them. This allows you to make informed decisions about how the restrictions should be applied.

GUIDELINE 13.6 The design team will require some analysts with knowledge and experience of the business area.

GUIDELINE 13.7 Understand the reasons for each audit requirement. Only implement those that are genuinely required for legal, company and security reasons.

GUIDELINE 13.8 Avoid creating covert channels that inadvertently make information about data available.

GUIDELINE 13.9 Views will be necessary in any data warehouse, but they have performance overheads and their usage should be minimized.

GUIDELINE 13.10 Be sure you fully understand any restrictions imposed on views. Not only can they disallow certain operations, but they may affect query optimization.

GUIDELINE 13.11 Increase the complexity estimate for any piece of software that requires security code to be added.

14 BACKUP AND RECOVERY

GUIDELINE 14.1 It is imperative that the backup strategy, the database and the data warehouse application all be designed together.

GUIDELINE 14.2 Your chosen tape medium must be scaleable at an affordable price.

GUIDELINE 14.3 Ensure that you have control of any shared backup resource.

GUIDELINE 14.4 Ensure that the SLA for the use of the Silo is sufficiently tight that you cannot lose any backups due to contention for its resource.

GUIDELINE 14.5 Ensure that your chosen backup software supports any media you are likely to use.

GUIDELINE 14.6 Evaluate and decide on your backup software and hardware together.

GUIDELINE 14.7 The design of the backup strategy and the database must be performed hand in hand.

GUIDELINE 14.8 Backup read only data twice to protect against failure in the backup media.

GUIDELINE 14.9 Clearly document the backup strategy and any likely recovery scenarios.

GUIDELINE 14.10 A data warehouse is a changing environment and you should perform regular backup testing.

15 SERVICE LEVEL AGREEMENT

GUIDELINE 15.1 A data warehouse is not an Operational system.

GUIDELINE 15.2 Ensure that the data warehouse does not indirectly become an Operational system.

GUIDELINE 15.3 Ensure you gather the requirements of every group of users. Any group could have requirements that differ from the others.

GUIDELINE 15.4 Always ask questions the right way round. Ask users what they need not what they want.

GUIDELINE 15.5 The SLA(s) must cover all the dependencies that the data warehouse has on the outside world.

16 OPERATING THE DATA WAREHOUSE

GUIDELINE 16.1 Keep all log and trace information, relevant to any problems or issues still under investigation, in a separate location to avoid the information be removed by regular and automated housekeeping.

GUIDELINE 16.2 Always try to shutdown systems, applications or database cleanly.

GUIDELINE 16.3 Thoroughly test any upgrades on the test system before upgrading the live system.

GUIDELINE 16.4 The data transfer and load processes need to be designed to work on subsets of the daily data, even if the data is expected to arrive as a single set.

17 CAPACITY PLANNING, TUNING AND TESTING

GUIDELINE 17.1 Do not allow cost or budget considerations to affect capacity estimates.

GUIDELINE 17.2 Remember to allow for resilience in your disk space capacity planning. Any Mirroring or RAID 5 overheads need to be counted.

GUIDELINE 17.3 Do not attempt to size the database until the database schema is complete.

GUIDELINE 17.4 Allow for period variations when sizing partitions.

GUIDELINE 17.5 Use the formulae in this section carefully. They are intended as guidelines not as a panacea.

18 TUNING THE DATA WAREHOUSE

GUIDELINE 18.1 Ensure that everyone, from the data warehouse designers to the users and senior management, have reasonable performance expectations.

GUIDELINE 18.2 Limit, to the absolute minimum required, the number of integrity checks that need to be applied on the data warehouse. Where possible integrity checks should be performed on the source systems.

GUIDELINE 18.3 Spread the load source files and the load destination files to avoid and I/O bottlenecks.

GUIDELINE 18.4 Store the expected execution plans for know queries.

GUIDELINE 18.5 You need to turn an unpredictable query mix to a predictable query mix.

GUIDELINE 18.6 Get queries to run against aggregations rather than against the base data itself.

19 TESTING THE DATA WAREHOUSE

GUIDELINE 19.1 Sufficient testing needs to be performed to establish that queries scale with the data.

GUIDELINE 19.2 Full scale testing requires a comprehensive test plan.

GUIDELINE 19.3 Double the amount of time you would normally allow for testing.

GUIDELINE 19.4 If the test data is generated, ensure the data has the correct balance and skew. Make sure the ratio of fact to dimension is correct and so on.

GUIDELINE 19.5 Schedule the recovery tests last, as a failed test can cause considerable delays.

GUIDELINE 19.6 Every backup test should be verified by performing recovery using the backed up data.

GUIDELINE 19.7 Test I/O operations for different stripe widths.

GUIDELINE 19.8 Test scheduling software and processes thoroughly.

GUIDELINE 19.9 Many of the tools, such as the system manager and the backup recovery manager, are best tested by their use during the system tests.

GUIDELINE 19.10 Take the time to test the most complex and awkward queries that the business is likely to ask against different index and aggregation strategies.

GUIDELINE 19.11 Ensure that the data warehouse design scales as the data scales.

GUIDELINE 19.12 Test everything twice.

APPENDIX B

ACCESSING THE DATA WAREHOUSE

GUIDELINE B.1   Do not design the data warehouse around a specific tool or tool type.

GUIDELINE B.2   To fully understand the user requirements and round them out, you must gain an understanding of the business.

GUIDELINE B.3   Make sure that period information is captured by department, group and any other organisational divisions.

GUIDELINE B.4   It is imperative to get the level of detail at which data must be stored correct. If this decision is made incorrectly, the data warehouse will need to be completely reorganized at some future date.

Glossary

3GL   Acronym for 3rd generation language. These are standard computer programming languages such as *C*, COBOL, FORTRAN and so on.

aggregation   A summary. Specifically, in data warehouse terms, an aggregation is a summary table built on one or more fact tables.

archiving   The storage of data offline. In a data warehouse environment it is common to keep online only the data required by the business. Legal and other requirements often mean that older data needs to be stored over a longer period. This data needs to be in a format that can quickly be restored to the data warehouse if required.

archive log file   A copy of a *redo log file* taken for backup and to ensure the database can still do roll forward recovery after the redo log file is reused.

ASCII   Acronym for American standard code for information interchange. This is an encoding scheme that maps alphanumeric and other characters on to an 8 *bit* code.

base data   See *fact data.*

bit(s)   Acronym for binary digit. A unit of computer storage that can store 2 values, 0 or 1.

byte   A standard unit of storage. A byte consists of 8 *bits*. Basically, a byte is sufficient to store a single character.

C   A computer programming language. This is the standard language in the UNIX environment.

C++   A computer language that is an extended object-oriented variation of *C*.

canned query   A term used to describe a standard query that is preprepared and frequently used.

Cartesian product   A join of two tables, where every possible combination of each row from the first table with rows from the second table is returned. This is necessary if there are no join criteria specified that allow rows from each table to be matched.

cluster   A tightly coupled group of *SMP* machines, with shared disks.

cold backup   A database backup taken while the database is shut down.

Control file   An Oracle term, but used generically throughout the book to refer to any file external to the database that contains mapping information needed to start the database.

CPU   Acronym for central processing unit.

daemon   A UNIX background process. Daemons are monitor and server processes used by applications and the operating system.

data dippers   A data dipper is a variety of query tool used to dip into the data in the data warehouse. They are designed for use as general-purpose query creation and browsing tools.

data mart   A data mart differs from a data warehouse in the scope of the data that it deals with. Typically, it is focused on a specific department or business process rather than being a corporate data repository. A data mart can be standalone or fed centrally from the corporate data warehouse.

data mining   A particular type of data analysis. The aim of data mining is to unearth any hidden trends and associations in a set of data.

data shipping   The opposite of *function shipping*. In a multi-*node* environment this is where the data for an operation is shipped to the node where the operation is being performed.

data warehouse   The definitions of what constitutes a data warehouse are many and varied. Most definitions concentrate on the data, saying it should be subject oriented, be consistent across sources, and so on. In our definition the data warehouse is more than just data, it is also the processes involved in getting that data from source to table, and in getting the data from table to analysts. In other words, a data warehouse is the data (meta/fact/dimension/aggregation) and the process managers (load/warehouse/query) that make information available, enabling people to make informed decisions.

DBA   Acronym for database administrator.

degree of parallelism   When applied to any process, such as a query, an index build or an update, that can be parallelized, the degree of parallelism is the number of parallel streams of processing that will be used to process each component of the job. In other words, it is the number of processes involved in any single component of a parallelized job.

dimension   A dimension of a piece of data is any part of that data on which it can be usefully viewed, divided or summarized. Typical dimensions are items such as `time`, `date`, `region` or `account_id`.

dimension data   Data stored externally to the fact data, which contains expanded information on specific dimensions of the fact data.

dimension table   Part of a *star schema*. A table which holds *dimension data*

disk controller   Piece of hardware that acts as the interface between I/O devices, such as disks and tape drives, and the machine. A controller has the ability to manage many devices simultaneously.

disk layout map   The mapping of the data warehouse *tablespaces* and all the areas external to the database onto *logical volumes* or disks.

distributed lock manager   The piece of software that coordinates access to items in memory in a multi-*node* machine. The distributed lock manager ensures that no item can be updated in multiple different locations at the same time.

drill down   The operation of moving from summarised data to detailed data is called drilling down.

EBCDIC   Acronym for extended binary coded decimal information code. This is another data encoding scheme and is an alternate to *ASCII*. Used primarily in mainframe environments.

ELDB   Acronym for extremely large database. We define an ELDB to be any database that is 100 + TB in size.

EPOS   Acronym for electronic point of sale. This is where sales data is captured electronically at the point of sale, and downloaded periodically to a central system.

fact data   The fact data is the basic core data that will be stored in the data warehouse. It is called fact data because it will correspond to business-related facts such as call record data for a telco, or account transaction data for a bank. The fact table(s) generally contain only information pertinent to the fact: that is, there are no operational fields, no derivable fields and no summarizations.

fact table   Part of a *star schema*. The central table that contains the *fact data*.

file system   An area of space set aside to contain files. The file system will contain a root directory in which other directories or files can be created.

foreign key   A field or set of fields in a table that reference a primary key in a second table. Note that the second table does not have to be different from the first table; in other words, a foreign key may reference the primary key in its own table.

FTP   More correctly it should be FTP/IP, but commonly abbreviated to FTP, this is an acronym for file transfer protocol, and is a standard network protocol for transferring information.

function shipping   The opposite of *data shipping*. In a multi-*node* environment this is where the operation is shipped to the node where the data resides.

gigabyte   A gigabyte is 1024 *megabytes*.

GUI   Acronym for graphical user interface.

hot backup   See *online backup*.

I/O bus   The communication path that connects a machine to its peripheral I/O devices, such as *disk controllers*.

journal file   See *redo log file*.

kilobyte   A kilobyte is 1024 *bytes*.

LAN   Acronym for local area network.

legacy system   An older system on hardware or software that is either being phased out or is no longer part of current IT thinking.

logical database design   A database description that contains definitions of logical entities, their attributes and their relationships. The logical entities will correspond to entities within the business being mapped.

logical volume   A portion of a disk or set of disks that is to be treated as a single logical entity for I/O. The logical volume can be used as a *raw device* or to hold a *file system*.

megabyte   A megabyte is 1024 *kilobytes*.

metadata   Data about data. Metadata is data that describes the source, location and meaning of another piece of data.

middleware   A term used to describe a piece of software that sits between other pieces of software and coordinates access in both directions.

MOLAP   Multidimensional online analytical processing.

MPP   An acronym for massively parallel processing. These are large multi-*node* machines with large numbers of *CPU*s.

node   A node is a semi-independent processing unit that forms part of an *MPP* or *cluster* system.

node affinity   If an operation is confined to or has a preference for running on a specific *node*, it is said to have node affinity.

NUMA   Acronym for non uniform memory architecture. A NUMA machine is composed of multiple *nodes*, but unlike *cluster* or *MPP* machines, it has a shared memory address space.

OLAP   Online analytical processing.

OLTP   Online transaction processing. An OLTP system is designed to handle a large volume of small predefined transactions.

online backup   A database backup taken while the database is open and potentially in use. The RDBMS will need to have special facilities to ensure that data in the backup is consistent.

overnight processing   Any processing that needs to be done to accomplish the daily loading, cleaning, checking, aggregation, maintenance and backup of data, in order to make that new data available to the users for the following day.

petabyte A petabyte is 1024 *terabytes*.

physical database design A description of the database that contains definitions of all tables, indexes and other database objects. It also contains definitions of the *tablespaces* and which objects reside in them.

primary key The field or set of fields in a table that uniquely identify any row in that table.

raw device In UNIX, a *logical volume* that is addressed directly rather than via the standard file system addressing. Access to raw devices bypasses any I/O caching that the operating system uses.

RDBMS Relational database management system.

redo log file An Oracle term, but used generically throughout the book to refer to a journal file that allows transactions to be replayed. They are used in recovery scenarios to roll the database forward from an old backup.

ROLAP Relational online analytical processing.

schema A set of database objects that logically belong together. A schema has an owner that can grant access to objects in the schema to other database users.

SCSI Acronym for small computer system interface. This was a protocol standard originally defined for connecting devices to small systems. The standard has been extended and enhanced, and is now widely used in the UNIX world as the standard connection protocol, even on enterprise-size systems.

shell script An interpreted programming language. A shell script allows you to combine standard user commands with processing logic.

SKU A standard retail business acronym, it stands for stock keeping unit.

SLA An acronym for service level agreement.

SMP An acronym for symmetric multi-processing. An SMP machine consists of many *CPU*s which share memory and disk.

snowflake schema A variant of the *star schema* where each dimension can have its own dimensions.

SQL An acronym for standard query language. This is the standard *RDBMS* query interface.

star query A query on a *star schema* where the dimensions are first reduced by using the where predicates and then joined (with a *Cartesian product* if necessary) before the join to the much larger fact table is performed.

star schema A logical structure that has a *fact table* in the center with *dimension tables* radiating off of this central table. The fact table will generally be extremely large in comparison to its dimension tables. There will be a *foreign key* in the fact table for each dimension table.

starflake schema This is a hybrid structure that contains a mix of *star* and *snowflake schemas*. Some dimensions may be represented in both forms to cater for different query requirements.

tablespace An Oracle term, but used generically throughout the book to mean an area of space allocated in the database to hold tables (or indeed any database object that requires space, such as index, hash cluster, and so on). A tablespace is a logical entity, and as such can cross datafile boundaries.

telco Common abbreviation used for telecommunications companies.

terabyte A terabyte is 1024 *gigabytes*.

timebox A project management term, that means to place a strict limit on the amount of time that can be spent on a specific activity.

top cover A project management term. To top cover a project means not being involved in a project on a day-to-day basis, but being available on a regular schedule to check that the project stays on course. This is normally a role fulfilled by a consultant that is an expert in the specific field he/she is top covering.

TPC Transaction Processing Council. This is a standards body that defines, audits and publishes the standard IT industry benchmarks.

trace file A file used to capture information about a running process. This information can be used later to trace that process's progress: hence the name.

VLDB An acronym for very large database. What constitutes a very large database is a moving target, but for our purposes we define a VLDB as any database between 100 GB and 100 TB. Anything larger than that is called an *ELDB*.

WAN Wide area network.

Index